W9-CSH-414

SHRUBS AND HEDGES

The American Horticultural Society
Illustrated Encyclopedia of Gardening

SHRUBS AND HEDGES

The American Horticultural Society
Mount Vernon, Virginia

For the American Horticultural Society

President
Dr. Gilbert S. Daniels

Technical Advisory Committee
Everett Conklin
Mary Stuart Maury
Dr. John A. Wott

Shrubs and Hedges Staff for The Franklin Library/Ortho Books

Editorial Director
Min S. Yee

Supervisory Editor
Lewis P. Lewis

Editor
Ken Burke

Art Directors
John Williams
Barbara Ziller

Creative Director
Michael Mendelsohn

Assistant Creative Director
Clint Anglin

Written by
A. Cort Sinnes

Shrub Selection Guide Written by
Michael McKinley

Illustrations by
Raul del Rio

Special Consultant
Dr. Joseph E. Howland
Professor of Horticulture
University of Nevada

Production Director
Robert Laffler

Production Manager
Renee Guilmette

Production Assistant
Paula Green

For Ortho Books

Publisher
Robert L. Iacopi

For The Franklin Library

Publisher
Joseph Sloves

The cover photograph shows two handsome rhododendron hybrids at the height of flowering. Photograph by Derek Fell.

Horticultural Consultants
Fred Galle, Curator
Callaway Gardens
Pine Mountain, GA

Richard Hildreth, Director
State Arboretum of Utah
Salt Lake City, UT

Paul W. Meyer, Curator
Morris Arboretum
Chestnut Hill, PA

Acknowledgments
Burlingame Garden Center
Burlingame, CA

Orchard Nursery
Lafayette, CA

Jane Wilson

Contributing Photographers
(Names of photographers in alphabetical order are followed by page numbers on which their work appears. R = right, C = center, L = left, T = top, B =bottom)

John Bryan
24M, 84B, 104T

Josephine Coatsworth
13MR, 19, 22T, 41

David Fischer
75

Fred Galle
14BL

Pamela Harper
14BR, 15B, 80T,B, 82LT, 85B, 86B, 87T, 88L, 89, 92B, 95, 96M, 97T, 98, 100T,M, 102T, 103T,B, 104B, 107T,M,B, 108T,B, 109T,B, 110B, 111T,B, 112T,M,B, 114B, 115, 117T, 118B, 119T,M,B, 120T, 122M, 125B, 126B, 127B, 131T,TM,BM, 132T,BR, 133T,B, 134TL,TR,B, 136T,B, 139B, 140B, 141RM

Horticultural Photography/Pictures Library
14ML, 61, 106B, 110M, 118T

Elvin McDonald
13RT, 29B

Michael McKinley
2, 12TR, 13TL, 14MR, 15M, 17, 20, 21L, 23T, 24B, 28, 29M, 31, 34, 36, 37T,B, 38, 39, 40T,B, 55, 66L,R, 71TL,B, 72B, 77, 81T, 82R, 85T, 88R, 93T, 96T, 99, 101T, 104M, 105, 106T, 117B, 121T, 122T, 123, 124T, 125T, 132M, 135T, 138B, 140T, 141B

James K. McNair
11, 21M

Paul W. Meyer
15T, 141TL

John Neubauer
12TL, 27, 91

Ortho Photo Library
13LB, 14T, 22B, 23M,B, 24T, 29T, 69, 83L,R, 85T, 86T,M, 87B, 94T, 110T, 114T, 116B, 121B, 128, 129, 130T, 134M, 135B, 137T,B, 141RT

Ray Rogers
130B, 132BL

Martin Schweitzer
43, 51, 59

Michael D. Smith
63, 64, 71TR, 74TL,TR,M

George Taloumis
92T, 93B, 102B, 126T, 139T

Ron Taven
81B, 82LB, 84T, 94B, 96B, 97B, 100B, 101B 103M, 116T,M, 120B, 122B, 124B, 127T, 131B, 141TR

Tom Tracy
12B, 13RB

University of California
72T

Wolf von dem Bussche
52, 138T

Produced under the authorization of The American Horticultural Society by The Franklin Library and Ortho Books.

Copyright © 1980 by Ortho Books. Special contents © 1982 by The American Horticultural Society. All rights reserved under International and Pan-American Copyright Conventions.

Every effort has been made at the time of publication to guarantee the accuracy of the names and addresses of information sources and suppliers and in the technical data contained. However, the subscriber should check for his own assurance and must be responsible for selection and use of suppliers and supplies, plant materials, and chemical products.

No portion of this book may be reproduced in any form or by any means without permission first being requested and obtained in writing from The American Horticultural Society, c/o The Franklin Library, Franklin Center, Pennsylvania, 19091. Portions of this volume previously appeared in the Ortho Book *How to Select & Care for Shrubs & Hedges*.

Library of Congress Catalog Card Number 81-71121
Printed in the United States of America

12 11 10 9 8 7 6 5 4 3 2 1

A Special Message from
The American Horticultural Society

Shrubs are one of the gardener's key materials. They offer a wide spectrum of floral hue, plus a more subtle but no less varied range of leaf color; in winter certain plants delight us with their bright stems or berries. Like an artist with his palette, you as gardener can fill in broad areas of color or opt for particular highlights, and this book will give you the most attractive plant choices available to achieve these ends. You will also learn the many basic forms that shrubs take—such as pyramidal, columnar, weeping— and how you can use them to add interest and shape to your landscape. Hedges, which are shrubs planted and (usually) trimmed to form an unbroken line, are one of the principal ways of doing this. And not only do they let you carve up your space in pleasing patterns, but they can provide privacy, and protection against wind, dust, and noise. If you wish literally to sculpt a plant into geometrical or animal form, try the specialized technique of topiary explained in the chapter devoted to pruning.

Gardeners combine the skills of painter and sculptor, filling spaces with both color and three-dimensional forms. In addition, gardening is, and should be, an individual matter—a reflection of personal taste. You may prefer a formal garden, with neatly kept hedges, precisely delineated lawn areas, an overall symmetrical look. Or you may be more comfortable with an informal garden, where a more natural, relaxed feeling prevails. In either case, *Shrubs and Hedges* will help you realize the layout you want with detailed instructions on planning and designing; buying plants; planting and transplanting; watering, fertilizing, and otherwise maintaining your shrubs. Incidentally, one of the joys of owning shrubs is that, once properly established in their environment, they require so little upkeep.

Perhaps the secret to using shrubs and hedges successfully is a sense of balance. Or, to put it as a question: What is the proper mix of mass, color, and texture for your special gardening needs? The American Horticultural Society is confident that this handsome and informative volume will provide some stimulating—and lasting—answers.

Gilbert S. Daniels
President

CONTENTS

The Backbone of the Garden 10

Shrubs and hedges are integral to the structure of the garden. This chapter explains how they differ from each other, and shows you some of their many and varied uses—from ground cover to ornamental brilliance and formal display. Also explained is the distinction between deciduous and evergreen shrubs, and between broadleaved and coniferous evergreens.

Shrubs in the Landscape 16

In order to utilize shrubs to best advantage, it's important to know what to expect in terms of growth habits and fully mature appearance. In this chapter you will learn the eight basic forms of shrubs, as well as fundamental design concepts, practical uses for plants (such as noise and traffic control), and the ins and outs of container-shrub growing.

Planning Ahead 30

To make sure the plants you have selected are right for your particular garden area, it is essential that you assess both your soil and microclimates. This chapter shows you the easy steps involved, and how to make any modifications that may be necessary. It also tells you where to look, and what to look for, when buying shrubs and hedge plants.

Planting and Transplanting 42

This chapter describes and illustrates the 11 basic steps for planting shrubs. Also discussed are the special problems and techniques involved in setting out balled-and-burlapped and bare-root shrubs, and in transplanting small and large shrubs, as well as laying out hedges. The up-to-date information here provided is the key to the survival and healthy growth of your plants.

Care and Maintenance 50

Once your shrubs are established, and their root systems secure, how should you look after them? In most cases, attention to just four basic measures will ensure handsome, healthy plants, and in this chapter you will find many helpful tips on watering (including the different kinds of irrigation systems available), fertilizing, mulching, and climate protection.

 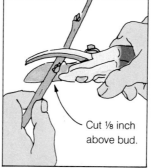 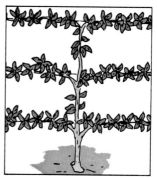

Cut ⅛ inch
above bud.

Pruning 58

As this chapter makes clear, the ancient art of pruning is alive and well. By using different cuts, you can achieve a natural look, make a formal hedge, create a topiary sculpture or an espalier; in addition, pruning can revitalize old shrubs and establish consistent renewal patterns. Rhododendrons, azaleas, and roses call for special treatment.

Pests and Problems 68

Regular tours of inspection, with an eye trained to spot trouble before it gets out of hand, are crucial in keeping your shrubs and hedges pest- and disease-free; so are the preventive-maintenance steps outlined in this chapter. Other sections deal with the problems to look for, and the specific solutions recommended to deal with them.

Plant Selection Guide 76

When it comes to choosing plants for special effects, for particular uses in the garden, or for problem locations, consult both the handy shrub selection lists and the more complete entries in the extensive "Gallery of Shrubs." Well over a hundred color photos bring the beautiful world of shrubs and hedges to life.

Index **142**

SHRUBS AND HEDGES

The lower-growing azaleas in the foreground
define the strong curve of the lawn as
well as provide colorful contrast to the
rhododendrons in the background.

THE BACKBONE OF THE GARDEN

Shrubs and hedges—what they are, and how they can work for you.

As a group, shrubs contain some of the most beautiful and dramatic plants available to the gardener. But because people take shrubs for granted, they tend to overlook many of their special traits.

Shrubs have an undeserved image as obscure masses of green plants that lack any of the flair or distinction of annuals, perennials, or bulbs. Shrubs, in fact, come in thousands of varieties, in every imaginable form and size, with an array of leaf shapes and textures that seems almost infinite. Some burst into seasonal bloom with exquisite, colorful flowers; others remain a steady, stately green all year long. Although shrubs are commonly used as backgrounds for other plants, they often deserve to be featured as garden highlights, with all their elegance on full display.

Shrubs can shape and define spaces, create privacy, accentuate doorways and entrances, and hide unsightly views. They can muffle noise, improve the climate of your yard, and even help to protect against burglary. And they can do all these things with natural grace and beauty and a minimum of maintenance. It is no wonder that landscape architects call shrubs "the backbone of the garden."

As for hedges, they have always been a part of gardening. In spite of their upkeep demands, not only are they integral to the most beautiful gardens, but also they provide many versatile ways to define, limit, or protect specific areas.

In this book you will find information about nearly every gardening situation—whether you are landscaping your entire yard from scratch, whether you are looking for a single shrub for a special place, or whether you simply want to know more about caring for the shrubs you already have. In the sections that follow, you will find out about the place of shrubs in the landscape, both as permanent plantings and in containers; planning the use of shrubs; how to plant and transplant shrubs; how to water, fertilize, prune, and spray for pests and diseases. The Plant Selection Guide tells you all the characteristics and requirements of specific shrubs so that you can make the best possible choices for your garden.

The photographs on the next four pages illustrate some of the more beautiful and practical ways to use shrubs, as well as some new possibilities for your own garden. Since shrubs represent such a superb overall value, there's no need to begrudge the time, expense, and effort required to purchase, plant, and maintain them—the returns will more than compensate you.

What Is a Shrub?

While there is no hard-and-fast definition of a shrub, this one is commonly accepted: *a woody plant with multiple stems or trunks that grows less than 15 feet high when mature.*

A *woody* plant has stems and branches that survive from one year to the

Shrubs can fulfill a variety of design functions in the garden. Top left: Azaleas provide masses of springtime color. Top right: A boxwood hedge eases the transition from large shrubs to the lawn area. Above: Juniper and Irish moss planted together provide a richly textured ground cover.

next; they don't die back to the ground after each growing season. It is this woody character that distinguishes shrubs from herbaceous plants, which are subject to winter damage and do die back to the ground each year.

The fact that shrubs have *multiple stems or trunks* sets them apart from trees, which usually have only a single stem or trunk. There are exceptions: many shrubs can be deliberately trained to have only a single trunk. Shrubs trained in this way are called *standards*; basically, they are miniature trees, often used for a formal effect. Some trees also have multiple trunks, but they usually grow higher than 15 feet.

The loosest part of the definition is that a shrub must be *less than 15 feet high when mature*. A shrub that grows taller than 15 feet doesn't automat-

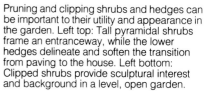

Pruning and clipping shrubs and hedges can be important to their utility and appearance in the garden. Left top: Tall pyramidal shrubs frame an entranceway, while the lower hedges delineate and soften the transition from paving to the house. Left bottom: Clipped shrubs provide sculptural interest and background in a level, open garden.

Below top: Topiary in whimsical forms can be a charming centerpiece for a garden area.

Below middle: Container-grown fuchsias left full at the bottom and trained as a standard at the top give form and color to a patio. Below bottom: Flowering hedges must be pruned at the appropriate time in order to flower well.

ically become a tree; in fact, the same plants reach widely varying mature heights in different regions of the country. To distinguish between shrubs and trees, common sense is your best guide. Most trees are capable of reaching impressive heights; shrubs remain comparatively small—usually under 15 feet.

What Is a Hedge?

Hedges are the special application of shrubs or other plants that have been planted close together so that they form an unbroken line, and in most cases they are trimmed carefully. Formal hedges resemble fences in their solid,

The versatility of shrubs allows them to be used for color, texture, and fragrance at all times of the year in all parts of the garden. Right: Azaleas provide a colorful border during the spring. Middle left: The brilliant autumn foliage of winged euonymus (*Euonymus alatus*) rivals the impact of any flowering shrub. Middle right: Different foliage colors provide texture and contrast in this formal design. Bottom left: Daphne flowers can fill a garden with fragrance as well as providing color. Bottom right: Pyracantha berries supply color and interest in the midst of winter.

Even without leaves, a Japanese maple contributes interesting form and contrast to a winter landscape.

even appearance. A hedge can delineate space, form a garden border, act as a boundary, or create a screen for privacy. Just about any shrub will make a hedge, but there are some that grow uniformly and lend themselves to regular trimming. A list of shrubs that are particularly good for hedges appears on page 87.

Hedge shrubs come in three basic heights: low, medium, and tall. *Low* hedge shrubs (12 inches or less) are used for bordering flower beds and walks; *medium* hedge shrubs (up to 6 feet) are used for property borders and as backdrops for other plants; *tall* hedge shrubs (over 6 feet) are used for controlling wind and sun and for screening out objectionable views.

A good-looking hedge may require some effort to establish and maintain, but many people consider such effort well spent. Later chapters will tell you how to plant, trim, and maintain hedges. However, when reading the general discussions of shrubs, bear in mind that the information refers to *all* shrubs, including those that are not commonly used for hedge plantings.

Deciduous and Evergreen Shrubs

Shrubs may be deciduous or evergreen. *Deciduous* plants are those that lose their leaves in the fall and grow new ones in the spring. Cold winters are a decided boon: deciduous shrubs best known for their spring flowers, such as lilacs, need sufficient winter chilling to put on an optimum spring display. Mild-winter areas will support the successful growth of the same plants, but the spring display may be somewhat diminished.

Evergreen plants, in comparison, are always green, keeping their leaves the year around. There are two major categories of evergreens: broadleaved and coniferous (needleleaved).

The *broadleaved evergreens* generally tend to be more delicate than deciduous shrubs and are most adaptable to areas with reasonably mild winters. *Coniferous evergreens* grow satisfactorily in most climates—you will see them nearly everywhere in the United States and Canada.

Despite these broad generalizations about where to grow deciduous and evergreen shrubs, a determined gardener can often prove the rules false. If your winter temperatures say "No" but you want certain plants in your garden, see page 57 for ideas about winter protection and pages 27 to 29 for information on growing shrubs in containers. The surest way to grow shrubs successfully, however, is to choose varieties that are hardy for your climate. To find out which ones suit yours, check the Plant Selection Guide starting on page 76.

Broadleaved evergreens retain their leaves all year. Shown here is a boxwood (*Buxus sempervirens*) hedge, with pruned Japanese privet (*Ligustrum japonicum*) behind.

Coniferous evergreens, such as this false cypress (*Chamaecyparis* species), have inconspicuous flowers, but are available in a variety of shades of foliage.

These mature shrubs and hedges create an enclosed green and private space.

SHRUBS IN THE LANDSCAPE

Use plants to shape, color, and protect your space. The possibilities are almost endless.

To pick the right shrub for each garden area, you should know beforehand what mature form to expect. Often a shrub looks one way in a 5-gallon can and quite another after it has been in your garden for a few years. Most shrubs have a naturally occurring form, so don't try to force them to be something they're not; instead, be aware of what forms to expect and let each plant develop in its own way.

Basic Forms

Commercial shrub growers have divided shrubs into eight forms:

- ☐ pyramidal
- ☐ low-branching
- ☐ round-headed
- ☐ prostrate or spreading
- ☐ columnar
- ☐ compact or dense
- ☐ open
- ☐ weeping

These basic forms are indicated in the shrub descriptions in the Plant Selection Guide. The accompanying drawings will give you an idea of what these categories look like. One plant may combine several of these characteristics, but most often one form predominates.

Any plant can be pruned and trained into almost any shape. But keep in mind that when you direct a plant's growth into a shape that differs from its natural one, you create more work for yourself. It's easier to select shrubs that, on their own, will grow into the forms you want.

The form a shrub takes depends not only on its species and on the way it is pruned but also on where it is placed in the garden. If you want a shrub to be compact, or dense and full, plant it in full sun. If you want it to have a lacy, *open* look, plant it in the shade. In general, then, a shrub's shape is changed by the amount of light it receives, but the extent of this change depends on the particular plant. Some shrubs are barely affected by the light levels they receive, while others show a dramatic change. Japanese maples, for instance, are open, spreading, and graceful when grown in a shady location, but when grown in the sun the same variety is compact and globular.

In nature, shrubs form much of the *understory* of forests: the plants that grow under the tree canopy. These understory plants spread their branches to better catch the little light that penetrates through the trees above. Leaves are arranged in horizontal planes, with no leaf under another. Their habit is open, delicate, and graceful. Shrubs that grow in full sun—in meadows or brushland—grow smaller and are more closely knit, with smaller, tightly packed leaves and short, thick stems. The determining factor here is not shortage of light; it is exposure—to sun, wind, rain, and snow.

Forms of Shrubs

Pyramidal. This neat shape is common to many conifers. Use it in the formal garden without pruning frequently.

Low-branching. The lowest branches reach, or nearly reach, the ground. Use it as a filler for low-maintenance areas.

Round-headed. This shape gives a casual, natural look to the landscape. Use it as a specimen plant.

Prostrate. The branches either grow horizontally, or are weak and lie on the ground. Use it as a ground cover.

Designing With Shrubs

The design basics discussed in this chapter will help you to make most general design decisions.

There are two extremes in landscape style—formal and informal. Many people think that the choice of plants is largely responsible for creating these styles. But that isn't so: the same plants can be used in either setting without disturbing the formal or informal feeling. It is *how* plants are used that makes the difference. A garden's overall style is established by lines, shapes, spaces, and enclosures. Plants, materials, and structures are chosen to complement and enhance the desired effect.

Formal design. The earliest recorded garden designs—in Egypt in 2200 B.C.—were laid out along formal lines. The ancient Greeks, and the Romans after them, also fashioned gardens in this style. Much later, during the Renaissance, the classical formal garden was revived in Europe. As a type of design, the formal garden has been with us ever since. It has survived for thousands of years because it is basically simple and pleasing to the eye. Considering this venerable history, it is not surprising that the guidelines for establishing such gardens have become highly refined. However, they have not necessarily become complex; in many ways, a formal garden is the easiest to lay out.

Choosing Shrub Heights to Match Situation

1 foot

Use this height for a low ground cover or as an edging for the planting bed or path.

1½ feet

A hedge this height is difficult to step across. Use it to direct traffic.

3 feet

Use as a barrier, hedge, or deep ground cover.

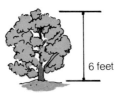

6 feet

A hedge this height gives privacy without a "walled-in" feeling.

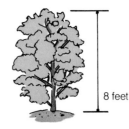

8 feet

Use as a background planting, a windbreak, or a screen for privacy and security.

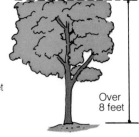

Over 8 feet

Use as a background for a large garden, a wind or sound screen, or a small tree.

Columnar. The branches angle upward sharply, creating a narrow outline. Use it for dramatic emphasis in the landscape.

Compact. The leaves grow close together, making the shrub dense and opaque. It is typical of shrubs grown in full sun. Use as a screen.

Open. You can see through this shrub, making its framework visible. It is typical of shrubs grown in the shade. Use as a specimen.

Weeping. The stems and branches are strong, but new twigs are weak and bend toward the ground. Use for a solemn, graceful touch.

Symmetry is the key to a formal garden—take a look at the photograph below. A symmetrical garden is usually laid out on straight lines, with whatever appears on the left side repeated on the right. The outermost dimension of the garden is frequently rectangular, and this shape is repeated in other parts of the plan—pools, patios, flower beds, and so on. The center of interest often revolves around a single object—a statue, pool, sundial, or outstanding specimen plant. For optimum effect, it is usually placed to the rear of the garden.

Traditionally, a formal garden relies heavily on compact evergreen plants that are often pruned and kept trimmed to various well-defined shapes. In its extreme form, this method of pruning is called topiary (see page 61). Neatly trimmed rows of privet or coniferous evergreen plants are the most common type of formal hedge planting, and descend from time-honored design concepts.

Informal design. Informal gardens are frequently considered more "natural," and in a sense they are. The curved lines give a relaxed feeling, and plants are allowed to develop their own shapes. If you prefer the informal look, don't mistake it for lack of design: you will still need clear ideas about planting patterns. The best informal gardens are laid out every bit as carefully as their formal counterparts.

The formal design of this garden is based on the rectangular shape of the whole area, with a few semicircular curves added to provide interest and contrast.

SHRUBS IN THE LANDSCAPE / 19

The gentle curves of the informal design of this landscape invite the visitor to explore the farther reaches of the garden.

Both deciduous and evergreen plants grow well together in informal settings, with as many different combinations as there are gardens. Because no precise rules govern the informal garden, more design freedom is possible every step of the way.

Most of the common flowering shrubs, such as lilac, viburnum, abelia, or hibiscus, make very attractive hedges for informal gardens. They produce the most flowers, and require less frequent and less drastic pruning than does, say, the privet; consequently, flowering hedges usually have a less even appearance than do the more formal types.

Broadleaved plants (both evergreen and deciduous) may not be as compact or finely textured as traditional hedge plants, but they can still make good hedges. These less uniform, more sprawling hedges are often referred to as "informal" hedges. But can any hedge be considered strictly as informal planting? Plants of a single variety in a straight line will give a structured, formalized feeling, no matter how they are pruned. If you want a truly informal effect, plant a variety of shrubs and avoid straight lines, similar to what might occur in nature. The result will be more like a barrier than a traditional hedge, but it will be more in keeping with an informal, naturalistic garden.

The less your garden emphasizes order, the more your chores are reduced—at least partly. Plants will need less pruning, leaves can be left where they fall, and a tricycle or hammock will be viewed as part of the whole.

Balanced plantings. Whether your garden is to be formal or informal, good design requires *balance*. In a formal garden the balance seems obvious, although there may be more to it than immediately meets the eye. In an informal garden the balance is not as obvious, but is every bit as important. Balance leads to a sense of continuity among different kinds of plants. No matter what the garden style, balance can be achieved in these time-honored ways:

☐ *Plant taller-growing varieties behind shorter-growing ones.* There's no sense in planting short plants behind tall ones unless you intend to keep the tall ones severely pruned.

☐ *Place plants with lighter-colored foliage in front of those with darker foliage.* The arrangement of light leaves in front of dark ones is more pleasing, and dramatic, than the other way around. When the sun shines down on lighter green leaves against a dark backdrop, the color is particularly intense and striking.

☐ *Select background plants for their dark foliage, their base-branching form, and their leaf texture.* Background plants are just that—backgrounds for more showy plants in front. They often perform the same function as hedges, but are pruned less regularly and are allowed to reach greater heights. To minimize confusion, it is usually wise to make a background out of the same variety, or out of two similar varieties in an alternating pattern.

☐ *Limit the number of plant varieties.* This applies not only to the background but to the whole garden as well. There are sound reasons for this approach. Grouping one plant variety makes a stronger design statement than planting individual specimens of assorted, unrelated varieties. Plants with an "open" growing habit will look more substantial when planted in a group. Also, gardens composed of a few select varieties have an organized, purposeful look and tend to be more easily maintained than gardens sporting a mixture of several plants.

Granted, a landscape with only a few kinds of plants may not be your idea of a garden. So don't feel obliged to follow this plan if you like a lot of variety. An English cottage garden, for example, has a deliberate and charming confusion: plants are added at the gardener's whim without reference to a formal design. After all, style is a personal matter. Your garden should reflect your taste, no one else's.

Balance in your garden design will result in more dramatic displays of your plant materials. Left: Massed shrubbery gives structure and visual containment to the garden. Middle: A splashy hedge of blooming azaleas is set off by the dark green foliage of the hedge behind. Right: A tall, finely textured hedge serves as the perfect foil for a border of roses.

This cottage garden at Sissinghurst Castle in England combines in an informal way a profusion of lower-growing plants against a background of taller-growing flowering shrubs.

Color. When most people think of color in the garden, they think only of flowers or flowering shrubs. Leaf color, however, exists in truly amazing variations. For example, there are many shades of green: gray-green, blue-green, yellow-green, brownish-green, bright green, and dull green. There are so many different shades of green, in fact, that you would be hard put to find a nursery with five different shrubs of an identical color.

Besides the many shades of green, shrubs also come with gray, red, purple, yellow, and variegated foliage. Put any of these beside a green shrub and judge the effect for yourself. And don't overlook the colors the seasons bring—the bare bark and branches of winter, the bright new growth and flowering of spring, the more muted tones of summer, and the fruits and changing foliage of fall.

Some gardeners like the understatement of an all-green garden, while others want more variety. Before you select a shrub, think about what kind of seasonal show you prefer. Do you want a totally green display, or do you want other colors as well? If you live in an area with extended winters, consider that shrubs with colorful bark and twigs, persistent fruit, and interesting leaf texture may actually give as much character to the garden as shrubs with flowers and green leaves. When choosing flowering shrubs, find out what colors the flowers are and when they bloom. Then plot their locations so that the colors will complement one another rather than clash. This formula applies to foliage, too. Try to imagine in advance whether a new shrub with gray-green leaves will look attractive next to an existing shrub with yellow leaves, and so forth.

In mild-winter climates camellias will produce colorful blooms from winter to early spring.

Texture. When selecting shrubs, notice the different kinds of texture produced by a plant's leaf size and pattern. And don't forget the texture produced by the pattern of the bare branches, twigs, and bark during the dormant season. Are the leaves small and compact, giving a neat, clipped appearance? Or are they large and uneven, creating a bold, informal feeling? Is their pattern coarse or fine? What does the shrub look like in winter?

Judge the texture of a plant close up, then look at it again from 40 feet away. Does the texture still look the same? Some shrubs lose their pleasing effect when they are planted too far away from a favorite viewing area. Similarly, the texture of a large-leafed shrub may be out of scale in a confined space or when viewed only at close range.

In general, plant more finely textured plants in front of more coarsely textured varieties—a pleasing pattern of graduated textures that follows tried-and-true theories of proportion and scale. If you favor a dramatic effect, choose coarsely textured, large-leafed shrubs. If you like a more tailored, formal landscape, look for compact shrubs with comparatively

The fine texture and blue-green foliage of juniper make a pleasing contrast with evergreen euonymus.

Left top: The magnificent display of this specimen azalea is framed by a border of dark green foliage.

Left bottom: A contrasting but coordinated display of color and texture is provided by this planting of reddish purple Japanese barberry (*Berberis thunbergii* 'Atropurpurea'), the dark green of bird's nest spruce (*Picea* species), the silvery foliage of Japanese pieris (*Pieris japonica* 'Variegata'), and the brilliant yellow of fullmoon maple (*Acer* species).

The difference in foliage texture—the form and size of the leaves—complements the different colors of Japanese barberry 'Atropurpurea' and Japanese pieris 'Variegata'.

small leaves. Many of the conifers can also contribute to the formal effect, depending on how they are used.

Special effects. You can easily achieve special effects with shrubs known as *specimen plants*, or just *specimens*. Specimen plants draw attention to themselves: they usually have some feature or combination of features that sets them apart from other shrubs. A specimen plant's uniqueness may derive from its flowers, berries, shape, color, texture, or rarity, as well as from its personal significance.

The number of specimens used in a single landscape is usually limited to one or two—any more than that and the special quality would be diminished. The very specialness of these plants has a great deal to do with their location in the garden. They should be carefully placed where they can command center stage. For example, if a specimen's unique features need close viewing, place the plant by the front door or walkway so that it receives the attention it deserves.

Practical Considerations

As you design your ideal garden, keep in mind that shrubs can be practical as well as attractive. By shielding your yard from the wind, cutting down on noise, hiding an ugly ground area, or camouflaging part of an oddly shaped building, you can vastly improve the general environment. Here are some of the ways in which shrubs and hedges can do double duty.

When planning color in your garden, consider the season when the shrubs will be colorful. Right top: Spring-blooming shrubs such as forsythia complement bulbs and perennials. Right bottom: The stems of red-osier dogwood (*Cornus sericea*) have a striking winter color.

Noise reduction. Shrubs absorb noise. For the best noise reduction, plant the shrubs—preferably the tall-growing kind—as densely as possible. Plants with compact, leafy foliage deter noise better than the more open varieties. University tests have shown that thick shrub plantings can reduce noise up to 20 percent, compared with unplanted areas. If noise is a year-round problem, choose an evergreen variety.

Wind protection. Place shrubs designed as a windbreak on the side of the yard from which the wind usually blows. (Sometimes windbreaks are needed on more than one side.) A single hedgerow of shrubs will stop the wind, but a double row, planted on staggered centers, will work even more effectively.

Experiments using anemometers have shown that maximum wind reduction occurs within a space of from four to seven times the height of the windbreak. Using this calculation, a hedge that will eventually grow 6 feet high should be planted a maximum of 24 to 42 feet away from the area you want to protect.

Privacy. Shrubs can set off secluded areas within a garden as well as define the public/private boundary at your property's edge. Perhaps you want to block off a street view, or want a green barrier between your yard and your neighbor's. And within your own landscape, you may want to isolate an area set aside for sunning from major traffic.

Noise Reduction

An unbroken, dense row of shrubs can significantly reduce noise levels from traffic, a playground, or a neighboring commercial district. In addition, the hedge acts as a baffle for dirt and debris, keeping your yard cleaner and more pleasant.

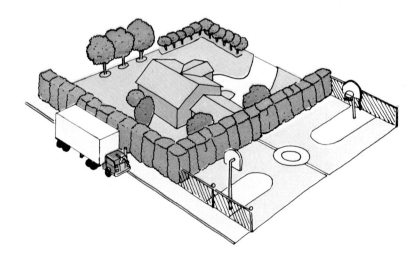

Wind Protection

The wind-control properties of hedges and rows of trees have been known by gardeners and farmers for centuries. When the force of the wind is broken and diffused, the microclimate of your yard is improved. If afternoon winds are a common occurrence in your area, a hedge can do a great deal to increase your enjoyment of your garden.

Privacy

There are many ways to achieve privacy in a garden, but the most attractive is a wall of leafy green, perhaps with occasional splashes of color. Choose formal, trimmed hedges, or put in less formal plantings of shrubs, and leave them to grow in their own way. In localities with height limitations on fences between neighboring yards, a hedge is a good way to get the maximum in privacy.

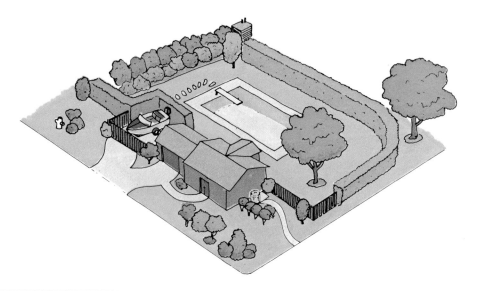

Guides and Barriers

Shrubs can do a great deal to direct pedestrian traffic. They can also act as barriers, keeping people, bicycles, and cars from entering areas where you don't want them. Don't use delicate plants; plants with thorns or prickly foliage are best. If you live on a street with heavy automobile traffic, you will probably want to choose dense shrubs to help deflect glare from streetlights and headlights.

Guides and barriers. Shrubs have still another practical property: their ability to act as barriers. Homeowners often overlook this attribute, but it's worth your attention. Barrier plantings can keep people out of areas where you don't want them and guide them to areas where you do.

When using shrubs as guides or barriers, think of them as architectural forms rather than as plants. Select barrier plants with an eye for their density and sturdiness. If you really want to keep people out of certain areas, look for thorny or prickly varieties. (See list on page 87.)

The thornier shrubs also work well under windows to deter prowlers. But make sure that the shrub grows *tightly* against the house. If there is access space between the house and the shrub, the shrub will actually aid the prowler by acting as a screen while he jimmies the window.

Dust reduction. A solid row of shrubs can reduce dust considerably. According to a test conducted in one large city, the dust accumulation on the leeward side of a planted area was reduced by 75 percent. Shrubs also trap larger pieces of debris that could otherwise litter your yard. If you live in a dusty, sooty area, select pollution-resistant species, and give the leaves of barrier plantings a good shower now and then to keep them healthy. A list of pollution-tolerant shrubs is included in the Plant Selection Guide on page 76.

Structural aids. If your house has some unattractive architectural features, carefully placed shrubs can help disguise the problem. Houses with uneven proportions, oddly shaped windows, or tall foundation walls are all good candidates for shrub rehabilitation. These kinds of custom corrections require only a relatively small investment of time and money, but they can make a big difference.

When selecting shrubs as structural aids, it's again best to view them as architectural forms. Think about the form needed to correct a proportion problem or to balance out a poorly placed window. You might even try photographing the outside of your house, then drawing in the shape needed. Take the picture to your local garden center and see what suggestions the staff has to offer.

Growing Shrubs in Containers

The minute you plant a shrub in a container, you give it a singular importance that can turn it into a prized specimen. A row of shrubs in the garden may not get a second glance, but a potted shrub is hard to overlook. Shrubs in containers often turn out to be the favorites in a garden, and the extra attention they receive often results in spectacular plants. For a list of shrubs that do well in containers see page 86.

Mobility. Aside from their specimen qualities, container shrubs also have practical benefits:

- ☐ If you move frequently, your shrubs can go along with you.
- ☐ Containers allow you to have shrubs that wouldn't ordinarily grow in your native soil.
- ☐ You can grow shrubs that wouldn't survive a cold winter outdoors. Just roll the containers to protected areas before cold weather begins.
- ☐ The right container shrubs can easily enhance your patio or entranceway; you can also change their positions in these areas.
- ☐ You can move shrubs in full bloom to a prominent spot for a few days, then return them to their usual locations after the show.
- ☐ You can shift your shrubs around as the seasons dictate. Species that don't normally do well in your climate will thrive if you provide the right protection at the right time.

The thorny stems of this flowering quince (*Chaenomeles speciosa*) trained against a house wall can be an effective deterrent to prowlers.

Planting in Containers

1. Check drainage holes.
Drainage holes should be large (at least ¾ inch) and numerous (maximum 1 foot apart). If necessary, make more holes. There should be enough room between the container and the ground surface it sits on for water to escape from the holes in its bottom. If necessary, nail 1-inch cleats to the bottom, or improvise some sort of stand.

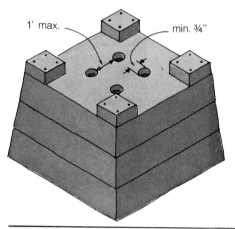

1' max.   min. ¾"

2. Cover drainage holes.
Place a piece of broken crockery over each hole or spread a piece of window screen across the bottom of the container to keep the soil from washing out.

3. Place soil in container.
Put enough planting mix in the container so that the top of the shrub's rootball will be 2 to 3 inches below the rim of the container.

4. Remove shrub from can.
See Step 5 of Planting Steps on page 46.

5. Place shrub in container.
Orient the shrub so that the stem is at the center of the container and is not leaning (even if you have to tilt the rootball to accomplish this).

6. Add soil.
Pour soil around the rootball until it is level with the top of the rootball. Do not plant the shrub deeper than it was in the nursery container. The soil level should be 2 to 3 inches below the edge of container.

7. Water.
Water the shrub a number of times. This will help leach out excess salts in the soil, and also wet the soil thoroughly and settle it around the rootball.

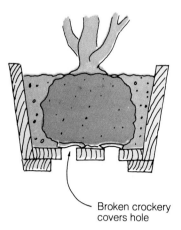

Broken crockery covers hole

Choosing appropriate shrubs.

Size. The intermediate size of most shrubs makes them good candidates for container culture. If you are familiar with only those shrubs grown in open ground, you might think it impractical to grow wisteria, boxwood, or lilac in a container. But remember all those plants growing very well in containers at your local nursery.

Growth. Any shrub will grow in a container, but those that grow somewhat slowly and have a compact plant habit will do best. Fast-growing shrubs will need repotting more often and will require more pruning. Because dwarf shrubs are naturally small, they make ideal subjects for container culture. Pay special attention to these unusual plants on your next trip to the nursery. For more information on dwarfs, see page 89.

Hardiness. Container plants are particularly prone to winter damage, so use species that are hardy to at least one zone (10°) colder than your area. Or you can attach movable bases to the containers so that you can move the plants to a protected location—under the eaves of the house, for example.

Maintenance procedures. Growing shrubs in containers is not that different from other forms of gardening. However, a few of the plants' requirements are more critical.

Soil requirements. The soil used to fill the containers makes a difference. If your containers are not overly large or if you have only a few of them, consider using one of the lightweight packaged soil mixes. Container-grown plants demand proper drainage, and these mixes provide about the best drainage possible.

If you use garden soil to fill your containers, be sure to mix in large quantities of soil amendments—compost, peat moss, nitrogen-stabilized sawdust, leaf mold, ground fir bark, or pine bark. Blend the soil amendments with the soil; do not simply apply them as a surface layer. Add perlite to lighten the mix and improve drainage. Amendments should constitute at least one-half of the final mix. Common proportions are: 1 part garden soil, 1 part perlite or sand, and 1 part organic material.

When you fill a container with soil, be sure to leave 2 or 3 inches between the top of the soil and the top of the pot. This space holds the water while it soaks through the soil to the bottom, and enables you to water in a single

Dwarf varieties are particularly suited for growing in containers. Compare the growth habits of *Pittosporum tobira* 'Wheeler's Dwarf' (upper left) with the original species (lower right).

Left: With proper training even a large, spreading vine such as wisteria can be an unusual and dramatic container plant.

Below top: Remember that container plants need more frequent watering than those planted in the garden.

Below bottom: Rhododendrons are long-time favorites for container shrubs.

application rather than having to return to the container several times before the soil is thoroughly soaked.

Watering and feeding. A container shrub's roots are very restricted: they do not have the free run of a good garden soil from which to draw moisture and nutrients. Thus, a container plant depends almost totally on the gardener. To compensate for this restricted root space, never let your plants wilt from lack of moisture. Water on a regular basis; nurseries commonly water container plants every day during the summer. To wet the soil evenly from the top of the pot to the bottom, apply enough water to run out of the drainage hole.

This increased amount of water flushes nutrients through the soil much more rapidly than with plants growing in the ground. To compensate, lightly feed container plants with a complete fertilizer; during the active growing season of spring and summer, this may be as frequently as every two weeks. Or you can use a slow-release fertilizer. Many gardeners prefer to feed container plants with liquid fertilizer because it is so easy to apply. For information about fertilizers, see page 54.

Caring for roots. Over a period of years, the roots may fill the container so that the plant becomes rootbound. If this occurs, you can do either of two things: transplant the plant into a larger container, or shave off a portion of the roots and add some new soil to the container. If you decide on the latter, lightly prune the top of the plant to compensate for root loss. Repeat this revitalization process every few years, or whenever the shrub seems to have diminished in vigor despite regular waterings and feedings.

Changing locations. If you want to move container shrubs from one spot to another, do it gradually. A radical change in environment can injure plants if it is made too abruptly. Be especially careful about moving a plant grown in the shade into a sunnier location; leaves that have grown in the shade can be badly burned if moved directly into the hot sun. Make the change in a succession of moves, allowing the shrub a few days to adjust to each stage.

Many flowering shrubs can be moved inside the house for a few days of special attention during the blooming period. With any outdoor shrub, however, an indoor stay of more than a few days to a week is not recommended. While outdoor shrubs are inside, keep them in as cool a location as possible; above all, keep them away from direct blasts of dry furnace heat or cold air from an air conditioner.

Selecting plants at your local nursery is the
easiest way to judge their attractiveness, but
remember to consider each plant's cultural
requirements as well as its visual relationship
to other plants in the garden.

PLANNING AHEAD

*To save yourself the trouble and
disappointment of planting the wrong
shrub, take the time to assess both
your garden's growth potential and
your buying options.*

No matter what style you choose for your garden, vigorous and healthy plants are essential for an attractive landscape. Plants become vigorous and healthy by receiving proper care and by being planted in a congenial environment. The importance of matching a plant's needs with the conditions of a particular spot in your yard cannot be overemphasized.

You may admire a shrub in a catalog, a nursery, or a friend's garden, but don't plant it in *your* garden unless you have a strong conviction about it. And before planting anything, learn about its requirements. Does it need full sun, filtered shade, or morning sun only until 11 o'clock? In what kind of soil does it grow best—an acid peat soil, a deep garden loam, or a quick-draining, sandy soil? Will this shrub tolerate "wet feet" and grow next to a leaking hose bib, or will regular applications of water from a nearby sprinkler system cause it to curl up and die?

A pleasing, balanced planting of shrubs requires forethought and care. When you are at the nursery or garden center, take your time. Remember that once you get the shrubs in the ground, they are going to be there a long time. (However, they can be moved with relative ease the first year or two, if necessary.)

If you plan to buy more than one shrub, place your candidates together in one place at the nursery as they will appear in your garden. How do they look together? Do their textures, forms, and colors complement one another? A certain amount of diversity is necessary to create interest. For example, a dark green, needled evergreen shrub may look attractive with a finely textured, broadleaved shrub. Or a plant with spiky, swordlike foliage may combine well with a compact, leafy shrub.

If you are adding new shrubs to established plantings, bring sample leaves of your existing plants with you to the nursery. As you pick out new plants, mentally reconstruct your garden as it is now. Will the additions fit into the picture, creating an interesting, balanced scene?

It's easy to get carried away at the nursery or garden center and buy shrubs on the basis of looks alone, but if the plants you buy won't grow in the locations you have in mind, they'll produce nothing but needless aggravation. So find out about plant requirements by talking to the clerks, or take along helpful descriptions (such as those found in the Plant Selection Guide). Then match those requirements to the sites available in your yard. Not all shrubs, however, have strict cultural and climatic requirements. Except for the fussiest varieties, shrubs will tolerate a considerable range of environments. Just make sure that your yard suits the climate zone for the particular shrub, and don't ask it to grow in conditions alien to its needs.

Even if the right spot doesn't occur naturally in your garden, you can make many modifications to create a more suitable site. Information on the following pages will tell you how to change the growing conditions, including the climate, to match your particular plants' needs.

Assessing Your Soil

In general, shrubs are very adaptable. If given the proper care, they will grow well in most soils. However, you will be far ahead of the game if you are aware of what type of soil you have. Most soils fall into a wide middle range that provides a healthy environment for many plants. But if your soil happens to be representative of one of the extremes of soil conditions, knowing that fact will enable you to select plants that adapt particularly well to that type of soil, or to determine how to improve the soil. Every generalization about soils has exceptions; nevertheless, some general comments will give you perspective on the vast amount of information available.

Every soil has *depth*, *fertility*, *texture*, and *structure*. Picture this portrait of the ideal garden soil: its topsoil is several feet deep; it is reasonably fertile; it has a good balance of sand, silt, and clay particles (texture); and it has just the right amount of air space between those particles to promote both good drainage and water retention (structure). In addition, it has an acceptable acid/alkaline balance conducive to the healthy growth of most plants.

In actuality, there are very few ideal soils. In most cases, however, soil problems can be solved with relative ease. And because soil is complex in nature, improving one aspect of it usually eliminates several other problems as well.

Soil testing. The most accurate way to find out about your soil is to take samples from the areas in which you intend to plant and have them tested in a soil laboratory. For information on where to go, call your local county extension agent and find out whether your state offers a soil-testing program.

Meanwhile, you can do some relatively simple but helpful things on your own. First, ask your neighbors, local nursery, garden center, or county extension agent about your area's general soil type. Then test your own soil.

Testing for texture (the relative proportions of sand, silt, and clay particles). Dig several holes 6 to 8 inches deep in the general area where you expect to plant new shrubs or hedges. (If you intend to plant many shrubs in different parts of the yard, do this experiment for each individual area.)

Fill a quart jar about two-thirds full of water and add soil until the jar is almost full. For the clearest stratification, also add about ½ teaspoon of detergent per quart of water. Screw on the jar lid and shake vigorously. Then let the soil settle. In a short time the heaviest sand particles will sink to the bottom, making the sand layer visible. Then the silt layer will form. Finally, the extremely small clay particles will settle on the top. These particles are so small that the molecular action of the water alone may keep them in suspension indefinitely. The results of the experiment should be ready to read in two or three hours.

Determining Soil Texture

Shake some garden soil in water with a little dish detergent. The larger particles (sand) will settle out in the first minute, the silt will settle out in the next 2 hours, and the clay over the next several weeks.

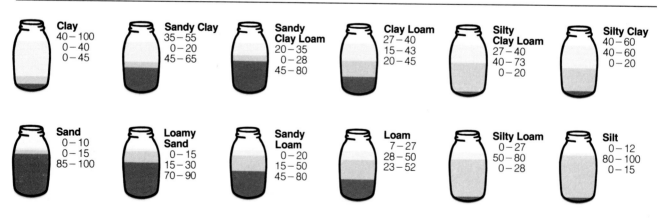

Clay 40–100 / 0–40 / 0–45	Sandy Clay 35–55 / 0–20 / 45–65	Sandy Clay Loam 20–35 / 0–28 / 45–80	Clay Loam 27–40 / 15–43 / 20–45	Silty Clay Loam 27–40 / 40–73 / 0–20	Silty Clay 40–60 / 40–60 / 0–20
Sand 0–10 / 0–15 / 85–100	Loamy Sand 0–15 / 15–30 / 70–90	Sandy Loam 0–20 / 15–50 / 45–80	Loam 7–27 / 28–50 / 23–52	Silty Loam 0–27 / 50–80 / 0–28	Silt 0–12 / 80–100 / 0–15

Carry out this same test using soil from different places in your garden. Then chart each test by holding a piece of paper up to the jar and marking off the layers. Compare the proportions of the elements with the illustrations on the opposite page.

☐ Your soil is *sandy* if there is over 45 percent sand and no more than 30 percent silt.
☐ Your soil is *sandy loam* if there is 45 to 80 percent sand and 15 to 50 percent silt.
☐ You have a *medium loam* if there is 23 to 52 percent sand and 28 to 50 percent silt.
☐ Your soil is *clay loam* if there is 20 to 45 percent sand, 15 to 43 percent silt, and 27 to 40 percent clay.
☐ You have a *heavy clay* soil if there is over 40 percent clay.

Loam soils are the best garden soils, but both sandy and clay soils can be dramatically improved by adding organic matter. It may be compost, rotted manure, nitrogen-stabilized bark or sawdust, ground corn cobs, or other locally available material. You can add the organic matter to the entire yard or only to the areas about to receive new shrubs, but in either case be sure to add enough. Organic matter should comprise from one-third to one-half of the final mixed soil. This means that if you cultivate to a depth of 8 inches, you should add 3 to 4 inches of organic matter over the top of the soil before you mix it in.

Testing for drainage (how fast or slow water moves through the soil). Remove both ends from a coffee can. In the area you want to test, push the can into the soil to a depth of 4 inches. Fill the remainder of the can with water and let it drain through. Fill the can again and time how long it takes for the water level to drop 1 inch. If it takes longer than two hours, you probably can expect to have problems with plants "drowning," especially those plants intolerant of "wet feet."

The way a soil drains relates to its structure—how the various soil particles are held together. The same methods for improving the soil's texture also work to improve its structure; this improvement, in turn, helps drainage. Whether there is too much air space (as in sandy soils), or too little (as in clay soils), adding organic matter will help correct the problem. If areas of your property have standing water, you have a more serious problem, and you may want to install drainage tiles.

Testing for fertility. Even professional soil laboratories have difficulty testing soil fertility accurately. Because levels of specific nutrients are so difficult to determine, most gardeners simply add a complete fertilizer to the soil at prescribed intervals during the growing season to make up for any deficiencies. Whatever product you use, be sure to read and follow all label instructions.

Testing for hardpan. Hardpan is a cementlike layer of soil, a few inches thick, that is sometimes found a foot or two beneath the surface of porous soil. Hardpan stops the downward movement of water, thus causing drainage problems. To test for hardpan, dig a hole about 2 feet deep (a posthole digger works well). If you hit hardpan, the simplest way to provide drainage is to break up the hardpan under each plant with a pick or crowbar. You do not have to remove or replace hardpan—just provide a way for the water to pass through it.

Soil pH—how important is it? You may have heard about soil pH and wondered what it is and if it is really important. The pH of soil *is* important, but pH problems are easy to correct.

The pH (potential Hydrogen) is a chemical term that indicates acidity or alkalinity. The pH scale shows relative acidity or alkalinity. The scale runs from 0 (extremely acid) to 14 (extremely alkaline); the middle of the

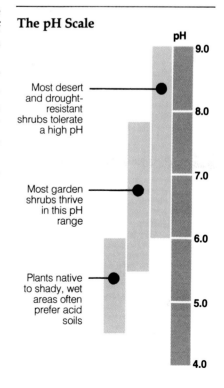

The pH Scale

pH

9.0

Most desert and drought-resistant shrubs tolerate a high pH

8.0

7.0

Most garden shrubs thrive in this pH range

6.0

Plants native to shady, wet areas often prefer acid soils

5.0

4.0

scale—7—is the neutral point. Most shrubs do best in a slightly to very slightly acid soil, down to a pH of about 6.

Adjusting the pH. Among the popular plants that thrive in acid soil are rhododendrons, azaleas, daphne, pieris, blueberries, gardenias, camellias, and nandina. To make soil more acidic, most gardeners simply add considerable quantities of sphagnum peat moss. However, if your soil is already too acidic for the shrubs you want to plant (a condition common in areas with heavy rainfall), add ground limestone for the most reliable cure. Check with your nursery staff or county agent for application rates and the best time of year.

If alkalinity is the problem—particularly in some of the arid soils of the West and in the limestone soils of the East and Midwest—correct the condition with garden sulfur or ferrous sulphate (both available at your nursery). If you tell the county agent or nursery staff the present pH of your soil, the type of soil you have, and what pH level you are trying to achieve, they will be able to tell you how much sulfur to add.

Testing for pH. It's easy to test for pH when you use an inexpensive kit available at most nurseries and scientific supply houses. Or, if you have a soil test done for you, the pH reading will automatically be included in your report. (See the other information about pH on this page.) You can also use a meter to check the pH of your soil. Just insert the electronic probe into the soil, and the meter will indicate the level of acidity or alkalinity.

Assessing Your Microclimates

The positions of your house, fences, and slopes all help modify the climate in your yard. Make it a point to know all the different climates there. Then, when you see an attractive plant that likes cool soil and diffused sunlight and tolerates excessive moisture, you'll know if you've got a place for it.

So before you buy any new shrubs, take an inventory of the microclimates in various parts of your yard. Each plant has its optimum climatic requirement: shrubs that grow well on the north side of the house will probably find conditions on the south side intolerable.

Your house as regulator. Your house is a constant climate regulator, with almost perpetual shade on the north side, full sun and the most radiation on the south, half shade and hot sun on the west, and half shade and milder sun on the east. The walls themselves radiate heat to varying degrees, and roof overhangs conserve outgoing radiation, warming the air under the eaves on frosty nights. With only this basic information you can assess areas in your yard and match them with plant requirements.

The evergreen oak over these azaleas shelters them from sun and wind and creates the ideal microclimate in which they thrive.

Tips for Climate Modification

Once you know about the microclimates in your garden, you may want to change them. Here are some pointers for increasing or decreasing certain climate characteristics.

Preserving warmth
☐ Plan for maximum flat surfaces—paved areas, patios, untilled ground, rock or masonry areas. These surfaces absorb large amounts of the sun's radiation and, in turn, give off heat to surrounding areas.
☐ Plan for a "ceiling" in your yard, such as a patio cover or an overhead lath, which traps the warm air that reradiates from other surfaces at night.
☐ Plant or build windbreaks and cold-air diverters. Cold air sinks to the lowest part of the yard. If you can divert its path with a hedge or fence, you can keep the shielded area warmer.
☐ Plan sun pockets that trap the sun on cool spring mornings. A two-sided fence or screen can create a warm climate that differs radically from the climate in the rest of your yard.

Providing coolness
☐ Grow vines on overhead structures and plant shade trees.
☐ Plant untilled ground with ground cover, lawn, or other plant material. This deflects summer heat, which can affect the temperature of adjoining areas.
☐ Prune the lower growth of trees and large shrubs for increased air circulation.

Reducing the effects of wind
☐ Plant or build windbreaks, baffles, or diverters. To find out about the best placement of hedges and fences, see the information on pages 24 to 27.
☐ Make semienclosed outdoor living areas with fences and solid overhead coverings.

Decreasing humidity
☐ Provide maximum ventilation by pruning trees and shrubs in an open manner.
☐ Make sure the drainage of the entire yard is sufficient; no spot should have standing water.
☐ Make maximum use of paved or decked areas—flat areas encourage drying winds.

Increasing humidity
☐ Plant for thick overhead vegetation, which slows evaporation and adds water through transpiration.
☐ Use plenty of ground covers.
☐ Add a pool or fountain—it can have both a real and an imagined effect in making a yard seem less arid.

Nurseries and Garden Centers

Nurseries and garden centers are usually delightful places to shop, and once there, most people have a little extra time to spend "just looking around." While you're strolling, keep your eyes open for clues about the nursery and the plants that grow there. Are the growing beds well ordered and easy to walk through? Do the plants look well watered? Are the signs and plant labels legible and informative, and do they give both common and botanical names? Most important, is the sales staff helpful and well informed? A short talk with a good nursery professional can give you much information that would be difficult to get elsewhere. (A clerk who doesn't know the answer to a specific question can probably find someone else who does, or locate the information in a reference book.) Because the information you receive from your nursery is localized—and the result of many years' individual

Attractive displays, well-tended merchandise, and informative signs are indications that a nursery stocks dependable plants.

experiences—knowledgeable staff can be a valuable and continuing source of trustworthy information.

While it's fun to stroll through the nursery to see what's new, if you're an impulsive shopper you had perhaps better forego the temptation. Before you leave home, in fact, make a list of those plants you have room for and are ready to plant *now*. If you follow the design suggestions on pages 18 to 27, you'll know what sizes, shapes, colors, and textures are worth your consideration.

Mail-order Nurseries

Mail-order nurseries offer a good alternative to a local nursery or garden center. Their colorful catalogs, which arrive during the cold days of winter, offer an enticement to garden-hungry readers. Mail-order nurseries often have a limited shipping season and limited supplies of certain plants; on the other hand, they are often good sources for the rare or unusual plants unavailable at your local nursery.

Many of these mail-order nurseries have been in business for generations and offer the highest quality plant material. Don't be bothered if your order is sent from some distance away; most local nurseries also receive their plants from outside the area. Nonetheless, plants that are shipped through the mails undergo a degree of stress and need to be "babied" as soon as they arrive. Take them out of the shipping containers and plant them as soon as you can. See pages 45 to 47 for planting instructions, and follow carefully.

If you're ordering plants from a mail-order firm for the first time, it's a good idea to limit your order. Find out how you like the plants, whether they arrive in good condition, and whether they perform well in your yard. Then, if all goes smoothly, you can order more. Most reputable mail-order nurseries will stand behind their stock with a reasonable guarantee.

How Shrubs Are Sold

Containers. Shrubs are most commonly sold in containers, which may be metal, plastic, or wood, and which are available in many sizes. Most shrubs

Careful inspection of the health and condition of shrubs before you buy will ensure that your plants will get off to a good start in your garden.

are planted in 1- or 5-gallon containers. Specimen shrubs are sometimes sold in 15-gallon containers. How do you know what size shrub to buy? The key is patience: if you buy a smaller size, you will have to wait longer for the shrub to grow to ideal proportions. For this reason many people choose the 5-gallon-size shrub, even though it costs considerably more.

When it's time to make a choice, keep this formula in mind: It takes approximately one to one and a half years for a 1-gallon-size shrub to reach 5-gallon size. But in two and a half to three years, shrubs that started out in both 1-gallon and 5-gallon containers will have reached about the same size.

Plastic cans allow you to slip the shrubs out easily, without damaging the root system; as an added bonus, you can reuse the plastic container. To get plants out of metal cans (except for those with straight or crimped sides), the cans must be cut. You can either cut them yourself or have them cut at the nursery. Wooden containers holding large specimen shrubs must be dismantled before planting time.

No matter what the container is made of, make sure it's in good shape before you buy any shrub. Rusted metal, split plastic, or disintegrated wood usually means that the plant has been in the nursery for a long time. That in turn means that the plant's roots may have grown into the ground soil at the nursery or the plant has become badly potbound and may have developed girdling roots that may eventually kill it. Avoid such plants.

Checking the root system. The shrub should be well anchored in the container, but not rootbound. Try lifting the plant gently by the trunk: if the soil moves at all, the plant has not had time to develop roots throughout the rootball. If the plant has been in the container too long, however, growth will have stopped, and will be difficult to start again. Check for thick masses of roots on the soil surface or around the sides of the soil ball. If you don't prune and straighten the roots when you put the plant in your garden, they will go on growing in the same circle and never expand into the garden soil. Heavy winds may topple the plant because it is so poorly anchored in the soil. And even if it remains upright, the plant will just struggle along with a small ball of soil the size of the original container, despite the good garden soil surrounding it.

A Mexican orange (*Choisya ternata*) in a 1-gallon plastic container.

Buying Container Plants

A container plant in a nursery should be moved to a larger container before it gets too crowded, and then offered for sale only when its roots are established in the new soil.

If the roots are thick and exposed, it has been in the container too long.

Tug gently to see if it is well rooted in the container.

Buying Balled-and-Burlapped Plants

Balled-and-burlapped plants are raised in the field, then dug up with a ball of soil around their roots. The twine and burlap hold the rootball together. Open the top of the wrapping and lay it back so you can inspect the rootball.

A broken rootball means that many roots are damaged.

Roots that circle tightly around the trunk can eventually strangle the shrub, restricting its growth or even killing it.

Buying Bare-Root Plants

Bare-root plants also are grown in the field, but they are deciduous plants that are dug up in the winter, when they are out of leaf and dormant. They can remain out of the ground until they begin to grow again in the spring. Bare-root plants are usually cheaper than container or balled-and-burlapped plants, but they are available only in the winter or early spring.

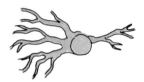

The root system should be symmetrical and evenly balanced. A lopsided root system will not provide a good anchor in the soil.

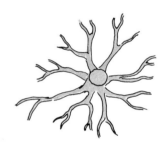

The size of these India hawthorns (*Raphiolepis indica*) is in good proportion to their 1- and 5-gallon containers.

Roots tightly wrapped around the stem are called *girdling* roots. These will restrict growth by slowly choking the shrub. Avoid this shrub, or else make sure to cut the girdling root when you plant.

Avoiding the wrong container. A small plant in a 5-gallon can is as poor a buy as a large plant in a 1-gallon can, but for different reasons. The small plant in the 5-gallon container was no doubt recently moved from a 1-gallon can—in effect, you are paying a 5-gallon price for a 1-gallon plant. There's nothing wrong with nurseries transplanting 1-gallon stock into 5-gallon containers, but before they are offered for sale, the plants should be held in a growing area until they reach 5-gallon size. Telltale signs that plants have recently been potted into larger-size containers include: the relatively small size of the plant; a small rootball (disclosed by probing a little); and unusually soft and loose soil in the container (it has not yet been packed down by repeated waterings).

An oversize plant in a small can is sure to be rootbound. It may even have sent its roots past the can, down into the soil below. In either case, don't buy the plant.

Balled-and-burlapped shrubs. Balled-and-burlapped shrubs can be bought and planted any time, but spring is the preferred season. To pick a balled-and-burlapped plant, untie the tip of the burlap and look carefully at the rootball. It should have a well-developed network of small, fibrous roots. Don't choose a shrub with a ball of soil that is loose, cracked, broken, or bone dry. In addition, check for roots circling back around the trunk—they

Inspecting the Shrub

The following list contains some sound advice that will help you make the best selections.

Branches

The shrub branches should be evenly spaced. Such spacing indicates that the plant has had continuous growth under good growing conditions. New shoot growth should be uniform all the way around the plant. This indicates that the plant has a fully developed root system.

Pruning Cuts

When you inspect a plant before buying it, make sure there are no signs of recent severe cutting back. All pruning cuts should be to outside buds so that the plant will keep its natural shape and not grow crisscrossed branches. There shouldn't be any short stubs left from pruning: they invite disease and insect attacks as they die back.

Check the Label

Make sure that you are buying the variety you set out to buy. Plants within a species usually look similar, while species within a genus can be widely dissimilar and yet look surprisingly alike when they are small plants at the nursery. After planting your shrubs, remove the labels attached by wires to prevent later girdling of a branch or the trunk.

can girdle the trunk after the shrub has been planted in the soil. Check for girdling roots by brushing away the soil on top of the rootball or sticking your finger into the top 2 or 3 inches of soil near the trunk. You can usually see or feel girdling roots in the top of the rootball.

After you have selected the shrub you want, retie the burlap and carry the plant by holding the rootball from underneath—don't use the trunk as a handle. Balled-and-burlapped plants are top-heavy and not very stable, so keep them from falling over by tying or by leaning them against a wall or fence. Until planting time, store the shrub in the shade, and keep the rootball moist by watering slowly from the top. If the weather is warm, also wet the foliage occasionally.

Although many other materials are used as wrap, burlap has the advantage of rotting readily. This allows you to leave it under the shrub when you plant. (See page 48.) Synthetic material does not rot, and must be removed before planting.

Bare-root shrubs. Bare-root plants offer good value if you know what to look for, and if you're willing to garden when others are still shaking off the winter doldrums. Bare-root plants are less expensive; they don't have to make the transition from nursery container soil to your garden soil, and they tend to establish themselves more rapidly.

Bare-root plants are available only during the dormant season, and should always be planted before growth begins. For the best selection, shop at the beginning of the bare-root season—late winter or early spring. Many varieties of deciduous shrubs are available bare root, particularly roses and shrubs commonly used as hedge plants.

At one time, when bare-root trees and shrubs arrived at the nursery, they were "heeled in" (temporarily held) in raised beds of bark or sawdust. Customers then picked out the plants they wanted, pulled them out of the beds, and had them pruned. Today, however, bare-root plants often go

A balled-and-burlapped azalea.

A bare-root rose.

directly from the delivery truck into individual cans. These plants can still be considered "bare root" as long as the new, little white roots have not started to grow when the plants are removed from their containers. If roots and leaves have sprouted, the plants are sold as container plants—at increased prices.

Before you buy a bare-root shrub, examine its root system carefully. Look for several large brown-colored roots going in different directions at different levels from the main root. In most cases, the upper portion of the plant should be pruned before it leaves the nursery. If you cannot plant the shrub right away, cover the roots with sawdust or damp earth to keep them from drying out. Dried roots quickly lose their ability to continue growing. Store the plants in a cool place to keep the buds from opening too early.

Selecting Hedge Plants

The deciduous plants commonly used for hedges are often available as bare-root plants. One of the most popular and best-looking among these is the privet, botanically known as *Ligustrum*. There are many varieties of *Ligustrum*, but the one offered bare root at your garden center is probably the one that's best adapted to your climate. Good-quality bare-root privets are usually from 12 to 24 inches tall, and should have sturdy stems and well-developed root systems.

If no bare-root plants are available when you want to start your hedge, buy 1-gallon-size plants. Avoid the expense of the 5-gallon size—the largest plant is not always the best buy, since you will immediately be pruning the plant heavily to force as many new shoots as possible from the base. Look for vigorous, well-branched plants.

Slow-growing evergreen shrubs, such as yew (*Taxus*), holly (*Ilex*), and the various varieties of boxwood (*Buxus*), are among the most preferred varieties for hedges. Their slow growth may be a drawback if you want quick privacy. In the long run, however, slower-growing plants make a denser hedge, and one that needs less pruning maintenance than some of the faster-growing choices, such as privet.

These slow-growing boxwoods (*Buxus sempervirens*) have been planted for a year and are already filling in well. Note the spacing between plants.

If you want a neatly trimmed hedge, keep in mind that smaller-leafed varieties demand less specialized care than plants with large leaves. The English laurel (*Prunus laurocerasus*) is a handsome broadleaved evergreen shrub sometimes used for hedges. Because its leaves are large, however, this hedge must be pruned selectively, not sheared. (See the list on page 87.) Shearing plants with oversize leaves will cause an abundance of imperfect, cut-up leaves.

These mature boxwood hedges in the gardens of Sissinghurst Castle, England, define the boundaries of the flower beds and add interest to an intersection of two paths. Slow-growing boxwood requires less clipping to maintain its tailored look than other faster-growing shrubs.

Bringing Your Plants Home

When you purchase new shrubs, be sure to follow these next two bits of advice:

☐ Because cut metal cans are almost impossible to water correctly, don't have a can cut unless you are going to plant the shrub that same day.

☐ Don't attempt to bring a shrub home in a car in which the plant does not comfortably fit. Any plant, but especially a leafy one, can become rapidly windburned if left exposed in a speeding automobile. If you must take your new shrub home with you, protect it by wrapping it securely in cloth or some other protective material. Most nurseries and garden centers will deliver purchases free of charge. Take advantage of this service, and both you and your new plant will benefit.

PLANTING AND TRANSPLANTING

It's important to get a shrub started right—whether you bring it home from the nursery or move it from one location to another.

Planting a seed, bulb, shrub, or tree in the ground is an important event. It's significant for the plant or plant-to-be, and special for the gardener as well. It has been said that you cannot plant a garden without being an optimist. Many positive thoughts are affirmed on planting day: the desire for a more beautiful environment; the anticipation of flowers, shade, fruit, or privacy; and the recognition that you will enjoy the future rewards season after season. To ensure that such optimism is well founded, this chapter makes clear each of the basic planting steps.

The best ways to plant shrubs and other plants have remained essentially the same for centuries. However, some recent changes in nursery methods have caused a few modifications of these techniques. And the information available about planting continues to grow through continuing research.

Transition Soil

As discussed in the section on soils (pages 32 to 34), most shrubs adapt well to the large middle range of native soils available to most gardeners. Nursery shrubs, however, are grown in a lightweight, porous soil formulated to keep the plants healthy while they are in containers. Consequently, these shrubs go through a transition period when placed in garden soil, which is usually quite different from container soil. Some plant experts feel that the plant's transition is eased by the use of *transition soil* during planting. This simply means that before you replace the soil from the planting hole, you mix in amendments to approximate the container soil.

But according to recent research, while plants started out in transition soil do better initially, after five years they are not as healthy as those planted with *un*amended backfill soil. If your soil has real problems, select plants that are particularly adapted to that soil. But if your soil is fairly ordinary, your plants are likely to thrive using either method of planting. Plants in transition soil may grow a bit faster at first, but eventually the roots must penetrate the native soil; research indicates that their doing so sooner rather than later may actually help establish a stronger root system.

The Planting Steps

If you carefully follow the 11 steps outlined on pages 45 to 47, success is practically guaranteed. The steps pertain to shrubs bought in containers. The procedures for planting bare-root and balled-and-burlapped plants are essentially the same; the few other things you should know about planting them are discussed in the sections that immediately follow the basic steps (page 48).

Transplanting

Transplanting means moving an established shrub from one spot in the garden to another. Transplanting any shrub, whether large or small, rep-

resents some danger to the plant. The worst problems are caused by root loss, either because some of the roots are mechanically broken off while the shrub is being dug out of the ground, or because the rootball is allowed to dry out before the shrub is safely placed in its new location. Here are a few tips for transplanting:

☐ Try to transplant during cool, moist weather; roots will dry out quickly on warm, windy days. Just before transplanting, you may want to spray both broadleaved and coniferous evergreens with an antitranspirant (a chemical that prevents leaves from losing water through transpiration).

☐ Move a shrub when it is dormant or as inactive as possible.

☐ Dig as large a rootball as you can handle to minimize root loss, and be careful not to break it. For best results, the soil should be fairly moist but not muddy. If you lose roots during the digging process, compensate by pruning the top of the shrub proportionately. It is usually advisable to prune by thinning out rather than by cutting back tips. (See page 60.)

Small shrubs. For the purpose of transplanting, a *small* shrub is one that can be carried on a shovel or spade after it has been dug out of the ground.

The first step is to dig a hole in the new location, as in planting step 1 on page 45. Then, with a sharp spade, cut around the entire shrub you want to transplant. On the last downward cut, tip the spade back and lift the shrub out. Carry it gently on the spade to the new location and lower it into the hole. Next, follow planting steps 7 through 11, on pages 46 and 47, for filling the hole, building a basin, and watering the shrub.

Large shrubs. In transplanting a large shrub, first dig the new hole and have it ready to receive the plant. Next, prune away or tie up the low branches of the shrub to permit easy access to its base. Dig a ditch around the plant, as shown in the illustration on page 49. Using a sharp shovel, undercut the rootball from one side until the shrub is about to topple over. Have a piece of burlap ready—a gunny sack cut so that it spreads open is fine—and push it down evenly on the undercut side of the rootball. Continue digging on the opposite side until you can topple the shrub onto the burlap. Wrap the burlap around the rootball and tie with twine to keep the rootball together. Lift the shrub onto a piece of heavy plastic so that you can slide the shrub to its new location, or put it on a wheelbarrow or handtruck. Plant according to the instructions for balled-and-burlapped shrubs on page 48.

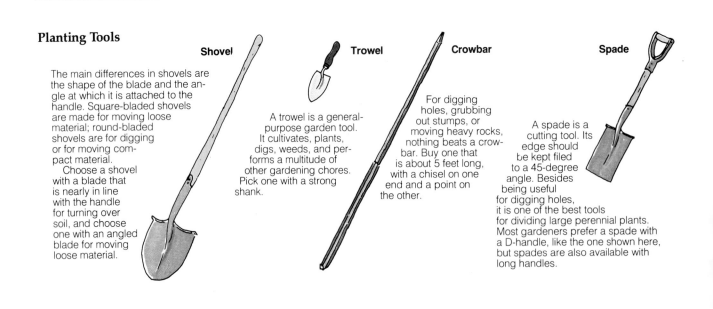

Planting Tools

Shovel

The main differences in shovels are the shape of the blade and the angle at which it is attached to the handle. Square-bladed shovels are made for moving loose material; round-bladed shovels are for digging or for moving compact material.

Choose a shovel with a blade that is nearly in line with the handle for turning over soil, and choose one with an angled blade for moving loose material.

Trowel

A trowel is a general-purpose garden tool. It cultivates, plants, digs, weeds, and performs a multitude of other gardening chores. Pick one with a strong shank.

Crowbar

For digging holes, grubbing out stumps, or moving heavy rocks, nothing beats a crowbar. Buy one that is about 5 feet long, with a chisel on one end and a point on the other.

Spade

A spade is a cutting tool. Its edge should be kept filed to a 45-degree angle. Besides being useful for digging holes, it is one of the best tools for dividing large perennial plants. Most gardeners prefer a spade with a D-handle, like the one shown here, but spades are also available with long handles.

The Basic Planting Steps

1. Plant at the right time.

Traditionally, early spring and early fall were said to be the ideal times for planting shrubs. Recent information suggests that this may be too limiting. Actually, you can plant at any time, with these exceptions:

Don't plant before the soil is workable. If the soil resists a spade or cultivator, wait until it dries out somewhat.

Don't plant immediately preceding a period that will cause the shrub climate-related stress. Late spring and late fall are usually times when the approching heat or cold will place newly established plants under stress.

2. Dig the hole.

Dig the planting hole approximately twice as wide and as deep as the rootball, or 1 inch shallower. Plants tend to sink after they have been planted, so if the hole is deeper than the original rootball, later on the plant may suffer from crown and root rot. The rootball should be sitting on firm, undisturbed soil. See page 33 for information on drainage.

3. Amend the backfill soil (optional).

If you are going to make a transition soil, this is the time to do it. The soil that you take from the hole is called *backfill soil*. Keep the backfill in one pile, and make a rough estimate of its volume. Next, add a slow-to-decompose organic soil amendment to the pile. See pages 55 and 56 for a description of types of organic matter. The proportion of soil conditioner to backfill soil is flexible, but approximately 25 percent of the final mix should be conditioner.

4. Add nutrients.

If you are planting your new shrub in early spring or when you expect leaf growth to begin, now is a good time to add a complete fertilizer. To add a dry type, throw in a small amount of fertilizer, according to the manufacturer's recommended ratios—as a rule of thumb, use 1 to 2 tablespoons if you are planting a shrub from a 1-gallon container, and ¼ cup for plants in 5-gallon containers. Stir it into the soil, so that the rootball does not come into direct contact with straight fertilizer.

5. Remove the shrub from the container.

If the plant has been grown in a plastic container, it will slip out easily, especially if the rootball is damp. Whatever you do, don't break the rootball when trying to get it out—you may permanently damage the root system. If the container is a straight-sided metal can and you are going to plant the shrub the same day you buy it, have the can cut at the nursery. If you are going to wait, even for a day or two, leave the can intact, and cut it at home with a large pair of tin snips or a can cutter like the type used at the nursery.

6. Place the shrub in the hole.

First check the rootball. Cut or pull away any circled, matted, or tangled roots so that all roots radiate out from the rootball. Shorten the roots to match the width of the planting hole so they will not be bent when they are planted. Shrubs planted with matted roots often stay that way, not venturing into the surrounding soil. To compensate for damaged or cut roots, lightly trim the top of the shrub. Now check the rootball's depth in relation to the planting hole depth, and in it goes.

7. Fill the hole.

Fill the hole with backfill soil to the level of the surrounding soil.

8. Build a basin.

Build a shallow basin around the shrub so that irrigation water will be concentrated in the area where it is needed most. Be sure to build it so that the water drains *away* from the stem of the plant. Thoroughly water the soil around the root zone. Apply water until the soil is loose and muddy. Gently jiggle the plant until it is positioned exactly how you want it. This action will eliminate any remaining air pockets. Check again to be sure water drains away from the stem of the plant. Use the basin for primary watering until some roots have had a chance to expand into the surrounding soil—usually around six weeks later. If dry weather conditions require continued irrigation, enlarge the basin at this time. However, if you live in an area with sufficient summer rain or if you have installed another irrigation system, now you can break down the basin.

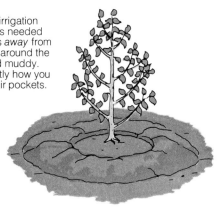

9. Stake, if necessary.

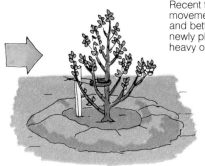

Recent tests have shown that some back-and-forth movement of the tops of plants actually results in faster and better-quality growth. The only reason to stake a newly planted shrub is if the plant is extremely top-heavy or if it is planted in an area of high winds. If a stake is necessary, place it on the side of prevailing winds, or use two stakes on either side of the shrub and tie them loosely for support with something that will not damage the surface of the stem, such as an old bicycle inner tube or a piece of old garden hose. Check the ties frequently to make sure that they are not cutting into the growing plant. Remove the stake after the plant is securely rooted in its new location, usually after the first year.

10. Prune, if necessary.

Shrubs planted from containers rarely require any pruning immediately after planting, except for cosmetic purposes. For the methods appropriate for your particular kind of shrub, see the chapter on pruning beginning on page 58.

11. Water.

Watch the plant to see how much water it requires. If a newly planted shrub wilts during the hottest part of the day, the rootball is not getting enough water, even though the surrounding soil may appear wet. Even if it rains or if the plant is in the path of a sprinkler, you may need to water it by hand several times a week for the first few weeks, if the soil seems dry. But do not overwater. Too much water is as bad as too little.

Planting Balled-and-Burlapped Shrubs

To plant balled-and-burlapped shrubs, follow the steps for planting containerized plants on pages 45 to 47, and then follow these extra procedures.

Handle the ball carefully, and set it in the hole with the burlap still on. Adjust the height of the rootball, as you would with a shrub from a container. If the burlap has been treated to retard rotting (ask at the nursery), it will have to be removed or have large holes cut in it.

Once the rootball is in the hole, untie the burlap from the trunk of the plant and pull it away from the top of the rootball. If the strings pull away easily, discard them; if not, leave them to rot in the soil. (Remove synthetic twine, since it does not rot.)

Cut or fold the burlap back so that it will be below the surface of the soil. Because any exposed burlap acts like a wick, drawing water out of the soil, bury all edges. If the plant is wrapped in synthetic material instead of burlap, remove it completely.

You may want to do a little pruning to compensate for the roots that were lost when the shrub was dug up by the grower. Sometimes a little extra fertilizer and water will compensate for any roots that were pruned away earlier.

Planting Bare-Root Shrubs

The nursery will usually prune a bare-root shrub for you after the shrub has been pulled from the holding bed. Sometimes one-third or more of the growth is cut back, but this results in a stronger, better-looking shrub.

Unless they are planted immediately after their purchase, bare-root shrubs should be stored in a cool spot with their roots in moist soil, sawdust, or bark to prevent them from drying out.

Dig a hole large enough to accommodate the span of the roots without bending them. Also, prune off any broken or very long roots, and place the plant in the hole with the top root 1 inch under the soil level. Work the backfill soil between the roots with your hands, getting rid of any air pockets.

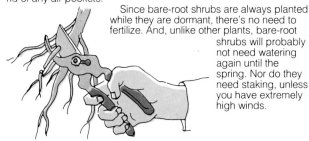

Since bare-root shrubs are always planted while they are dormant, there's no need to fertilize. And, unlike other plants, bare-root shrubs will probably not need watering again until the spring. Nor do they need staking, unless you have extremely high winds.

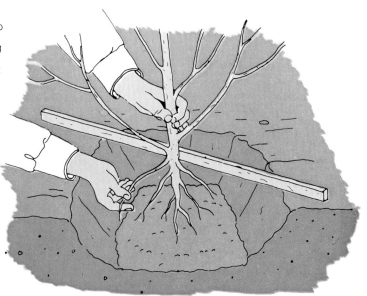

Planting Hedges

There are two basic ways to plant a hedge—you can dig a trench the length of the hedge or you can dig individual holes. Although the methods are interchangeable, the trench method generally works best for bare-root plantings, and the individual hole method works best for plants from containers. With either method, the eleven basic steps of planting apply. Generally speaking, the width of the trench should be two times the width of the rootball.

A double, staggered row of shrubs results in the more rapid growth of a thicker, denser, and wider hedge, but involves more initial expense and effort. If you plant a double row, stagger the plants so that no two plants are directly opposite each other.

The width of the spacing between individual plants will depend partly on the potential branch spread of the shrub variety and partly on how fast you want the hedge to fill in. Spacing can be from 18 inches to 30 inches apart. Most gardeners recommend a spacing of 18 to 20 inches within the row to avoid root crowding. Some dwarf varieties are planted 12 inches apart. Ask at your nursery for advice on your particular plant variety.

Transplanting Small Shrubs

Moving a small shrub is a simple and usually quick process. First, dig a new planting hole. Then cut the roots on all sides of the shrub with a sharp spade. On the last cut, push the spade as far under the shrub as you can and lift it up.

Carry the shrub on the spade to the hole you dug previously and gently lower it into place. Fill the hole with soil, then build a basin and puddle the plant in with a thorough irrigation. Prune to compensate for the roots you have cut.

Transplanting Large Shrubs

This is a more complex process than for small shrubs. Give yourself room to work by pruning away the lower branches or tying them out of the way.

Dig a ditch all the way around the shrub, as deep as you wish the rootball to be. A mattock and shovel or spade are best for this job. Be careful not to break the rootball with the mattock.

Undercut the ditch on one side with the spade. Cut gently, by chopping with the spade until the rootball begins to loosen. You will probably cut more than halfway through, leaving a narrow neck of soil and roots.

Tuck burlap into the cut you have made under the rootball. Try to wad as much material into the cut as you will need to wrap the other side of the rootball. Spread the rest of the burlap on the ground.

Cut the neck of soil from the other side of the shrub, lowering it gently onto the burlap. Reach under and pull the wad of burlap toward yourself. Wrap the rootball in burlap and tie it tightly with twine before lifting it from the hole.

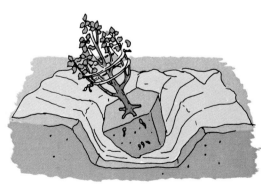

The easiest way to move a heavy shrub is to slide it on a piece of plastic or cardboard. Plant it in the new hole according to the directions on pages 45 to 47.

CARE AND MAINTENANCE

Back to basics: tried-and-true techniques that will keep your plants flourishing.

Most shrubs require very little maintenance—one of their primary advantages. While newly planted shrubs need a little extra attention to assure their establishment, after the first year you can simply sit back and enjoy them.

Once a shrub is established, its roots spread out through many cubic feet of soil. They may extend far beyond the limits of the branches, and many feet down into deep ground layers. Because shrubs draw on a large volume of soil for water and nutrients, their maintenance needs are more flexible than those of flowers or vegetables.

Shrubs may need no extra water or fertilizer at all. This is either because their roots extend under the vegetable garden or the lawn, which you water and feed regularly, or because their roots cover such a wide area that they can find enough naturally occurring food and water.

Slow-growing shrubs are particularly independent of fertilizers. Camellias often do well on the nutrients released as a mulch decomposes, and need no extra fertilizers.

Nevertheless, most shrubs need proper maintenance to be beautiful year after year. Here are the main things to remember:

☐ When you water, water thoroughly.
☐ To keep roots and soil healthy and to help retain moisture around root zones, add a layer of mulch.
☐ For spectacular and healthy growth, give shrubs the added nutrients they need at the right times.
☐ Protect your shrubs from severe weather conditions.

The only other requirement is occasional pruning. The chapter entitled "Pruning" covers this aspect of shrub gardening.

This chapter focuses on watering, fertilizing, and protecting shrubs. If you give your shrubs the care outlined on these pages, they will continue the healthy growth they started when you planted them.

Watering

Getting shrubs established. A shrub selected to suit its site will be easy to maintain, making demands for special care only during the first few months after planting. During this period of initial establishment, a shrub's roots will grow only about an inch into dry soil. A plant can die of thirst even though plenty of water is available just a couple of inches away from the root tips. Therefore, if you want a shrub to develop a healthy, extensive root system, make sure the root-growth area is kept moist.

If you don't have an irrigation system, the most efficient way to water a newly planted shrub is to create a basin around it. (See page 47 for details about how to make basins.) It's rarely sufficient to fill a basin only once, especially in hot weather. And few people are patient enough to water a shrub properly with a hand-held hose turned on to a moderate trickle. The

Frequent regular inspections of your plants enable you to spot potential problems and take corrective steps before they become major and troublesome.

Tools for Watering

Garden hose. Choosing a good hose is like buying tires for your car—the more your hose is reinforced, the less likely it will be to have a "blowout" or any other defect. Look for nylon (tire cord) reinforcement in both vinyl and rubber hoses; some have a radial design for added strength.

The best hose to buy is a vinyl one that is treated to stay flexible in cold weather. Check the inside diameter measurement (ID) when selecting the water volume necessary for your gardening needs. A hose with a ⅝-inch diameter, or one with a ¾-inch diameter for long distances, is fine for average gardening use.

best bet is to fill a basin twice, allowing the water to drain into the soil between waterings. If you have a number of shrubs to water, fill each basin, then start at the beginning again and repeat the process. Or, if you would rather be doing something else while you water, put the hose in a basin and turn the water on to a trickle. Set a kitchen timer for however long it takes to wet the soil thoroughly.

Your new shrub will be settled in its new place in the garden after about six weeks, but for the first year you should watch its development carefully. Make sure it gets sufficient amounts of water, especially during that crucial first summer.

After shrubs are established. Once a shrub is well developed, your watering worries are virtually over. Except in arid parts of the country, you will seldom need to water your shrubs at all! Even if you have a prolonged drought, you should still water infrequently but thoroughly. Established shrubs need little or no water from the ground surface because their root systems are deep and extensive.

When you do water, do it slowly to let the water soak deeply into the soil. Avoid frequent light waterings, since these lead to a shallow root system.

Testing for wetness. To find out how wet your soil is, cut into it with a shovel or trowel and check below the top 4 inches. Or use a soil-moisture tester— see the illustration on page 53. If you are watering a newly planted shrub, make sure the rootball is moist; it can be dry even though the surrounding soil is wet. Check by poking your finger into the rootball area—ideally, every day—until you know how much watering your new shrubs need to maintain the proper moisture level. For established plantings, make sure the deeper levels of soil get enough moisture.

Watering problems. It doesn't take long to discover that "watering problems" really mean "*soil* problems" (see the soil section on pages 32 to 34). Because *clay* soils absorb water slowly, drainage is very slow. The air in the soil so necessary for healthy root growth is minimal in this kind of soil, especially after watering. If water fills too many of the air spaces for too long, roots may die—causing top growth to die as well. *Sandy* soils, on the other hand, allow water to drain through rapidly; this leaves plenty of air but little water. The middle range of *loamy* soils have good water retention and drainage.

If you don't have a natural loam, you can improve your soil. The secret is *organic matter*, and lots of it. You get the best and most immediate results when you amend all the soil in the area you intend to plant. But if you are planting in a spot that has established plants, you can mulch with organic matter and improve the soil gradually. However, unless your soil is extraordinarily bad, which is rare, you can compensate for drainage difficulties by watering clay soils a little less and sandy soils a little more.

Irrigation systems. Shrubs don't require regular watering, but if you install an irrigation system for your other plants and trees, you will probably want to include watering devices for your shrubs as well. Many kinds of systems are available, from the conventional sprinkler systems to the more sophisticated drip systems (see page 54). Any system will save you work; the one you choose will depend on the type of gardening you do and the terrain of your garden.

Shrub border irrigation. If you have a shrub border around a lawn area, plan to have one system for shrubs and another for the lawn, with a different type of sprinkler head for each. Hooking the two systems together will get the shrubs watered every time you water the lawn—which is fine for the grass but too frequent for the shrubs. Ask your nursery or garden center staff about the sprinkler heads that are best for shrubs. Even with an automated sprinkler system, remember that infrequent but deep irrigation is better than light watering, and less wasteful of water.

Drip irrigation. In drip irrigation, small plastic tubes are installed directly next to the plants to be watered. Outlets (emitters) located at appropriate points along the tubes deliver water to the plants slowly, a drop at a time. The amount of water the plant needs is supplied on an almost constant basis. This method differs radically from conventional irrigation methods, which provide quantities of water followed by periods of drought. Drip systems cost about as much as conventional sprinkler systems but use much less water.

Here's how drip irrigation works. Emitters control the amount of water reaching the soil. Emitter models vary: some have porous walls, others are more complex mechanical units that deliver water to a specific point. The latter are most often used for shrub plantings (see page 54). Emitters reduce the flow of water so that it is released drop by drop. The flow rate, which is fixed, ranges from ½ to 2 gallons per hour.

The emitters are connected to lateral lines, which are usually made of plastic and have relatively small diameters—⅜ to ¾ inch. Lateral lines can cover long distances without losing pressure (a problem with conventional watering systems) because the flow rates are so low.

The main lines are also plastic, and can be installed above or below ground. Their size depends on the number of lateral lines and the flow of water needed. One cautionary note: Even when buried, main and lateral lines are frequently gnawed by gophers and ground squirrels.

Because foreign matter may plug the emitters, water used for drip irrigation must be free of sand and other small particles. To ensure water cleanliness, various types of sand or cartridge filters are used. Most systems also require some kind of pressure reduction, using a pressure regulator valve. The manufacturer will indicate the pressure needed by the particular emitter you choose. Some emitters require only 2 to 3 pounds of pressure, while others may need as much as 30 to 40 pounds.

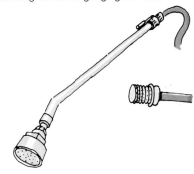

Hose nozzles. In addition to a good hose, special nozzle attachments will help you to water your shrubs properly. The nozzles illustrated here are examples of bubblers—nozzles that will supply maximum amounts of water without disturbing the soil or gouging the roots.

Water timer. Many types of water timers are available, from the simple to the sophisticated. Pictured here is a simple model that will turn a hose or sprinkler on for a preset length of time, then turn the water off. Other, more elaborate models can be programmed to water on a permanent schedule or to turn on automatically whenever the soil needs water. Check at your local garden center for more details.

Soil moisture tester. A soil moisture tester lets you know if your shrubs need water. The amount of moisture in the soil activates an electrical charge: the more moisture in the soil, the higher the electrical response. A combination light and moisture meter reads the amount of light that is reaching your plants, and also tests for moisture.

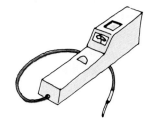

Soaker hose. A soaker hose oozes water along its entire length. Older types are made of canvas and last only one season, but newer ones are of plastic and last for two or more watering seasons.

The "head" is the control station where the water flow is measured and filtered and the pressure is regulated. If an automatic time clock is included in the system, it is installed as part of the main control.

Drip systems can be customized by adding a variety of equipment. Some of the most popular extras are fertilizer injectors, time clocks, and moisture sensors. Check at your local nursery or garden center for details on specific drip systems and accessories.

Fertilizing

The majority of soils contain most of the nutrients shrubs need. Fertilizers act as a supplement, making up for any possible deficiencies. Shrubs demand little fertilizer compared with the amount required by lawns or vegetables. Light applications at regular intervals greatly increase growth and stimulate optimum flower production. Experienced neighbors, nursery men, or your county extension agent can tell you which nutrients are generally needed in your area. One nutrient—nitrogen—is needed in almost all areas, and is usually added routinely.

Nutrients. Commercial fertilizers contain three primary nutrients— nitrogen, phosphorus, and potassium (NPK)—and are labeled by percentages of these nutrients. The percentages differ, but they are always listed in the same order. They reveal two important things. First, they tell how much of a nutrient the fertilizer contains, by weight. In a 5-pound box of 5–10–10 fertilizer, 5 percent of those 5 pounds is nitrogen, 10 percent is phosphorus, and 10 percent is potassium. Furthermore, 5 pounds of 5–10–10 contain only half as much nitrogen as 5 pounds of 10–12–16. Second, the numbers tell the relative proportions of the three major nutrients. Ratios of 2–1–1 (like 10–5–5 or 20–10–10) indicate that there is twice as much nitrogen as phosphorus and potassium, and ratios of 1–2–2 (like 5–10–10) indicate the opposite.

Each nutrient tends to stimulate a different type of growth. Nitrogen promotes leafy growth, while phosphorus and potassium promote flowering and fruiting. Ratios of 2–1–1 are normally used to encourage leafing when plants are growing actively; ratios of 1–1–1 or 1–2–2 work best when plants are forming flower buds or growing new roots (in late summer).

When to fertilize. Because shrubs need nitrogen most when they are growing rapidly, make the heaviest application just before or during active spring

Drip Irrigation

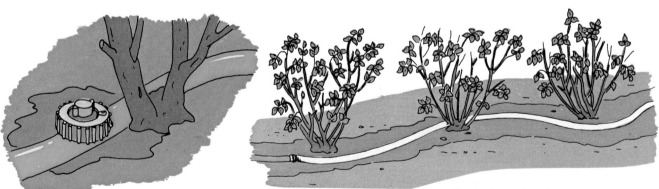

Point emitter. Emitters apply water from a specific point. One or more emitters are placed around each plant. As the plant grows and its need for water increases, more emitters are added. Their small openings may cause plugging; look for self-cleaning or nonclogging types.

Soaker hose. A soaker hose waters a strip, rather than a point. Lay the hose beside a hedge or row of shrubs. Many people leave soaker hoses in place for the entire season.

growth. In areas where the ground freezes in winter, nitrogen is sometimes applied in the fall as well, after top growth has stopped. This stimulates root growth, which continues into the winter and resumes in early spring. Do not make heavy applications of nitrogen in late summer or you'll start new top growth that won't have time to harden off by winter. Since nitrogen stimulates leaf growth, use it in moderation on any shrub that requires regular pruning. Extra nitrogen on a hedge will only mean more frequent shearing for you.

If you want to promote flower or fruit production on shrubs that bloom in early spring, fertilize before the buds set in late summer. The fertilizer should have a low proportion of nitrogen (such as the 1–1–1 or 1–2–2 ratios): too much nitrogen can divert energy from setting flower buds and making fruit to leaf production. Shrubs need phosphorus and potassium all during growth, but since these nutrients persist in the soil for long periods, timing their application is important only if you specifically want to stimulate flowers or fruit.

The nitrogen-deficient leaves (top) of this camellia are easy to spot when compared with healthy leaves (bottom).

Types of fertilizers. There are two basic types of fertilizers: inorganic and organic. Inorganic fertilizers are made up of mixtures of minerals and chemicals. They may be applied directly to the soil in dry form or they may be designed to be applied as a liquid form dissolved in water. As inorganic fertilizers dissolve in the soil, they are in a form that is directly usable by plants.

Dry inorganic fertilizers are available in powders, granules, and pellets. Generally, dry fertilizers are the most convenient: They can be scattered on the ground and watered in, cultivated into the soil, or buried deep in the root zone. Some dry fertilizers are relatively soluble in water and become instantly available to plants. These types usually leach from the soil in a few weeks and must be reapplied regularly.

Other dry varieties—known as slow-release fertilizers—are relatively insoluble in water, but become available to plants over a period of time. With urea formaldehyde, the most common slow-release fertilizer, bacterial action in the soil gradually frees nitrogen into soluble form. Other slow-release fertilizers release nitrogen in different ways. Depending on the type, these fertilizers remain effective in the soil for six weeks to two years. You can apply them less often than the soluble forms, but they are more expensive.

One type of slow-release nitrogen is called *water-insoluble nitrogen* (WIN). It is often shown on the label as a separate part of the nitrogen analysis. A fertilizer with 10 percent nitrogen might contain 8 percent water-soluble nitrogen and 2 percent water-insoluble nitrogen.

Liquid inorganic fertilizers are sold in liquid or powder form, but each must be mixed in water before use. You can mix either kind in a watering can and apply it directly to the root zone, or meter it into a hose and spray it on with irrigation equipment.

Liquid fertilizers are often preferred for container plants that need light, frequent feeding. They are also useful in drip irrigation systems, where they can be metered into the system and fed to the plants along with regular irrigations.

Liquid fertilizers are also used for *foliar feeding,* a method that sprays a dilute fertilizer solution directly onto the leaves. Useful when very quick results are desired, or when a soil problem keeps the roots from absorbing nutrients, foliar feeding is time-consuming and its effects are temporary. Use it only as a curative, not as a regular method of fertilizing.

Organic fertilizers are derived from plant or animal sources. Manure, compost, seed meals, blood meal, and fish meal—all are organic. Fish emulsion is a liquid organic fertilizer; most of the rest are sold in a dry form. Although the majority are expensive, they last for a long time in the soil, as

Nutrient Content of Fertilizers

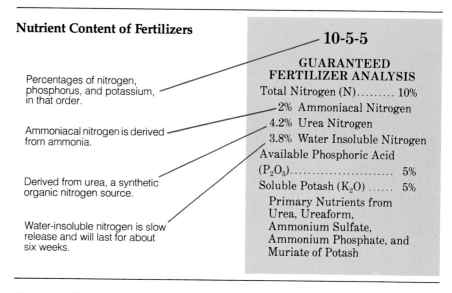

Percentages of nitrogen, phosphorus, and potassium, in that order.

Ammoniacal nitrogen is derived from ammonia.

Derived from urea, a synthetic organic nitrogen source.

Water-insoluble nitrogen is slow release and will last for about six weeks.

10-5-5

GUARANTEED FERTILIZER ANALYSIS
Total Nitrogen (N)........ 10%
  2% Ammoniacal Nitrogen
  4.2% Urea Nitrogen
  3.8% Water Insoluble Nitrogen
Available Phosphoric Acid
(P_2O_5)..................... 5%
Soluble Potash (K_2O) 5%
Primary Nutrients from Urea, Ureaform, Ammonium Sulfate, Ammonium Phosphate, and Muriate of Potash

they must be slowly broken down into inorganic molecules before they can be used by the plant. The non-nutrient part of organic fertilizers improves soil structure.

Before buying a fertilizer, take the time to read the various labels. If you know what you are fertilizing for and when to do so, you can purchase just the right fertilizer at the right time. And the directions on the package will help you determine how much to apply.

Mulches

Any of the organic materials used as soil amendments (see page 55) can also serve as a mulch—the difference lies in how you apply it to the soil. A mulch is intended to stay on top of the soil, usually in a layer about 3 inches thick; a soil amendment is incorporated into the soil.

A layer of mulch over a shrub's root zone has many beneficial effects. Tests have shown that mulches:

☐ keep the soil temperature cooler, which is helpful for root growth
☐ keep the soil moisture at a more even level, thus reducing the amount of watering needed
☐ keep weeds from taking hold
☐ encourage the long-term development of good soil structure

For the greatest effect, renew organic mulches once or twice a year. A layer of mulch is especially useful around newly planted shrubs. Since most organic mulches float in water, the best time to add them is after you break down the water basin—usually about six weeks after planting. Spread the mulch evenly over the shrub's root area, but keep it a couple of inches away from the stem. Moist mulch against shrub stems encourages crown rot, the growth of various fungi, the breeding of insects, and the burrowing of mice and other rodents.

While any organic material can serve as a mulch, certain kinds do better than others, including finely ground fir or pine bark, pine straw, compost, well-rotted manure, and, where available, redwood soil conditioner. Peat moss, however, makes a poor mulch: it forms a crust on top, making it difficult to water. Check with your nursery or garden center for good mulching materials that are readily available in your area.

Climate Protection

If the shrubs in your garden are climatically adapted to your area, they will rarely need protection from weather extremes. Only if there is an occasional extreme cold snap or heat spell will you have to protect sensitive plants. But if you grow shrubs outside their natural environment—for example, trying a frost-tender plant in an area that gets regular frosts—the microclimate surrounding these plants will need to be modified more extensively. In the majority of gardens, wind, heat, and cold are the most likely reasons for damage.

Wind. If your garden is exposed to high winds, one of the best remedies is to plant a windbreak (see page 25). A living windbreak will make your garden's climate more pleasant, both for people and for plants. High winds not only accelerate water evaporation but, even worse, they also damage the roots of newly planted shrubs: plants that have not yet become established can easily be toppled, harming tender new roots. If high winds pose a problem for you, see page 47 for information on staking new plants.

Heat. During periods of unusual heat, the most important protection you can give your shrubs is to keep them well watered. Do not let the soil around the plants dry out. Mulch to keep the soil cool and moist. For plants with particularly tender foliage, erect a simple, temporary structure of four stakes covered with a burlap shade. To provide emergency relief for larger shrubs, sprinkle the leaves with water—it *will* help, despite what you may have heard to the contrary. There are a few plants whose foliage might be damaged by a quick sprinkling, but generally the benefits far outweigh the drawbacks.

One simple way to protect shrubs from excessive heat is to plant them suitably in the first place. For example, most shade-loving shrubs will tolerate morning sun until 11 o'clock or so and afternoon sun during the winter. But don't expect a shade plant to thrive in a location where it receives afternoon sun in the summer, especially if the heat reflects off a wall or if searing winds prevail.

Cold. If occasional hard frosts damage sensitive plants in your area, pay attention to the weather reports. If you know in advance that the early morning temperatures will be unusually cold, you can take protective measures the night before. If the shrubs are in movable containers, move them close to the house, where the eaves will protect them. If the shrubs are in the ground, cover them with burlap, cardboard, or plastic. (Be sure to remove this protection the following morning.)

To protect tender plants in an area that has regular frosts, build a lightweight structure that can be used from year to year. Cover the structure tightly with fabric; this will trap warm air rising from both the ground and the plant during the night.

In areas of extreme cold, tender deciduous shrubs need special protection to make it through the winter. A coarse mulch, such as leaves or straw, should be packed around the crown of a plant, or, if necessary, around the entire plant. Hold the mulch in place with a wire cylinder.

Winter damage to broadleaved evergreens is frequently the result of leaf transpiration; when the soil freezes solidly, water is unavailable to the plants. To prevent this kind of damage:

☐ Water thoroughly if the soil is dry in the late fall. Water holds heat, and a moist soil freezes more slowly than a dry soil.
☐ Mulch heavily.
☐ Spray an antitranspirant, available at garden centers and nurseries, on the leaves to retard drying.

Snow can damage shrubs, particularly needled evergreens, by packing on the branches and breaking or flattening them from the accumulated weight. You can protect against snow damage by tying up such plants with cord before the first snow (see illustration). Applying an antitranspirant to coniferous shrubs will also give them some measure of winter protection.

Sun Protection

During heat waves, protect sensitive shrubs with this simple shelter made of four posts driven into the ground and covered with a sheet of fabric.

Evergreen Winter Protection

The weight of snow on their branches breaks or flattens evergreen shrubs. Protect the shrubs by tying them with cord.

PRUNING

Want to direct your shrubs' growth, even create living sculptures in your landscape? Here's how.

Pruning can direct shrubs' growth, improve their health, and increase their production of flowers and fruit. Pruning lets you direct growth to balance a shrub that is lopsided, keep a shrub small and compact, make one grow tall, or open up another.

The basics of pruning are really quite simple. You need to know *what* and *how* to prune, and *when* to do it. The information and drawings in this chapter are intended to remove any doubt that may surround the subject of pruning shrubs.

Pruning Styles

There are two basic styles of pruning: a *natural style*, which conforms to the natural pattern of a shrub's growth, and a *formal style*, which includes espaliers, topiaries, hedges, and other severely shaped specimens.

The natural look is achieved by exploiting the natural growth habit of the shrub. Take a look at the Plant Selection Guide beginning on page 76; the natural form is included in each shrub description. The type of pruning that improves a natural shape is called *thinning*. See page 60.

A formal effect can be achieved either by using your pruning shears ambitiously or by planting varieties of shrubs that grow neat and compact on their own. If the shrubs in your garden are not naturally compact, you'll need to do occasional *heading back* (see page 60) or frequent shearing to create a tailored, formal look. If you shear plants, do it frequently enough to remove only a little bit of growth each time. It's like getting haircuts: if you have them frequently, it's difficult to tell when you've had one; if you get one only every six months, however, the effect is very noticeable.

When to Prune

Pruning time for a particular shrub depends on what type of shrub it is. The timing is more critical for shrubs that are grown primarily for their flowers than it is for evergreen shrubs, whether coniferous or broadleaved.

Flowering shrubs divide into two groups: those that flower on new wood and those that flower on old wood. On this basis alone, you can determine when to prune your flowering shrubs.

How can you tell whether a shrub blooms on new or old wood? First, you need to know how to distinguish between the two types of growth. *New wood* is new stem growth produced during the current growing season. It is usually light green or pinkish in color and relatively soft. *Old wood* has been grown during a previous season. It is usually much darker in color than new wood, and much more brittle. While your plant is blooming, take a close look to see whether the flowers form on new wood or old.

If you've just bought a shrub and it isn't blooming yet, or if you've moved into a house that comes complete with an established but dormant garden, don't prune until you know whether the shrub blooms or not, and—if it does—on what type of wood.

Types of Pruning

Heading   **Thinning**

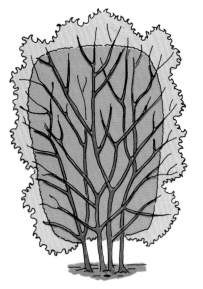

Pruning the end of a branch causes the dormant buds nearest the cut to begin growing. A shrub that has been pruned by heading is denser, has more growing points, and is smaller than an unpruned shrub.

Thinning removes an entire branch. Since no dormant buds are left under the cut, the energy that would have gone into that branch is spread throughout the shrub. The entire shrub will be larger and more open than an unthinned shrub.

Once you know what type of wood a shrub flowers on, it's easy to tell when to prune. Shrubs (and trees, for that matter) that bloom in early spring bloom on old wood. Prune these a week or two after the flowers drop—if you prune them during the dormant season, you will remove the already-formed flower buds. Pruned at the correct time, however—in the spring or early summer—the plants have the rest of the season to produce more flower buds for next year's display.

Shrubs that blossom in late spring or in summer produce flowers on wood that was grown during the same growing season. The time to prune these shrubs is during the dormant season, or just before growth starts in very early spring. This encourages more new stem growth, and therefore more flowers.

Types of Pruning

When you remove any part of a plant, you are pruning. The two basic pruning methods are thinning and heading. *Thinning*, or *thinning out*, removes entire branches back to a main trunk, or major branches to the ground. *Heading*, or *heading back*, removes only part of a branch.

The important difference between thinning and heading is their effect on plants. Thinning diverts the shrub's energy to the remaining branches; these, in turn, grow more vigorously. The long-term result of thinning a shrub is an open, natural look. Shrubs that are thinned also become larger than shrubs that are headed back.

Heading back a branch causes the plant to grow multiple branches where previously there was only one. Heading stimulates the growth of dormant buds closest to a pruning cut. Over the long term, heading creates a denser shrub that has more branches but is smaller than a shrub that has been thinned. Heading is usually associated with formal shapes.

Pinching

Shearing

A pinch removes only the growing point. This causes buds below the pinch to break dormancy and begin to grow, which produces a thicker plant. Since the pinch also delays growth for a couple of weeks as the buds break, it is used to retard growth in one part of a plant.

Shearing removes many growing points at once. Each shearing releases more buds from dormancy, resulting in a dense mass of growing points at the surface of the shrub. Sheared shrubs have a sculptured look.

Two special forms of heading are *pinching* and *shearing*. They have the same effect as other heading cuts, but are accomplished in special ways.

Pinching is done with the fingertips. A pinch removes only the growing point of a branch, allowing the lateral buds near the end of the branch to grow. This usually results in two, three, or four growing points where before there had been only one. Pinching is used to make a small plant bushy and thick or to redirect energy within the plant, and to guide its growth.

Shearing, or clipping, resembles pinching in that only the growing points are removed. The difference is that shearing removes growing points *en masse*, using hedge shears or power trimmers. The plant responds by increasing its number of growing points. Shearing is used for a formal effect, as in hedges or topiary, and produces a dense, sculptured shape. Thinning, in contrast, produces a natural, open shape.

Topiaries. When plants are shaped into geometrical and animal forms, they become topiaries—living garden sculptures. The plant most suitable for topiary work is a finely textured hardy evergreen—most often, boxwood or yew. Start with a young, 1-gallon plant with plenty of low branches that will fill out close to the ground. Topiary requires patience. For example, creating a simple double-balled shape will take five years for boxwood and ten years for yew. A more complex animal form will take twice that long.

The easiest topiary to shape is the double ball, or "poodle." First, prune the lower portion into a ball shape. Then, select several strong branches. Wait until these have grown at least 2 feet above the first ball. Next, strip the foliage off the bottom foot to form the separating stem, and start shaping the top foot of growth into the second ball.

Espaliers. Espaliers are shrubs or trees that are trained to grow flat against a solid vertical plane. Almost any shrub with fairly limber growth can be

A shrub pruned to a "poodle" shape is an easily achieved topiary effect.

Pruning Tools

Pruning shears

There are several models to choose from, but those with a scissors action are better than those with a blade and anvil construction, which tend to crush the stems being cut. Keep your shears sharp, clean, dry, and well oiled, and they will last a lifetime.

Hedge trimmers

Electric hedge trimmers take most of the work out of the trimming process.

If no electric outlet is near, look for cordless electric trimmers that can be recharged—some models can be used for 35 minutes without stopping.

Hedge shears

Some hedge shears have a notch at the base for cutting through thicker branches, but they are really designed to shear light new growth. Use loppers for heavier pruning.

Pruning loppers

Heavy-duty loppers may be necessary to prune mature shrubs with sturdy branches. This tool can lop off limbs up to 1½ inches in diameter with little effort, leaving a cleaner cut than that of a saw.

Pruning saw

If you have large shrubs that need pruning, you may want to own a pruning saw. The teeth are designed to cut green wood without binding. Pruning saws cut with a pulling motion, which makes them very efficient for movable branches.

Pruning Cuts

Before leaves and new stems appear, *growth buds* form in small swellings on the stems and branches. Inside these buds await tiny, undeveloped leaves, branches, and flowers.

There are two types of buds: terminal and lateral. A *terminal bud* grows at the *tip* of a shoot; a *lateral bud* appears at the *side* of a shoot. These buds are the keys to making good pruning cuts.

When you prune, always cut *above* a bud. To place your cut near a lateral bud, select one that is pointing outward so that the new branch will grow away from the main trunk rather than crisscrossing with interior branches. Cutting above an outward-pointing lateral bud will also open up the plant to light, air, and orderly growth—important goals in pruning.

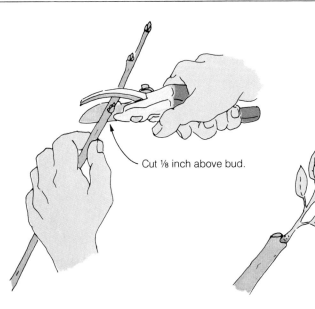

Cut ⅛ inch above bud.

Cutting off lateral buds or side branches forces the shrub's energy into the terminal buds, thus pushing the branches to grow in the directions they are already pointing.

When you get ready to make a pruning cut, hold the branch just below where you want the cut to be. Put the cutting blade of your hand pruners under the branch. Cut at an upward angle. The slant of the cut should be in the direction you want the new branch to grow. Never leave a budless stub of wood behind on the shrub. Unsightly stubs usually die and become an entry point for insects and diseases. *Think* about each cut before you make it. No pruning cut should ever be made without a good reason and a clear understanding of what the results are likely to be.

espaliered. There should always be 6 inches between the shrubs and the wall or fence. Place wire or wooden supports at that distance to allow for both air movement and room for the branches to develop.

Start by planting a shrub that has a strong central stem. Then run the wires (or supports) horizontally at 18-inch intervals, just below the height of the first wire. This will activate shoots to appear just below the cut.

During the first growing season, allow only three new shoots to develop. Train two shoots horizontally onto the wire, and let the other one grow vertically as an extension of the central trunk. Rub off all the growth from the lower trunk.

Later on, cut off the new leader (the vertical extension of the trunk) a little below the second 36-inch-high wire. This will activate a second set of shoots. Train these as you did the first set. Continue training the shrub in this manner until all the wires are covered with branches. When you have formed the frame you want, restrict new growth by pinching frequently during the summer.

Espalier

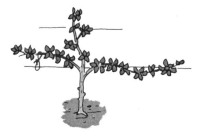

Pinch the young plant at the height of the first wire. Let three shoots develop from this pinch. Tie the middle shoot to the second wire, and train the other two along the first wire.

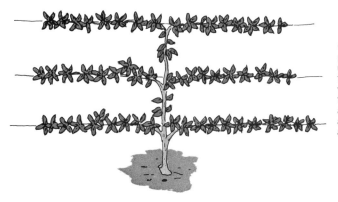

Continue this pinching and tying until six shoots are trained along the wires. Maintain this form by pinching any vigorous shoots as soon as they appear.

Hedges

Hedges are formed by repeated shearings. Each shearing of a fine-textured hedge should be ¼ inch higher than the previous one.

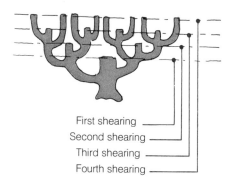

First shearing _____
Second shearing _____
Third shearing _____
Fourth shearing _____

Each time you shear a little higher, more buds break, increasing the density of the hedge. The surface is composed of fresh, new-growing points, even in an old hedge. The cut stubs are buried in foliage as the hedge grows.

Hedges. Hedge plants should be pruned heavily when they are first set out. Bare-root plants, intended to produce a dense hedge, should be pruned to about one-half their original height. Plants from containers, and other plants that will naturally produce an open hedge, should be pruned back by about one-third, both on the tops and on the sides.

Let a newly planted hedgerow grow without shearing for a full growing season to give the roots a chance to become established. The second year, trim the hedge lightly to keep its dense growth. Don't try to achieve the hedge height you want too quickly. Keep shearing lightly to keep the hedge thick, without gaps, as it grows to the desired height. Once the hedge is as tall as you want it, change your pruning technique.

Solving special problems. Shear *small-leafed hedges*, such as boxwood or yew, whenever they look ragged from uneven new growth, and take off almost all the new growth. Let the hedge retain just a little bit of new growth each time you shear—cut about ¼ inch farther out than you cut at the last shearing, to avoid bare spots and clusters of cut branches. When your hedge grows this slowly, it will always show a fresh new layer of leaves. After 10 or 15 years of this slow growth, the hedge will become too large, and you will have to cut it back very hard early one spring and let it begin its slow growth again.

Shearing a *large-leafed hedge* will cut the leaves in half and give the hedge a butchered look. So if you have the time, prune these hedges one branch at a time with a pair of hand shears. Make your cuts inside the layer of foliage so that they will be hidden, leaving only fresh, uncut leaves on the surface.

Solving common problems. Hedges that have been allowed to go their own way for a number of seasons develop several common problems. Usually they have grown too tall and spindly, have bare, unattractive spots, or lean into the neighbor's yard. Corrective pruning can take care of all these maladies.

A hedge that has grown too tall and floppy has usually been allowed to grow too fast. Hedges should be "built" carefully. Regular pruning to encourage a sturdy structure will strengthen a mass of wispy stems. If the hedge's

This properly sheared boxwood hedge makes a tailored enclosure for pieris shrubs.

The hole at the bottom of this pittosporum hedge is caused by the too-wide top, which shades the lower portion of the hedge.

structure is very weak, it can be cut back to the ground and allowed to grow up again at a more sensible rate of growth.

A hedge with bare, leafless undersides develops when there is not enough light at the bottom. In addition, the problem may be aggravated by a lack of water and nutrients. The solution? Cut the hedge back heavily to stimulate new growth at the bottom, then shape it properly as it grows. Water it regularly and see that it has enough fertilizer for vigorous growth.

To avoid *bare bottom*—to keep a hedge leafed out on the ground—shape your hedge so that the top is narrower than the bottom. This lets the whole side of the hedge receive light. Leaves that do not get enough light will drop off. It's especially important to shape a hedge in this way on the northern side, or on any portion that is in the shade.

A hedge that leans into the neighbor's yard often occurs when you keep your side of the hedge trimmed, while your neighbor lets his or her side grow. One solution is to dramatically reduce the height and width of the hedge, then let it grow back with an even, strong structure. Another is to use the 3- or 5-year system of renewal. See page 65. The best solution is to talk to your neighbor and jointly agree on how you will train and maintain the dividing hedge.

Bare spots in a hedge are caused by old age and repeated shearings that don't allow the hedge to grow. To alleviate the problem, cut away the dead twigs, branch by branch, and then in the future shear ¼ inch outside the last cut.

Revitalizing Old Shrubs

Many times, neglected shrubs need imaginative and dramatic pruning to make them attractive parts of the landscape again. This is often the case with a mature garden that you inherit with a house that has had a previous owner. But if you look at these shrubs as a natural resource (albeit one that you have to make the best of), you may be surprised. Sensitive pruning can transform many overgrown shrubs into valuable landscape assets.

To revitalize an older shrub, first clear away all weak, thin shoots, as well as any of the oldest trunks that have few side branches. This will open up the plant and allow sunshine to reach the center of the shrub, and leave behind the older, more massive, most interesting branches. Cut away any branches that point inward or cross other branches.

Now step back and take a look at the plant's new form. Does it make an interesting silhouette, or does it still need more trimming? Before cutting off any major branches, have someone pull the branch back as far as it will go without breaking. What does the shrub look like without it? Does the shrub need additional thinning out to make it less massive, or does it need trimming around the edges to give it a more compact, neat look?

Many older shrubs act like small trees, growing to heights never mentioned in catalogs and gardening books. Mature specimens can be the focal point of an entire landscape, especially if the foliage and branches that conceal the trunk are trimmed away. Follow-up thinning the next year can help revitalize an old specimen. Don't worry about taking growth away—you can make up for the missing foliage by planting new shrubs under the older ones. Or you may find the additional space desirable, particularly in a small garden.

If the top portion of a shrub looks hopelessly unattractive, cut the shrub completely to the ground. This will generate new growth from the roots rather than from older branches. As long as the plant has the strength to push out new shoots and leaves, it will have enough strength to replace what you cut off. The best time to take this drastic pruning action is in late winter or early spring. When new growth results, treat it like a new shrub.

However, cutting back some shrubs too far will kill them. If you don't know how a shrub will respond to a radical pruning, experiment by heading one branch back to a leafless stub. If the stub sprouts new growth, it is probably safe to cut the shrub back.

Renewal Pruning

Renewal pruning is a special form of pruning that can keep deciduous shrubs, particularly flowering varieties, young and vital, no matter how old they are. This method is responsible for the current health of many shrubs after more than a century of growth, particularly in the heritage gardens of the eastern states. This technique produces branches of no more than 3 to 5 years old on a plant that may be over 100 years old.

Every year or two, prune out a few of the oldest canes at ground level. This opens up the top to let light and air into the interior of the shrub and encourages growth from the base, which eventually renews the top of the plant.

Three-year renewal. Each year a deciduous shrub produces many shoots from the plant's base or roots. Prune the shrub so that one-third of the shoots will be one year old, one-third will be two years old, and one-third will be three years old. When you prune, remove crossing limbs or any dead or diseased branches. Then cut out most of the 3-year-old wood. This will induce new shoots to spring up, leaving the desired number to form the first-year shoots the following year.

One other type of pruning is necessary: reducing the shrub's total height to keep it within bounds and preserve its natural form. Removing the third-year wood every year after blooming will guarantee that you always have young, healthy wood to produce the biggest and healthiest flowers. As a bonus, this three-year renewal system also results in healthier plants—older wood is more susceptible to insects and disease than are young, strong shoots.

Five-year renewal. This approach is the same as the three-year system, except that you spread the steps over five years. Slow-growing shrubs respond well to the two additional years of thinning. However, this method will not produce as many new shoots each year as the three-year system will.

Flowering shrubs that have a moundlike habit of growth, such as summer-flowering spireas, hydrangea, and vitex, should be pruned yearly. Thin out some of the weakest canes and cut the rest back to varying heights so that the flowers will not all bloom at the same level.

Shrubs for Special Treatment

A few shrubs need special treatment. Three common ones are rhododendrons, azaleas, and roses.

Rhododendrons and azaleas. Rhododendrons and azaleas require more grooming than pruning. The spent flower heads of rhododendrons should be removed—this is called *deadheading*. Tips of azaleas should be pinched out to make the plants bushier. However, be careful not to take next year's flower buds.

For the most part, your fingertips are enough for pruning this group of plants. Only older plants that have become leggy, sparse, or damaged will require a few cuts from your hand pruners or loppers.

A rhododendron differs from an azalea in the placement of the buds; this difference causes them to need different types of pruning. Since a rhododendron bud is always found just above the leaf rosette, you must cut there, just above the bud (see the photograph, page 66). On an azalea, however, the buds are concealed under the bark along the entire branch. This means that you can cut anywhere along the branch and still be near a bud, which will then break into growth.

Rhododendrons must have their spent flowers removed. If seed pods are

Left: When deadheading rhododendrons, be careful not to break off the small buds behind the flowers. These buds will produce the next year's growth.

Right: When cutting roses, trim to just above a five-leaflet leaf. There will be a dormant bud at the base of this leaf that will produce the new growth.

left on the plant, they consume much of the energy that could go into flowers or leaves. With one hand, hold the branch with the faded flower; with the other hand, carefully snap off the flower head with a slight sideways pressure. Take care not to harm the growth buds below—they are next year's flowers and leaves. Injuring the flower buds means that there will be no flowers next year.

If your plant is too tall to handpick thoroughly, little harm will be done if some flower heads are left on. Try using a hose to wash away the dead petals. Many rhododendrons tend to bloom in alternate years if they are not deadheaded.

Azaleas require even less pruning than do rhododendrons. They should be tip pinched, particularly when young, to produce bushier plants. Do this within a couple of weeks after the plant blooms.

When azaleas get older, they may need stronger pruning. Because the buds are distributed along the entire branch, an azalea can be cut anywhere. It can even be sheared (although few people do so because it destroys the plant's natural shape). The result is a crop of flowers at the sheared surface.

To rejuvenate an older azalea that has grown too woody and leggy, prune it over a period of two or three years. The first year, cut back the oldest branches to within 10 to 12 inches of the ground. Do the same thing the second year, and again the third year. Never cut off more than one-third of the plant each year. In this way, you can safely transform the azalea into a compact, bushy plant that will produce an astonishing crop of flowers.

Roses. Roses are a varied lot, and their pruning needs vary with their growth patterns. For pruning purposes, however, these growing patterns can be grouped into two categories: roses that bloom all summer and those that bloom for only a couple of weeks in the spring.

Spring-blooming roses are pruned when they finish blooming. Prune fairly heavily to encourage new growth, which will bear next year's flowers.

Roses that bloom all summer are mostly the hybrid teas, floribundas, and grandifloras that are our most popular garden roses today. Prune them when they are dormant, usually in late spring just before they begin growth.

First, remove all dead wood and weak twigs. Then, open up the center of the plant by pruning out canes that have crossed inward. Next, remove any canes that have gotten too old to produce well. These canes produce weak, twiggy branches. The branches will be rough and dark with old bark, and may show signs of decay.

At this point you must decide how vigorous the rose is. If the new canes are ¾ inch in diameter or more, the rose is vigorous. Slender canes indicate a weaker shrub. The general rule is: The less vigorous the rose, the harder you prune it. This may sound backwards, but think of pruning as removing growing points (dormant buds) that will use up energy when the shrub begins growing in the spring. The fewer buds you leave, the more energy each growing point will have.

Leave about six canes on the most vigorous roses. On the least vigorous, leave only three. Head back the canes about one-third of their length. Heading them back more will make fewer, but larger, flowers. A lighter pruning produces more, smaller flowers and a more attractive shrub shape. Prune heavily if you want to produce flowers for cutting, lightly if you want a more attractive garden shrub.

As you pick each flower, cut its stem back to just above a leaf that has five leaflets. This leaf will have a strong dormant bud at its base to make a good replacement cane. If your rose bush gets too high by the end of the summer, or if you want cut flowers with long stems, cut each stem back so that only the two lowest five-leaflet leaves are left. This will slow the growth of the shrub.

Climbing roses have long canes that do not flower; flowers are produced on laterals. If the climber is on a trellis, untie it and lower it to the ground. Prune out all but the strongest three to five canes and cut all the laterals back to two or three buds. As for the remaining canes, don't cut them shorter—tie them back up on their trellis and arch them over at the top. This will stop their upright growth and encourage laterals to form.

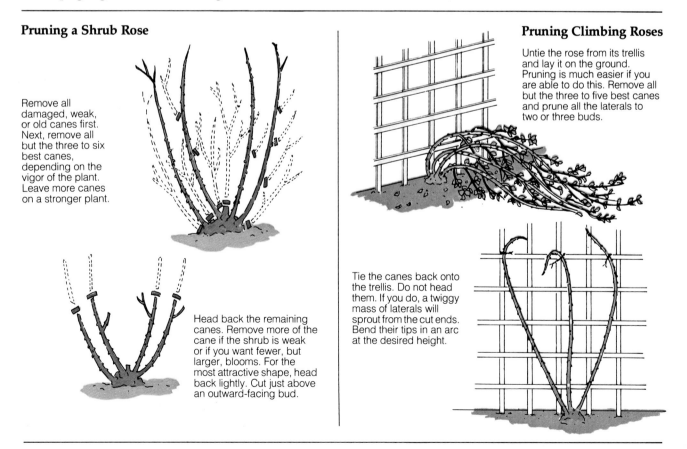

Pruning a Shrub Rose

Remove all damaged, weak, or old canes first. Next, remove all but the three to six best canes, depending on the vigor of the plant. Leave more canes on a stronger plant.

Head back the remaining canes. Remove more of the cane if the shrub is weak or if you want fewer, but larger, blooms. For the most attractive shape, head back lightly. Cut just above an outward-facing bud.

Pruning Climbing Roses

Untie the rose from its trellis and lay it on the ground. Pruning is much easier if you are able to do this. Remove all but the three to five best canes and prune all the laterals to two or three buds.

Tie the canes back onto the trellis. Do not head them. If you do, a twiggy mass of laterals will sprout from the cut ends. Bend their tips in an arc at the desired height.

PESTS AND PROBLEMS

Falling leaves may mean that trouble rather than the coming of fall. You can learn what to do about this and many other problems.

You can hold problems in the garden to a minimum if you are on familiar terms with the plants that grow there. Take a daily stroll, and keep an eye out for problems as well as beauty. This is the most pleasant and least time-consuming way to do your troubleshooting.

What do you look for? Anything that looks irregular: a chewed leaf, compacted soil, stunted foliage, a branch growing too far in the wrong direction. If you know your plants well, not only will you be quick to see obvious clues, but you'll be able to avoid trouble *before* it happens.

Checking Up on the Garden

You know things about your own garden that no book can tell you. Colors, textures, and vigor are all indicators of overall plant health, and only you know what's normal for your garden and what's not. If you make a point of getting into the garden as often as possible, you'll notice subtle but important changes that signal the current health conditions of your plants.

"At the first sign of attack" are the most important words in the business of pest and disease control. If you are in the garden on a regular basis, you'll be able to take care of the first aphids, the first brood of beetles, or the first attack of mildew.

Avoiding Problems

A vigorously growing shrub is less susceptible to injury from insects and diseases than one that is under stress from lack of water or nutrients—bark beetles, borers, and sucking insects, for example, do more damage during or after a drought than at any other time.

Plants have more to put up with than just insects and diseases; sometimes they suffer from the unwitting hand of the gardener. Sensitive gardeners are aware that plants have lives of their own. Someone who respects plants doesn't carelessly skin the bark from a trunk with a lawn mower, which could allow entrance to borers or fungi. The good gardener also makes sure that a plant is not being choked by a tie that has become too tight, and is careful not to cut the roots of nearby plants when power tilling.

Here are some common sense steps that will help to avoid problems in your garden:

☐ Keep old leaves picked up—they are often the breeding ground for various diseases and a safe hiding place for many damaging insects. (Composted leaves, however, pose no problem.)

☐ Keep your pruning shears *sharp*, and use them correctly (see page 62). Bark tears easily and heals slowly. Many insects and diseases will attack *only* if there is an opening in the bark.

☐ Pull weeds early, before they begin to compete with surrounding plants and distribute seeds for future generations of weeds. The best time to

pull them is when the ground is soft after rain or watering. (See the section on page 74 for weed control.)

☐ Spray at the first sign of disease or insect attack. The control you achieve will be more rapid and complete and the plant will suffer less damage from pests and diseases.

☐ Remove and destroy (by burning or throwing away) any diseased flowers or fruits. Disease spores can live on them from one season to the next.

☐ Practice a thorough cleanup before winter sets in. Remove debris and other likely homes for overwintering insects and diseases.

☐ To promote healthier plants and to keep the weed population to a minimum, keep a 3-inch layer of mulch on all open areas of ground. Cover the root zones of shrubs as well, but keep the mulch pulled back a few inches away from stems or trunks. See page 56 on mulching.

Local Help for the Asking

Local problems in the control of pests and diseases are under constant study by the research departments of your state university. Publications on the results of their studies are available to home gardeners at the office of your county extension agent. Many are available free, others at a nominal cost.

How do you tap this storehouse of regionalized information? The office of your county extension agent is listed in your telephone book, grouped under the county government offices. A phone call will bring you a list of available publications. Or you can write the state extension office for a list of publications and the addresses of the local county agents.

Local or regional arboreta and botanic gardens can also be valuable resources. You will find them listed in the Yellow Pages of your telephone book.

Problems to Look For

Small leaves. Leaves that seem unusually small indicate low vigor. This can be caused by a number of factors. The plant may be under stress from lack of water or nutrients; it may be planted in a location not suitable to its variety; or the soil may be compacted or poor in structure.

Sometimes the problem isn't caused by a deficiency, but merely by a response to light levels. Leaves that are exposed to the direct rays of the sun are smaller, thicker, and a lighter green than leaves that grow in the shade. Shade leaves tend to be large, thin, and dark green. In this case, the "problem" is a phenomenon of nature, and nothing to worry about.

Solutions. Aside from the quantity of light, small leaf growth derives from cultural practices. This means that good gardening practices will cause the symptoms to disappear. Pages 50 to 54 offer good advice on watering and fertilizing procedures. Before you purchase a plant for a specific location, be sure its needs match the site conditions. To match up plants and locations, check the Plant Selection Guide starting on page 76. And to avoid the problems that come with poor soil, read up on soil types and soil amendments on pages 32 and 33, and 54 to 56.

Sudden wilting. If a whole shrub suddenly wilts, the cause may be a gopher. Gophers eat roots, bulbs, and tubers. Occasionally, whole plants will disappear into their holes. Gophers tunnel 6 to 12 inches under the soil and push the excavated dirt out to the surface, leaving small mounds of finely particled earth behind.

If the sudden wilting of your plants is not due to gophers, make sure the water you apply is getting down to the roots. It's possible for the soil to look damp on the surface but be dry just a few inches below. See page 52.

If the shrub is healthy except for a single wilted branch, it may have been physically damaged in some way. Check to see if the branch is broken.

The damage may also be caused by insects that bore into stems and

Left: These leaves are from the same shrub. The smaller, lighter-colored leaf on the left is from a high, outside branch exposed to the sun. The leaf on the right is from a lower branch that never received full sun.

Right: Armillaria root rot has caused the leaves on this daphne to wilt.

trunks. Some plants, such as junipers and lilacs, are more susceptible to borer damage than others. If you suspect borers, look at the base of the damaged branch for small holes.

Certain wilt, crown rot, and root rot diseases also cause severe wilting.

Solutions. Gophers are best controlled by traps, which you can get at your local garden center. Follow the directions carefully. Gas bombs and poisoned bait are also available, but use them only with the greatest caution.

If a branch has been physically damaged but has not been completely broken off, it can often be saved. Mend the break with stretch tape or budding rubbers (used for grafting), available at your nursery or garden center. Or make a splint by tying a stick to the branch to hold the pieces together; you may even be able to nail the break closed. Then cover the broken area with a thick coat of grafting compound to keep the tissue from drying out. If the branch cannot be saved, cut it off. New branches will quickly grow to fill in the gap.

Control borers with sprays. Contact your local extension agent for recommended sprays and spraying times in your area.

If the problem is a wilt disease or root rot, a radical pruning will sometimes save the shrub. See pages 64 and 65.

Dead spots on tips and edges of leaves. Tan or light brown spots on the tips and edges of leaves are usually the result of a plant becoming so dry at one point that the extremities of the leaves become burned. If the dead tips and edges are dark or black, the burn is probably caused by excess fertilizer, de-icing salts, or other salts in the soil.

Solutions. If the problem has been caused by the plant drying out in the past, there is nothing that will restore the green color to the old, burned leaves. If the leaves are too unsightly, cut them off or trim them. In most cases, new leaves will replace the old ones. Avoid a recurrence of the problem by following a good watering program in the future.

The yellow leaves of this azalea are a symptom of an iron deficiency.

If burning is caused by a build-up of salts or too much fertilizer, apply unusually large quantities of water to the root zone, at a moderately slow rate, to leach the salts. Simply place a hose at the base of the plant and let it run slowly for several hours.

New leaves turn yellow. When new leaves are abnormally yellow, it's a clear signal that the shrub is not getting something it needs. The most common reason for yellow new growth is an iron deficiency. There usually is sufficient iron in the soil, but it may be fixed into insoluble compounds that the plant can't use. This problem frequently occurs with azaleas and other acid-loving plants that are growing in neutral or slightly alkaline soil, and with many other plants if you have strongly alkaline soil or water.

Solutions. Apply a chelated iron fertilizer. Chelating agents are synthetic organic substances that maintain copper, manganese, zinc, and iron in a water-soluble form so that they can be readily absorbed by plants. At the

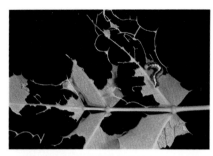

Top: A barberry looper caterpillar feeding on a mahonia leaf.

Bottom: At the first sign of snails, distribute snail and slug bait around the affected plants.

same time, apply sulfur or iron sulfate to help make the soil more acid. Use an acid-reaction fertilizer such as azalea food or ammonium sulfate to keep the soil from becoming alkaline again.

Holes in leaves. Holes are the telltale signs that a hungry insect has been feeding on your plant. Some of the most common pests are caterpillars, beetles, snails, and slugs.

Caterpillars are the larvae of moths and butterflies. They come in all sizes and colors, and are either naked or hairy (some are even decorated with tufts and spines). Their names usually correspond to their appearance, their hosts, or their way of life—leaf rollers, bagworms, leaf skeletonizers.

Leaf rollers are caterpillars that feed inside leaves that are rolled or tied together. The banded woolybear is the larva of the tiger moth—touch it and it rolls into a ball. Webworms and tent caterpillars build unsightly "tents" in forks and crotches of plants, and crawl from these protected places to feed on foliage. Or they web together needles or leaves, usually at the ends of branches, and feed beneath the webs. Loopers, inchworms, measuring worms, and cankerworms are all caterpillars with the same manner of movement. They double up or loop when they crawl. These worms usually feed on new foliage in the spring.

Beetles are a huge and diverse group of insects that includes many beneficial as well as destructive species. Ladybird beetles (ladybugs) and black ground beetles feed on aphids, grubs, and other harmful insects, and should be protected.

Most destructive beetles are general feeders on both ornamentals and vegetables. Three of the most harmful are the cucumber beetle, the flea beetle, and the blister beetle. Damage varies from small holes in leaves to complete defoliation.

If you can see the holes but cannot see what is causing the damage, this means either that the insects have left or that they do their eating at night. Check with a flashlight when it is dark to see if you can catch the pests in action. Prime suspects as nighttime marauders are *snails* and *slugs*, which hide in damp places during the day and feed at night or in wet weather.

Solutions. Spray with orthene or malathion. If snails or slugs are the problem, use snail and slug bait.

No flowers. A flowering shrub that doesn't flower is a real disappointment to its owner. Some shrubs may simply need to grow a few more years before they are mature enough to flower. Another cause is the lack of enough sunlight: most flowering shrubs bloom better when they receive more light. If the location is too dark, the foliage may look admirably healthy and lush, but there won't be enough light to promote flowering.

If some shrubs are overfertilized, or fertilized at the wrong time of year, their flower production goes down. The plant uses the nitrogen in a complete fertilizer primarily to promote green vegetative growth. The foliage may be lush, but it is thriving at the expense of the flowers. Shrubs that flower on the sides of branches, rather than at the tips, are most likely to respond in this way.

Another reason for fewer flowers is if plants are pruned during the wrong season, or simply if they don't receive enough water.

Solutions. If the plant is not receiving enough light, consider pruning overhanging branches that block the sun. If that isn't possible, you should probably move the shrub to a sunnier location. For transplanting techniques, see page 49.

Check to make sure that your fertilizer applications are timely—the general principles of when to add nutrients are discussed on page 54. If you suspect that the problem is too much nitrogen, switch to a fertilizer with a lower percentage of nitrogen, or use one without any nitrogen at all, at least for a year. Several different formulations (0–10–10, 5–10–10) are available specifically to promote better flowering. For more about fertilizer formulations, see page 54.

If you think you have been limiting flower production by pruning at the wrong time, read the section on when to prune your shrubs (pages 58 to 67), and check for the specific pruning needs of your plants in the Plant Selection Guide. As for watering, see pages 50 to 54 for helpful tips on watering practices.

Green or brown hopping insects. Pass your hand near a shrub infested with leafhoppers, and these little green or brown wedge-shaped pests will jump out at you. They have piercing mouth parts and feed on all kinds of plants and trees. Usually they suck the sap from the undersides of leaves, causing a loss of color; a stippled, wilted appearance; and a general loss of health and vigor. Some species inject a toxic substance as they feed, causing leaves to wilt. Leafhoppers, which also carry many plant viruses, are common in most parts of the country. A few do not usually harm a shrub, but if they swarm in great clouds when disturbed, they should be controlled.

Solutions. Spray leafhoppers with orthene or malathion.

White clouds of insects. When you shake or disturb a plant infected with adult whiteflies, what appear to be little clouds of snowflakes will billow out at you. Adult whiteflies are 1/16 inch long, wedge shaped, and pure white. But it's the pale green, brown, or black nymphs that do most of the damage. Whitefly nymphs are small, flat scales that suck juices from the undersides of leaves and secrete honeydew. In time, infested leaves become pale and mottled and may turn yellow and die. Whiteflies are a year-round pest in warm-winter areas, and a summer pest where winters are cold.

Solutions. To control the whitefly larvae in winter, use an oil-based dormant spray. Follow the directions on the label carefully. At other times, orthene or malathion is effective.

Oldest leaves drop off. Some shedding of the oldest leaves is natural, but an alarming rate of leaf drop may be caused by a number of factors. The most common one is insufficient sunlight. The location may not receive enough light, or the plant's shape may prevent the sun from reaching the bottom leaves. This is often the case with hedges that have been allowed to grow wider at the top than the bottom. Other causes include the stress caused by lack of water or insufficient nutrients.

It is normal for many evergreen plants in dry climates to lose some of their older leaves at the beginning of summer. After the new leaves have grown, older leaves turn yellow and drop, usually in May or June.

Solutions. If the plant just doesn't receive enough light where it is, move it. If the plant's shape is causing the problem, judicious pruning can make the difference. Selectively prune the top growth so that sunlight can reach the entire plant. Avoid plant stress with good watering practices and by fertilizing regularly. See pages 50 to 56.

Older leaves turn yellow. A lack of nitrogen causes the older shrub leaves to yellow. The growing tips usually remain green, but the new leaves are smaller than normal. During the growing season plants need an adequate supply of nitrogen in the soil to grow normally and to give leaves and stems their characteristic healthy, green color. Another possible source of yellowing is a lack of good drainage.

Solutions. If a lack of nitrogen is the cause, regularly fertilize the plants with a complete fertilizer (one that contains the three primary nutrients— nitrogen, phosphorus, and potassium). If poor drainage is the problem, you may have to move plants to another location. Follow carefully the transplanting directions on page 49.

Black smudges or a sticky secretion on leaves. Sooty mold, an unsightly black, sooty covering on branches and leaves, is not a leaf disease, and the

Left: Keno scale on a pyracantha.
Right: Aphids on a rose bud.

Below: Powdery mildew on rosebuds.
Bottom: Leaf spot on an ash leaf.

damage it does is chiefly to the leaf's appearance. Sooty mold is a secondary problem that comes with the presence of scale or aphids. This mold obtains its nourishment not from the plant but from a sugary secretion called honeydew that's left on the leaves and branches by aphids and scale insects.

Scales are tiny sucking insects that have shells. They can be white, red, brown, or black. Eventually, scale insects can seriously reduce a plant's vitality: foliage will pale and needles or leaves drop off prematurely. Heavy infestations may even kill branches, and sometimes an entire shrub.

Aphids, which are usually green or brown, frequently cluster at the growing tips of leaves to suck the plant's juices. The honeydew they secrete attracts ants. If nothing is done about them, aphids can be very debilitating.

Solutions. Because the mold is hard to wash off, most gardeners resort to pruning away affected branches and leaves. But the best defense against sooty mold is to get rid of scale and aphids before they can secrete quantities of honeydew.

Except when they are in their "crawler stage" (usually in the spring), scale insects are immobile, protected by their shells from predators and most insecticides. Scale can be smothered with an oil-based dormant spray under certain conditions: when deciduous plants are out of leaf; when the daytime temperature is above 50°F.; and when no frost is forecast for the next 24 hours. In some regions these conditions occur in the winter, but in colder areas oil spray may be applied in late fall or early spring. Whatever the season, don't spray unless the plants are completely dormant. Follow the directions on the label—some plants can be damaged by oil-based sprays. Scale can also be controlled with orthene or malathion during the crawler stage. Spray three times at 7- to 10-day intervals in May and June.

To control aphids, use orthene, diazinon, or malathion. Spray three times at two-week intervals to catch the eggs as they hatch.

Weeds around and under shrubs. Around mature shrubs, weed control is rarely a problem—the area under properly tended shrubs is usually too shaded for most weeds to grow. However, in parts of the garden that are newly planted, you may have a weed problem for the first couple of seasons.

Solutions. The best way to control most weeds that grow under shrubs is to keep a year-round mulch on top of the soil (see page 56 for mulching procedures). Any weeds that do push through will be easy to pull.

There are two kinds of herbicides that deal with weeds. One is used before weeds occur, or after you have cleaned the area completely of existing weeds; the other kills existing weeds. Follow the directions carefully when using weed-control chemicals. If misused, they can kill or damage your shrubs and other plants.

Chemicals that stop weeds from sprouting are called *pre-emergence* herbicides. They have no effect on existing weeds, but keep weeds from sprouting for up to a full growing season.

Sprays that kill existing weeds come in many formulations, and perform several different functions. Some products kill any vegetative growth they touch. They are called *nonselective* weed killers. Others are *selective* weed killers, which kill one type of vegetation but don't harm another. Read the label and know what you are doing before you use any herbicides around your shrubs.

White powder on leaves. Powdery mildew looks just like its name: a white, powdery mass that usually affects young leaves, shoots, and buds. Heavy infestations can distort young shoots and stunt foliage. The disease is spread by wind and encouraged by warm, humid days followed by cool nights. The fungus overwinters on fallen leaves, inside stems, and on bud scales.

Solutions. Sulfur dust or other fungicides will usually control powdery mildew. Start treatment at the first sign of the disease, and continue routinely. A thorough garden cleanup in the fall also helps. Rake up and destroy or dispose of fallen leaves and stems.

One way to avoid this problem is by not wetting leaves in the late afternoon or evening; give the plants a chance to dry off before evening settles in.

Spots on leaves. Spots on leaves can be symptomatic of a fungus disease or, more rarely, a bacterial infection. The spores of the fungus are carried by air currents or in water. Humid spring and summer weather are the worst times for this type of problem. The spots may be red, brown, black, or yellow.

Solutions. Leaf spot diseases usually are not serious; they can be controlled with fungicides applied on a regular basis, according to the manufacturer's directions.

Because the sources of some of these diseases live in plant debris—dead leaves, refuse, fruits, and the like—a thorough and regular garden cleanup can help to avoid leaf spot. Remove refuse from your garden and burn it or have it hauled away.

Fungus diseases can largely be prevented. Prune and space plants to allow for good air circulation, and allow enough time after sprinkler irrigation for plants to dry off before nightfall.

Precautions When Using Chemicals

Many pesticides, fungicides, and herbicides are available for the control of pests, diseases, and weeds. The two most important steps in pest and disease control are proper identification of the pest or disease and correct application of the product. Whenever you use a chemical spray, be sure to follow the steps outlined below.

Mixing. For your safety as well as for best results, read and be sure you understand the *entire* label before using any garden chemical. Then follow the directions faithfully.

When mixing these chemicals, always work on a clean, firm surface near a water source. Measure all products carefully to make sure they are diluted properly. Never make up more of a solution than you need at one time. Do not eat or smoke while mixing or spraying, and wash your hands thoroughly when you're done.

Spraying. With pesticides, application is half the battle. You must be sure to cover the pests and their hiding places adequately, as the label directs.

Never spray any plant that is suffering from a lack of moisture. Water deeply and thoroughly a day before spraying.

Avoid spraying altogether if the air temperature is above 85°F. or if it is exceptionally windy. In hot weather some chemical formulations may burn the foliage; and when it is windy, it is difficult to keep the spray from drifting to areas where it is not wanted.

The label will instruct you either to spray just enough to wet the foliage or to spray to the drip point (where the leaf surfaces are holding all the spray they can, and any more will drip off). In either case, be sure to cover all plant surfaces thoroughly. Don't forget the bottoms of leaves and both sides of stems and twigs.

Cleaning up. Thoroughly rinse the sprayer before putting it back on the shelf. Also, never burn empty chemical containers—rinse them out and dispose of them. Allow the sprayer to drain upside down for 30 seconds. Then rinse thoroughly with water and allow to dry before storing.

Spraying Equipment

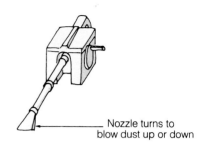

Nozzle turns to blow dust up or down

Dusters. A fan blows a stream of air that carries the dust into the foliage. Dusters are the simplest pesticide applicators, requiring no mixing or washing.

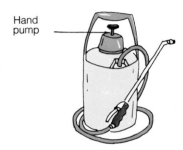

Hand pump

Pressure sprayers. An air pump builds up pressure in the tank that forces the spray from the nozzle. Because of the slow application, sprayers are best for restricted areas and small shrubs.

Spoons and bowls are needed for measuring and mixing concentrates. Use a sieve to strain lumps before pouring diluted wettable powders into the sprayer.

PLANT SELECTION GUIDE

One of the most valuable tools for a gardener is a good plant list. Here are twenty lists, plus detailed descriptions of favorite shrubs.

When faced with a new catalog, list, or encyclopedia of plants, the avid gardener is like a child at a candy store—breathless and overwhelmed at the variety of choices. There are well over six thousand shrubs in horticultural commerce, and more are being added to the list every day. To simplify this vast array somewhat, the Plant Selection Guide includes a mere five hundred or so shrubs that are considered the best or most popular. Flip through it to enjoy the breadth of beauty available to you, noting the selections that most catch your eye. Let the handy shrub selection lists guide you quickly to the best shrub for your particular environment. Turn to a single plant entry when you have a question about a particular shrub. Or read the Plant Selection Guide from beginning to end and become aware of the infinite variety in the beautiful world of shrubs.

Plant Names

Plants have two major types of names: common names and scientific names. Common names are sometimes more charming or easier to pronounce, but they lack a central authority to keep them straight. One plant can have many different common names, varying from region to region, and even from person to person. Or the same common name in one part of the country may refer to an entirely different plant in another.

Some standard is necessary to sort out the inevitable chaos. *The International Code of Botanical Nomenclature* is the worldwide authority for scientific names. The code ensures that every plant has one, and only one, correct identification: the scientific name. Always in Latin, this name is divided into two parts. The *genus* is like a human surname, indicating a general group of plants. For example, *Acer* is the generic name for a maple. The *species* is a more specific category within a genus, and is indicated by a specific epithet following the genus: *Acer palmatum* is a specific maple, Japanese maple.

A *variety* is a further subdivision of a species. It is a variation of the species that is found in the wild, and is distinguished by the ability to pass on its identifying traits through its seed. Botanical varieties are indicated in Latin, follow the species name, and are preceded by the abbreviation "var." *Acer palmatum* var. *dissectum* is the laceleaf Japanese maple.

A *cultivar* (which is a contraction of "cultivated variety") is similar to a botanical variety, except that it passes on its particular traits through either seed or vegetative reproduction (such as cuttings or grafting). It is usually the product of deliberate horticultural development. The naming of cultivars is controlled through *The International Code of Botanical Nomenclature*. Cultivar names are set off by single quotation marks (or the abbreviation "cv."), are rarely in Latin, and follow the name of either the species or the variety, as in *Acer palmatum* var. *dissectum* 'Crimson Queen'. When referring to a generalized group of plants, the term "varieties" often refers to both

botanical varieties and cultivars: "Many varieties of the Japanese maple are not shrubs."

One further variation in plant names is the use of the multiplication sign (×—pronounced "by") to indicate plants of hybrid origin. Often a collective name is given to indicate all plants with the same parentage. Thus *Abelia × grandiflora* refers to all the offspring of the hybrid *Abelia chinensis × Abelia uniflora*. Individual selections within the hybrid offspring would be indicated by cultivar names, such as *Abelia × grandiflora* 'Prostrata', which can also be shortened to *Abelia* 'Prostrata'.

In this book all plants are listed alphabetically by their scientific names. For cross-reference, common names are listed in the index. Don't be surprised, however, if you have difficulty finding a particular common name—it is impossible to list them all. Some plants have several hundred!

Selecting a Shrub

In the heading for each plant entry, you will find a range of hardiness zones: the northern and southern limits of the parts of the country in which the plant can be grown. A slightly modified version of the United States Department of Agriculture's Plant Hardiness Zone Map is shown below. Locate

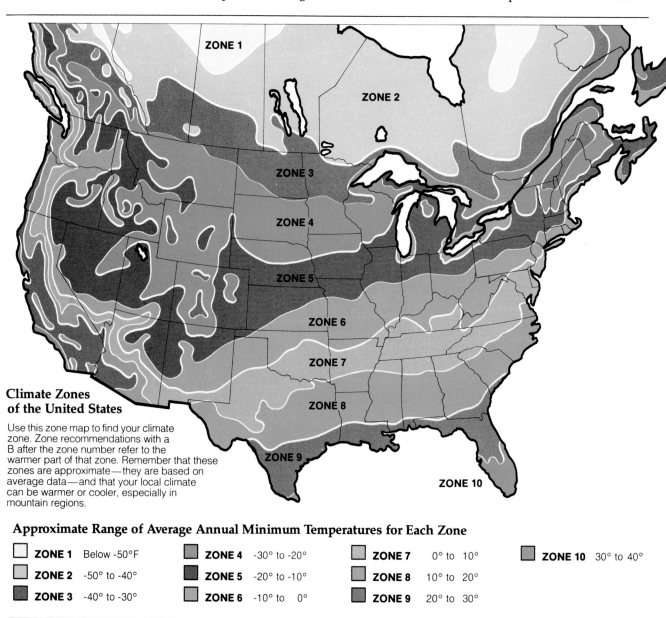

Climate Zones of the United States

Use this zone map to find your climate zone. Zone recommendations with a B after the zone number refer to the warmer part of that zone. Remember that these zones are approximate—they are based on average data—and that your local climate can be warmer or cooler, especially in mountain regions.

Approximate Range of Average Annual Minimum Temperatures for Each Zone

☐ **ZONE 1** Below -50°F	☐ **ZONE 4** -30° to -20°	☐ **ZONE 7** 0° to 10°	☐ **ZONE 10** 30° to 40°
☐ **ZONE 2** -50° to -40°	☐ **ZONE 5** -20° to -10°	☐ **ZONE 8** 10° to 20°	
☐ **ZONE 3** -40° to -30°	☐ **ZONE 6** -10° to 0°	☐ **ZONE 9** 20° to 30°	

your zone on it and use it as a reference when you consult the Plant Selection Guide. This kind of information should be used with discretion, however. Local conditions of temperature, rainfall, and other factors affecting hardiness can vary radically from the norms of the surrounding region. Even within a single garden, microclimates can differ as much as an entire zone.

To simplify shrub selection, a particular plant's range of cultivars is only touched on. Many plants (junipers and other dwarf conifers, for example) present such a huge number of cultivars that an entire volume might not even cover them all. Moreover, cultivars are best selected on a highly regional basis—preferably by using the expertise and experience of your local nursery, which stocks plants suited to the exact requirements of your area.

Most of the shrubs included in this guide are popular enough to be offered by most nurseries in regions where they can be grown. A few, however, may be too new, too difficult to propagate, or too expensive to be widely available; this is indicated in the description. In such cases, you may need to search a bit harder to find them. Your nursery may be able to special-order them for you (which is usually quite expensive), or you may be able to locate them in mail-order or specialty firms. Your local university, arboretum, or botanic garden may be further sources of assistance in locating rarer plants.

Shrub Selection Lists

When searching for that "just right" shrub to answer a particular problem or need, organized lists can be particularly helpful. Use the following lists to direct you to the appropriate description in this Plant Selection Guide.

Shrubs with Colorful Foliage

Bright golds, reds, purples, and blues can be available in your garden all year long if you shop for shrubs with colorful foliage. Deciduous plants are included in the list below, and evergreen species are marked with an asterisk (*). All should be located with care, since brightly colored leaves usually make a bold statement in the landscape.

Acer palmatum var. *dissectum* (Laceleaf Japanese maple)
  'Crimson King', reddish
  'Flavescens', yellowish green
  'Garnet', reddish
  'Ornatum', reddish
  'Ozakazuki', yellowish
  'Purpureum', deep red
  'Reticulatum', green, yellow, and pink
Aucuba japonica (Japanese aucuba)*
  'Crotonifolia', green and yellow
  'Picturata', green and yellow
  'Sulphur', green and yellow
  'Variegata', green and yellow
Berberis thunbergii (Japanese barberry)
  'Aurea', yellow
  'Crimson Pygmy', reddish
  'Sheridan's Red', red
  'Variegata', white and green
Berberis thunbergii var. *atropurpurea*
  (Japanese barberry), purple
Chamaecyparis lawsoniana (Lawson false cypress)*
  'Forsteckensis', gray-green
  'Pygmaea Argentea', yellow
Chamaecyparis obtusa (Hinoki false cypress)*
  'Mariesii', green tipped with white
Chamaecyparis pisifera (Japanese false cypress)*
  'Aurea Nana', yellow

  'Boulevard', gray
  'Golden Mop', yellow
  'Nana Variegata', green and white
  'Plumosa Rogersii', yellow
Cornus alba (Tartarian dogwood)
  'Argenteo-marginata', green and white
  'Spaethii', green and yellow
Cotinus coggygria (Smoke tree)
  'Daydream', purple
  'Velvet Cloak', purple
Daphne odora (Winter daphne)*
  'Marginata', green and yellow
Elaeagnus pungens (Silverberry)*
  'Maculata', green and yellow
  'Marginata', green and white
  'Variegata', green and yellow

Euonymus fortunei (Wintercreeper)*
  'Emerald and Gold', green and yellow
  'Emerald Gaiety', green and white
  'Golden Prince', green and yellow
  'Gracilis', green and white
Euonymus japonica (Evergreen euonymus)*
  'Albomarginata', green and white
  'Aureomarginata', green and yellow
  'Gold Center', green and yellow
  'Golden', green and yellow
  'Microphylla Variegata', green and white
  'President Gauthier', green and white
  'Silver King', green and white
  'Silver Queen', green and white
Hydrangea macrophylla (Bigleaf hydrangea)
  'Tricolor', green, white, and yellow
Juniperus chinensis (Chinese juniper)*
  'Armstrongii', gray
  'Blaaw', gray
  'Old Gold', yellow
  'Pfitzerana Aurea', yellow
  'Plumosa Aureovariegata', yellow
Juniperus chinensis var. *procumbens*
  (Creeping juniper)*, gray

Aucuba japonica 'Crotonifolia'

Juniperus chinensis var. *sargentii* (Sargent juniper)*, gray
Juniperus communis (Common juniper)*
  'Depressa Aurea', yellow
Juniperus conferta (Shore juniper)*, gray-blue
Juniperus horizontalis (Creeping juniper)*, gray or blue
Juniperus sabina (Savin juniper)*
  'Broadmoor', gray
  'Skandia', gray
  'Variegatus', gray and white
Juniperus scopulorum (Rocky Mountain juniper)*
  'Lakewood Globe', gray-blue
  'Table Top Blue', blue-gray
Kerria japonica (Japanese kerria)
  'Aureo-variegata', green and yellow
  'Aureo-vittata', green and yellow stems
  'Picta', green and white
Leptospermum scoparium (New Zealand tea tree)*
  'Gaiety Girl', reddish
  'Waringi', reddish
Leucothoe fontanesiana (Drooping leucothoe)*
  'Girard's Rainbow', green, white, and pink
Ligustrum × *ibolium* (Ibolium privet)
  'Variegata', green and yellow
Ligustrum japonicum (Japanese privet)*
  'Silver Star', green and white
Ligustrum ovalifolium (California or oval-leaf privet)*
  'Aureum', green and yellow
Ligustrum 'Vicaryi' (Golden privet), yellow
Myrtus communis (Myrtle)*
  'Compacta Variegata', green and white
  'Variegata', green and white
Nandina domestica (Nandina; Heavenly bamboo)*
  'Nana Purpurea', purplish
  'Variegatus', green and white
Osmanthus heterophyllus (Holly olive)*
  'Purpureus', purplish
  'Variegatus', green and white
Photinia × *fraseri* (Photinia)*, purplish
Pieris forrestii (Chinese pieris)*, red new growth
Pieris japonica (Japanese pieris)*, reddish new foliage
  'Variegata', green and white
Pittosporum tobira (Tobira; Japanese pittosporum)*
  'Variegata', green and white
Platycladus orientalis (Oriental arborvitae)*
  'Aurea Nana', yellow
  'Compacta', gray-green
Prunus 'Cistena' (Purple-leafed sand cherry), purple
Rosmarinus officinalis (Rosemary)*, gray
Taxus baccata (English yew)*
  'Aurea', yellow
  'Elegantissima', green and yellow
  'Washingtonii', yellow
Taxus cuspidata (Japanese yew)*
  'Aurescens', yellow
Thuja occidentalis (American arborvitae)*
  'Aurea', yellow
  'Lutea', yellow
  'Umbracilifera', gray-blue

Shrubs with Fall Foliage Color

Many deciduous shrubs are very striking in the fall when their foliage changes to various shades of red, orange, yellow, and bronze. Frequently, their colors are brighter and

Rhus copallina

longer lasting than those of many flowers. Consult the list that follows for some of the more spectacular choices.

Abelia × *grandiflora* (Glossy abelia)
Acer palmatum var. *dissectum* (Laceleaf Japanese maple)
Aronia arbutifolia (Red chokeberry)
Berberis thunbergii (Japanese barberry)
Clethra alnifolia (Summersweet; Sweet pepperbush)
Cornus alba (Tartarian dogwood)
Cornus sericea (Red-osier dogwood)
Cotinus coggygria (Smoke tree)
Cotoneaster divaricatus (Spreading cotoneaster)
Cotoneaster horizontalis (Rockspray cotoneaster)
Enkianthus campanulatus (Redvein enkianthus)
Euonymus alatus (Burning bush; Winged euonymus)
Fothergilla major (Large fothergilla)
Hamamelis species (Witch hazel)
Hydrangea quercifolia (Oakleaf hydrangea)
Lagerstroemia indica (Crape myrtle)
Mahonia aquifolium (Oregon grape)
Nandina domestica (Nandina; Heavenly bamboo)
Paxistima canbyi (Cliff-green; Mountain-lover)
Punica granatum (Pomegranate)
Rhododendron arborescens (Sweet azalea)
Rhododendron kaempferi (Kaempfer azalea)
Rhododendron Knapp Hill-Exbury Hybrids
Rhododendron schlippenbachii (Royal azalea)
Rhododendron vaseyi (Pinkshell azalea)
Rhus species (Sumac)
Rosa virginiana (Virginia rose)
Vaccinium corymbosum (Highbush blueberry)
Viburnum × *carlcephalum* (Fragrant snowball viburnum)
Viburnum dilatatum (Linden viburnum)
Viburnum × *juddii* (Judd viburnum)
Viburnum opulus (European cranberry bush)
Viburnum plicatum var. *tomentosum* (Doublefile viburnum)
Viburnum trilobum (American cranberry bush viburnum)

Shrubs with Evergreen Foliage

Evergreen shrubs, whether broadleaved or coniferous, add their own special warmth to the garden. Their presence is especially appreciated in the winter, when the landscape might otherwise feel bleak and uninviting. In the following list, the abbreviation SE following an entry indicates that a plant is semievergreen—partially or totally dropping its leaves in the northern limits of its hardiness range.

Abelia × *grandiflora* (Glossy abelia), SE
Arctostaphylos species (Manzanita)
Aucuba japonica (Japanese aucuba)
Berberis darwinii (Darwin barberry)
Buxus species (Boxwood)
Callistemon citrinus (Lemon bottlebrush)
Calluna vulgaris (Scotch heather)
Camellia species (Camellia)
Ceanothus (Wild lilac), western species
Chamaecyparis species (False cypress)
Choisya ternata (Mexican orange)
Cistus species (Rockrose)
Coprosma species (Coprosma)
Cotoneaster dammeri (Bearberry cotoneaster)

Cotoneaster horizontalis (Rockspray
    cotoneaster), SE
Cytisus × *praecox* (Warminster broom)
Daphne species (Daphne)
Elaeagnus pungens (Silverberry)
Erica species (Heath)
Escallonia species (Escallonia)
Euonymus fortunei (Wintercreeper)
Euonymus japonica (Evergreen euonymus)
Euonymus kiautschovica (Spreading
    euonymus)
Gardenia jasminoides (Gardenia)
Genista species (Broom)
Hypericum calycinum (Aaronsbeard
    St. Johnswort)
Hypericum × *moseranum* (Goldflower
    St. Johnswort)
Hypericum patulum (Goldencup
    St. Johnswort), SE
Iberis sempervirens (Evergreen candytuft)
Ilex cornuta (Chinese holly)
Ilex crenata (Japanese holly)
Ilex glabra (Inkberry)
Ilex vomitoria (Yaupon)
Juniperus species (Juniper)
Kalmia latifolia (Mountain laurel)
Leptospermum scoparium (New Zealand
    tea tree)
Leucothoe fontanesiana (Drooping leucothoe)
Ligustrum × *ibolium* (Ibolium privet), SE
Ligustrum japonicum (Japanese privet)
Ligustrum lucidum (Glossy privet)
Ligustrum ovalifolium (California or
    oval-leaf privet), SE
Ligustrum 'Suwanee River' (Privet hybrid)
Lonicera nitida (Box honeysuckle)
Mahonia species (Oregon or holly grape)
Myrtus communis (Myrtle)
Nandina domestica (Nandina; Heavenly
    bamboo)
Nerium oleander (Oleander)
Osmanthus delavayi (Delavay osmanthus)
Osmanthus fragrans (Sweet olive)
Osmanthus heterophyllus (Holly olive)
Paxistima canbyi (Cliff-green; Mountain-lover)
Photinia × *fraseri* (Photinia)
Photinia serrulata (Chinese photinia)
Picea species (Spruce)
Pieris species (Pieris)
Pinus species (Pine)
Pittosporum species (Pittosporum)
Prunus laurocerasus (English laurel)
Pyracantha coccinea (Scarlet firethorn), SE
Raphiolepis indica (India hawthorn)
Rhododendron carolinianum (Carolina
    rhododendron)
Rhododendron catawbiense (Catawba
    rhododendron)
Rhododendron Gable Hybrids (Gable
    hybrid azalea), SE
Rhododendron impeditum (Cloudland
    rhododendron)
Rhododendron Indica Hybrids (Indian
    hybrid azalea)
Rhododendron kaempferi (Kaempfer
    azalea), SE
Rhododendron keiskei (Kieske
    rhododendron)
Rhododendron lapponicum (Lapland
    rhododendron)
Rhododendron × *loderi* (Loder hybrid
    rhododendron)
Rhododendron maximum (Rosebay
    rhododendron)
Rhododendron obtusum (Hiryu or
    Kirishima azalea)
Rhododendron, P.J.M. Hybrids

Rosa wichuraiana (Memorial rose), SE
Rosmarinus officinalis (Rosemary)
Taxus species (Yew)
Thuja species (Arborvitae)
Tsuga canadensis 'Pendula' (Sargent's
    weeping hemlock)
Viburnum × *burkwoodii* (Burkwood
    viburnum), SE
Viburnum davidii (David viburnum)
Viburnum × *rhytidophylloides*
    (Lantanaphyllum viburnum)
Viburnum tinus (Laurustinus)
Xylosma congestum (Shiny xylosma)

Shrubs for Winter Interest

There are those who say you can never know
the true inner beauty of a plant until it drops
its leaves. A shrub's structure, bark, stem,
twigs, and buds offer a kaleidoscope of
winter textures to look at. The effects may be
delicate and subtle or bold and dramatic, but
the shrubs listed here are worth braving the
cold for—in a stroll through the winter
landscape.

Acer palmatum var. *dissectum* (Laceleaf
    Japanese maple)
Aronia arbutifolia (Red chokeberry)
Cornus alba (Tartarian dogwood)
Cornus sericea (Red-osier dogwood)
Corylus avellana 'Contorta' (Harry Lauder's
    walking stick)
Cytisus × *praecox* (Warminster broom)
Genista species (Broom)
Hamamelis species (Witch hazel)
Ilex decidua (Possum haw)
Ilex verticillata (Common winterberry)
Kerria japonica (Japanese kerria)
Lagerstroemia indica (Crape myrtle)
Magnolia species (Magnolia)
Myrica pensylvanica (Northern bayberry)
Rhus copallina (Flameleaf sumac;
    Shining sumac)
Rhus typhina (Staghorn sumac)
Rosa hugonis (Father Hugo rose)
Rosa virginiana (Virginia rose)

Shrubs with Showy Fruit

The wise gardener is aware of the all-season
values that shrubs can bring, a chief one
being attractive fruit. While flowers often last
only a week or so, the spectacular fruits of
many shrubs can last an entire fall or
winter. The following list presents some
of the more lavish examples of ornamental
fruits.

Arctostaphylos species (Manzanita)
Aronia arbutifolia (Red chokeberry)
Aucuba japonica (Japanese aucuba)
Berberis darwinii (Darwin barberry)
Berberis koreana (Korean barberry)
Berberis thunbergii (Japanese barberry)
Chaenomeles speciosa (Common
    flowering quince)
Cotoneaster dammeri (Bearberry
    cotoneaster)
Cotoneaster divaricatus (Spreading
    cotoneaster)
Cotoneaster horizontalis (Rockspray
    cotoneaster)
Cotoneaster multiflorus (Many-flowered
    cotoneaster)
Elaeagnus species (Elaeagnus)
Euonymus fortunei (Wintercreeper),
    selected varieties
Ilex cornuta (Chinese holly)

Pittosporum tobira 'Variegata'

Cornus alba 'Sibirica'

Pyracantha coccinea

Potentilla fruticosa 'Goldfinger'

Ilex verticillata (Common winterberry)
Ilex vomitoria (Yaupon)
Lonicera tatarica (Tatarian honeysuckle)
Mahonia species (Oregon grape;
    Holly grape)
Malus sargentii (Sargent's crabapple)
Myrica pensylvanica (Northern bayberry)
Nandina domestica (Nandina; Heavenly
    bamboo)
Photinia species (Photinia)
Prunus maritima (Beach plum)
Prunus tomentosa (Nanking cherry;
    Manchu cherry)
Punica granatum (Pomegranate)
Pyracantha coccinea (Scarlet firethorn)
Rhus copallina (Flameleaf sumac;
    Shining sumac)
Rhus typhina (Staghorn sumac)
Rosa hugonis (Father Hugo rose)
Rosa virginiana (Virginia rose)
Symplocos paniculata (Sapphireberry;
    Asiatic sweetleaf)
Vaccinium corymbosum (Highbush
    blueberry)
Viburnum davidii (David viburnum)
Viburnum dilatatum (Linden viburnum)
Virburnum × *juddii* (Judd viburnum)
Viburnum opulus (European cranberry bush)
Viburnum plicatum var. *tomentosum*
    (Doublefile viburnum)
Viburnum tinus (Laurustinus)
Viburnum trilobum (American cranberry
    bush viburnum)

Drought-tolerant Shrubs

In many parts of the United States, watering is the gardener's most time-consuming chore. Whether your garden is in the arid deserts of the Southwest, the Mediterranean, summer-drought climates of the West Coast, or the dry plains of the Prairie States, planting shrubs from the following list can help to make your gardening easier.

Arctostaphylos species (Manzanita)
Aronia arbutifolia (Red chokeberry)
Aucuba japonica (Japanese aucuba)
Berberis species (Barberry)
Callistemon citrinus (Lemon bottlebrush)
Caragana arborescens (Siberian peashrub)
Ceanothus species (Wild lilac)
Cistus species (Rockrose)
Coprosma species (Coprosma)
Cotinus coggygria (Smoke tree)
Cotoneaster species (Cotoneaster)
Cytisus × *praecox* (Warminster broom)
Elaeagnus species (Elaeagnus)
Euonymus japonica (Evergreen euonymus)
Genista species (Broom)
Hypericum species (St. Johnswort)
Juniperus species (Juniper)
Lagerstroemia indica (Crape myrtle)
Leptospermum scoparium (New Zealand
    tea tree)
Ligustrum species (Privet)
Myrica pensylvanica (Northern bayberry)
Myrtus communis (Myrtle)
Nandina domestica (Nandina; Heavenly
    bamboo)
Nerium oleander (Oleander)
Osmanthus species (Devilweed)
Photinia species (Photinia)
Potentilla fruticosa (Bush cinquefoil)
Punica granatum (Pomegranate)
Raphiolepis indica (India hawthorn)
Rhus species (Sumac)
Rosmarinus officinalis (Rosemary)

Tamarix species (Tamarix)
Xylosma congestum (Shiny xylosma)

Winter-tolerant Shrubs

If you live in the Northern Plains States, the mountains, or in northern latitudes where a more limited plant selection is the rule, the following list will direct you to the appropriate shrubs. You may be surprised to find a wider selection than you thought possible. The zone given is the hardiness limit for each shrub.

Arctostaphylos uva-ursi (Bearberry
    manzanita; Kinnikinick), Zone 2
Caragana arborescens (Siberian peashrub),
    Zone 2
Clethra alnifolia (Summersweet; Sweet
    pepperbush), Zone 3
Cornus alba (Tartarian dogwood), Zone 2
Cornus sericea (Red-osier dogwood), Zone 2
Genista tinctoria (Common woadwaxen),
    Zone 2
Ilex glabra (Inkberry), Zone 3
Juniperus communis (Common juniper),
    Zone 2
Juniperus horizontalis (Creeping juniper),
    Zone 3
Juniperus virginiana (Eastern redcedar),
    Zone 2
Lonicera tatarica (Tatarian honeysuckle),
    Zone 3B
Myrica pensylvanica (Northern bayberry),
    Zone 2
Picea species (Spruce), Zone 2
Pinus mugo var. *mugo* (Dwarf mugo pine),
    Zone 2
Potentilla fruticosa (Bush cinquefoil), Zone 2
Prunus 'Cistena' (Purple-leafed sand cherry),
    Zone 2
Prunus tomentosa (Nanking cherry;
    Manchu cherry), Zone 2
Rhododendron canadense (Rhodora
    azalea), Zone 2
Rhododendron lapponicum (Lapland
    rhododendron), Zone 3
Rosa rubrifolia (Redleaf rose), Zone 2
Rosa rugosa (Rugosa rose; Saltspray rose),
    Zone 2
Syringa vulgaris (Common lilac), Zone 3B
Tamarix ramosissima (Odessa tamarix),
    Zone 2
Thuja occidentalis (American arborvitae),
    Zone 2
Viburnum trilobum (American cranberry
    bush viburnum), Zone 3

Cytisus hybrids

City-tolerant Shrubs

Consider the following shrubs if you live in areas that have high atmospheric pollution. Most of these shrubs are also fairly tolerant of the restricted sunlight, reduced air circulation, and poor soils of many urban gardens.

Aesculus parviflora (Bottlebrush buckeye)
Aronia arbutifolia (Red chokeberry)
Berberis thunbergii (Japanese barberry)
Caragana arborescens (Siberian peashrub)
Chaenomeles speciosa (Common flowering quince)
Cornus alba (Tartarian dogwood)
Cornus sericea (Red-osier dogwood)
Elaeagnus species (Elaeagnus)
Forsythia species (Forsythia)
Hamamelis virginiana (Common witch hazel)
Hibiscus rosa-sinensis (Chinese hibiscus)
Hibiscus syriacus (Shrub althea; Rose of Sharon)
Hydrangea species (Hydrangea)
Hypericum species (St. Johnswort)
Ilex crenata (Japanese holly)
Ilex glabra (Inkberry)
Juniperus species (Juniper)
Kerria japonica (Japanese kerria)
Lagerstroemia indica (Crape myrtle)
Ligustrum species (Privet)
Lonicera species (Honeysuckle)
Magnolia stellata (Star magnolia)
Mahonia aquifolium (Oregon grape)
Malus sargentii (Sargent's crabapple)
Myrica pensylvanica (Northern bayberry)
Nerium oleander (Oleander)
Philadelphus coronarius (Sweet mock orange)
Pittosporum tobira (Tobira; Japanese pittosporum)
Potentilla fruticosa (Bush cinquefoil)
Pyracantha coccinea (Scarlet firethorn)
Rhus species (Sumac)
Rosa rugosa (Rugosa rose; Saltspray rose)
Rosa wichuraiana (Memorial rose)
Spiraea × bumalda (Bumalda spirea)
Spiraea vanhouttei (Vanhoutte spirea)
Syringa vulgaris (Common lilac)
Taxus baccata (English yew)
Taxus cuspidata (Japanese yew)
Vaccinium corymbosum (Highbush blueberry)
Viburnum opulus (European cranberry bush)

Shade-tolerant Shrubs

There are many qualities of shade, and some plants adapt especially well to a particular one. Most shrubs can tolerate the partial shade of high tree branches, even though they might prefer full sun. In the following list, however, you will find shrubs that do better in the shade than most. Most of these plants perform best in partial shade; the few that tolerate deep shade are marked with an asterisk (*). Realize that "deep shade" does not mean total darkness—all plants require some light to survive.

Aesculus species (Horse chestnut; Buckeye)
Aucuba japonica (Japanese aucuba)*
Calycanthus floridus (Carolina allspice; Strawberry shrub)
Camellia japonica (Common camellia)
Chamaecyparis species (False cypress)
Choisya ternata (Mexican orange)
Clethra alnifolia (Summersweet; Sweet pepperbush)
Coprosma species (Coprosma)
Cornus alba (Tartarian dogwood)

Cornus sericea (Red-osier dogwood)
Euonymus species (Euonymus)
Fuchsia × hybrida (Common fuchsia)
Fuchsia magellanica (Hardy fuchsia)
Gardenia jasminoides (Gardenia)
Hamamelis species (Witch hazel)
Hydrangea species (Hydrangea)
Ilex species (Holly)
Kalmia latifolia (Mountain laurel)*
Leucothoe fontanesiana (Drooping leucothoe)
Ligustrum species (Privet)*
Myrtus communis (Myrtle)
Nandina domestica (Nandina; Heavenly bamboo)
Osmanthus species (Devilweed)*
Pieris species (Pieris)*
Pittosporum species (Pittosporum)
Prunus laurocerasus (English laurel)
Rhododendron species (Rhododendron; Azalea)
Taxus species (Yew)*
Tsuga canadensis 'Pendula' (Sargent's weeping hemlock)
Viburnum davidii (David viburnum)
Viburnum × juddii (Judd viburnum)
Viburnum tinus (Laurustinus)
Viburnum trilobum (American cranberry bush viburnum)

Shrubs for Wet Soils

For many gardeners, a serious problem is having to work with heavy soil with poor drainage. Often, the low spots in such gardens collect water, which remains for a long time. The following list contains shrubs that perform well in standing water, along with other plants that tolerate a low amount of soil aeration.

Aronia arbutifolia (Red chokeberry)
Calycanthus floridus (Carolina allspice; Strawberry shrub)
Clethra alnifolia (Summersweet; Sweet pepperbush)
Cornus alba (Tartarian dogwood)
Cornus sericea (Red-osier dogwood)
Hamamelis vernalis (Vernal witch hazel)
Hypericum densiflorum (Dense hypericum)
Ilex glabra (Inkberry)
Ilex verticillata (Common winterberry)
Myrica pensylvanica (Northern bayberry)
Potentilla fruticosa (Bush cinquefoil)
Rhododendron canadense (Rhodora azalea)
Rhododendron viscosum (Swamp azalea)
Salix gracilistyla (Rosegold pussy willow)
Viburnum cassinoides (Withe-rod viburnum)
Viburnum opulus (European cranberry bush)
Viburnum trilobum (American cranberry bush viburnum)

Left: *Hibiscus rosa-sinensis*
Above: *Fuchsia × hybrida*

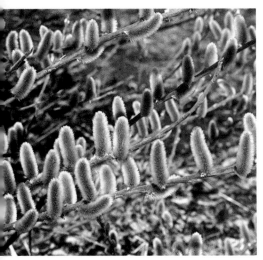

Salix gracilistyla

Shrubs for Acid Soils

While most shrubs will tolerate a moderately acid soil (a pH of 6), many shrubs *require* acid soil in order to thrive. The following shrubs should be considered only if you have, or intend to create and maintain, soil with a pH of 6 or less.

Arctostaphylos uva-ursi (Bearberry manzanita; Kinnikinick)
Calluna vulgaris (Scotch heather)
Camellia species (Camellia)
Choisya ternata (Mexican orange)
Clethra alnifolia (Summersweet; Sweet pepperbush)
Enkianthus campanulatus (Redvein enkianthus)
Erica species (Heath)
Exochorda species (Pearlbush)
Fothergilla species (Fothergilla)
Gardenia jasminoides (Gardenia)
Hydrangea macrophylla (Bigleaf hydrangea)
Hydrangea quercifolia (Oakleaf hydrangea)
Ilex species (Holly)
Juniperus communis (Common juniper)
Kalmia latifolia (Mountain laurel)
Leucothoe fontanesiana (Drooping leucothoe)
Magnolia species (Magnolia)
Mahonia species (Oregon grape; Holly grape)
Paxistima canbyi (Cliff-green; Mountain-lover)
Rhododendron species (Rhododendron; Azalea)
Tsuga canadensis 'Pendula' (Sargent's weeping hemlock)
Vaccinium corymbosum (Highbush blueberry)

Shrubs for the Seacoast

Seacoast gardens have their own unique problems—from harsh, constant winds to sandy soil and saline spray. The plants in the list below perform well under these conditions. Usually, they also make excellent choices for desert gardens; see the list for drought tolerance.

Arctostaphylos species (Manzanita)
Callistemon citrinus (Lemon bottlebrush)
Ceanothus species (Wild lilac)
Cistus species (Rockrose)
Coprosma species (Coprosma)
Cotoneaster dammeri (Bearberry cotoneaster)
Cotoneaster divaricatus (Spreading cotoneaster)
Cotoneaster horizontalis (Rockspray cotoneaster)
Cytisus × *praecox* (Warminster broom)
Elaeagnus species (Elaeagnus)
Escallonia species (Escallonia)
Genista species (Broom)
Hibiscus syriacus (Shrub althea; Rose of Sharon)
Hydrangea macrophylla (Bigleaf hydrangea)
Juniperus species (Juniper) especially *J. conferta* (Shore juniper)
Leptospermum scoparium (New Zealand tea tree)
Lonicera nitida (Box honeysuckle)
Myrica pensylvanica (Northern bayberry)
Pittosporum crassifolium (Karo)
Prunus maritima (Beach plum)
Raphiolepis indica (India hawthorn)
Rosa rugosa (Rugosa rose; Saltspray rose)
Rosa viginiana (Virginia rose)
Rosmarinus officinalis (Rosemary)
Tamarix species (Tamarix)

This well-tended azalea garden is complemented by other acid-soil-loving plants.

Shrubs That Are Easy to Care For

Any shrub is easy to maintain once the correct conditions for growth are met. The trick is in knowing and creating those conditions. Certain plants can ease that difficulty somewhat, because they are not very finicky. The shrubs listed here adapt to a wide variety of conditions and are pest resistant. While they can almost be left alone, even these plants will benefit from an occasional shot of fertilizer and deep watering during drought.

Abelia × *grandiflora* (Glossy abelia)
Aesculus parviflora (Bottlebrush buckeye)
Arctostaphylos uva-ursi (Bearberry manzanita; Kinnikinick)
Aronia arbutifolia (Red chokeberry)
Aucuba japonica (Japanese aucuba)
Berberis species (Barberry)
Callistemon citrinus (Lemon bottlebrush)
Calycanthus floridus (Carolina allspice; Strawberry shrub)
Caragana arborescens (Siberian peashrub)
Chaenomeles speciosa (Common flowering quince)
Cistus species (Rockrose)
Clethra alnifolia (Summersweet; Sweet pepperbush)
Coprosma species (Coprosma)
Cornus alba (Tartarian dogwood)
Cornus sericea (Red-osier dogwood)
Corylus avellana 'Contorta' (Harry Lauder's walking stick)
Cotinus coggygria (Smoke tree)
Cotoneaster species (Cotoneaster)
Cytisus species (Broom)
Deutzia species (Deutzia)
Elaeagnus species (Elaeagnus)
Euonymus alatus (Burning bush; Winged euonymus)
Exochorda species (Pearlbush)
Fothergilla major (Large fothergilla)
Genista species (Broom)
Hamamelis species (Witch hazel)
Hypericum species (St. Johnswort)
Ilex species (Holly)
Juniperus species (Juniper)
Kerria japonica (Japanese kerria)
Kolkwitzia amabilis (Beautybush)
Lagerstroemia indica (Crape myrtle)
Leptospermum scoparium (New Zealand tea tree)
Ligustrum species (Privet)
Lonicera nitida (Box honeysuckle)
Lonicera × *xylosteoides* 'Clavey's Dwarf' (Clavey's Dwarf honeysuckle)
Malus sargentii (Sargent's crabapple)
Myrica pensylvanica (Northern bayberry)
Myrtus communis (Myrtle)
Nandina domestica (Nandina; Heavenly bamboo)
Nerium oleander (Oleander)
Osmanthus species (Devilweed)
Paxistima canbyi (Cliff-green; Mountain-lover)
Philadelphus species (Mock orange)
Pinus species (Pine)
Pittosporum species (Pittosporum)
Potentilla fruticosa (Bush cinquefoil)
Prunus 'Cistena' (Purple-leafed sand cherry)
Prunus tomentosa (Nanking cherry; Manchu cherry)
Raphiolepis indica (India hawthorn)
Rhus species (Sumac)
Rosa species (Rose)
Rosmarinus officinalis (Rosemary)

Spiraea species (Spirea)
Symplocos paniculata (Sapphireberry; Asiatic sweetleaf)
Taxus species (Yew)
Thuja species (Arborvitae)
Viburnum species (Viburnum)
Xylosma congestum (Shiny xylosma)

Fast-growing Shrubs for Quick Solutions

Patience is one of the most difficult traits for a gardener to practice. The shrubs listed below can help ease the wait, since they grow more quickly than most. Don't expect them to leap up into their adult size overnight, however. Most will still take at least two seasons before they resemble a mature effect. Understand that many are not suitable for more permanent solutions: In general, the faster a shrub grows, the shorter it lives.

Abelia × *grandiflora* (Glossy abelia)
Berberis species (Barberry)
Callistemon citrinus (Lemon bottlebrush)
Caragana arborescens (Siberian peashrub)
Ceanothus species (Wild lilac)
Choisya ternata (Mexican orange)

Top: *Leptospermum scoparium*
Above: *Nerium oleander*

Rosa species

Rhododendron species

Erica species

Cistus species (Rockrose)
Coprosma species (Coprosma)
Cornus alba (Tartarian dogwood)
Cornus sericea (Red-osier dogwood)
Cotoneaster dammeri (Bearberry cotoneaster)
Cotoneaster divaricatus (Spreading cotoneaster)
Cytisus × praecox (Warminster broom)
Elaeagnus species (Elaeagnus)
Escallonia species (Escallonia)
Forsythia species (Forsythia)
Fuchsia × hybrida (Common fuchsia)
Hydrangea macrophylla (Bigleaf hydrangea)
Hypericum calycinum (Aaronsbeard St. Johnswort)
Kerria japonica (Japanese kerria)
Kolkwitzia amabilis (Beautybush)
Ligustrum species (Privet)
Lonicera species (Honeysuckle)
Nerium oleander (Oleander)
Philadelphus species (Mock orange)
Prunus laurocerasus (English laurel)
Pyracantha species (Firethorn)
Rhus copallina (Flameleaf sumac; Shining sumac)
Rhus typhina (Staghorn sumac)
Rosa species (Rose)
Salix species (Willow; Osier)
Spiraea species (Spirea)
Tamarix species (Tamarix)
Weigela florida (Old-fashioned Weigela)

Shrubs for Ground Covers

Many woody shrubs make excellent ground covers. The selections that follow represent the best of the low, spreading forms. Consider them for covering a steep bank where a lawn is difficult to maintain and where a solution to erosion is needed. Some of them do well in large beds, all to themselves. The list of dwarf shrubs on page 90 indicates by asterisks (*) which ones are also suitable for ground covers.

Abelia × grandiflora (Glossy abelia), 'Prostrata' 'Sherwoodii'
Arctostaphylos uva-ursi (Bearberry manzanita; Kinnikinick)
Berberis thunbergii (Japanese barberry), selected varieties
Calluna vulgaris (Scotch heather)
Ceanothus (Wild lilac), selected varieties
Chaenomeles (Flowering quince), selected varieties
Cistus species (Rockrose)
Coprosma × kirkii (Coprosma)
Cotoneaster dammeri (Bearberry cotoneaster)
Cotoneaster horizontalis (Rockspray cotoneaster)
Erica species (Heath)
Hypericum calycinum (Aaronsbeard St. Johnswort)
Iberis sempervirens (Evergreen candytuft)
Ilex glabra 'Compacta' (Inkberry)
Juniperus chinensis (Chinese juniper), selected varieties
Juniperus horizontalis (Creeping juniper)
Juniperus sabina (Savin juniper), selected varieties
Juniperus virginiana (Eastern redcedar), selected varieties
Leptospermum scoparium (New Zealand tea tree), selected varieties

Leucothoe fontanesiana (Drooping leucothoe)
Lonicera × xylosteoides 'Clavey's Dwarf' (Clavey's Dwarf honeysuckle)
Paxistima canbyi (Cliff-green; Mountain-lover)
Potentilla fruticosa (Bush cinquefoil)
Pyracantha coccinea (Scarlet firethorn), selected varieties
Rosa wichuraiana (Memorial rose)
Rosmarinus officinalis (Rosemary)
Spiraea albiflora (Japanese white spirea)
Xylosma congestum (Shiny xylosma)

Shrubs for Containers

Some shrubs adapt more easily to container culture than others. They may be naturally small, with a relatively contained root system. Or they may dwarf more easily by judicious pruning of roots and shoots. The shrubs that usually do best in containers already have a naturally neat and compact growth habit, or else can easily be kept that way. Use the following list as a guide for adding greenery and color to your deck or patio. Also see the list of dwarf shrubs on page 90 for more ideas about shrubs that are suitable for container gardening.

Acer palmatum var. dissectum (Laceleaf Japanese maple)
Aucuba japonica (Japanese aucuba)
Buxus microphylla (Littleleaf boxwood)
Buxus sempervirens (Common boxwood)
Camellia species (Camellia)
Chamaecyparis species (False cypress)
Corylus avellana 'Contorta' (Harry Lauder's walking stick)
Cotoneaster horizontalis (Rockspray cotoneaster)
Euonymus fortunei (Wintercreeper)
Fuchsia × hybrida (Common fuchsia)
Gardenia jasminoides (Gardenia)
Hydrangea macrophylla (Bigleaf hydrangea)
Ilex cornuta (Chinese holly)
Ilex crenata (Japanese holly)
Ilex vomitoria 'Nana' (Yaupon)
Kalmia latifolia (Mountain laurel)
Lagerstroemia indica (Crape myrtle)
Leptospermum scoparium (New Zealand tea tree)
Leucothoe fontanesiana (Drooping leucothoe)
Ligustrum species (Privet)
Lonicera nitida (Box honeysuckle)
Mahonia bealei (Leatherleaf mahonia)
Mahonia lomariifolia (Mahonia)
Myrtus communis (Myrtle)
Nandina domestica (Nandina; Heavenly bamboo)
Nerium oleander (Oleander)
Osmanthus species (Devilweed)
Picea species (Spruce), dwarf varieties
Pieris japonica (Japanese pieris)
Pinus (Pine), dwarf varieties
Pittosporum tobira (Tobira; Japanese pittosporum)
Prunus laurocerasus (English laurel)
Punica granatum (Pomegranate)
Pyracantha species (Firethorn)
Raphiolepis indica (India hawthorn)
Rhododendron species (Rhododendron; Azalea)
Rosmarinus officinalis (Rosemary)
Taxus species (Yew)
Thuja species (Arborvitae), dwarf varieties

Tsuga canadensis 'Pendula' (Sargent's weeping hemlock)

Thorny Shrubs for Barriers

Beware of these thorny shrubs. Use them wherever you want to keep people away—including yourself. Don't plant them near public places where they will scratch passers-by, lodge in the feet of barefoot children, or attack your knees and hands as you weed beds. As barriers, each of the following shrubs will prove to be impenetrable.

Berberis species (Barberry)
Chaenomeles speciosa (Common flowering quince)
Elaeagnus pungens (Silverberry)
Ilex cornuta (Chinese holly)
Osmanthus heterophyllus (Holly olive)
Pyracantha coccinea (Scarlet firethorn)
Rosa species (Rose)

Shrubs for Hedges and Other Formal Shapes

Consider the following shrubs when you plan a hedge, topiary, or other formal planting. All of them will take close shearing and clipping well.

Abelia × *grandiflora* (Glossy abelia)

Berberis thunbergii (Japanese barberry)
Buxus species (Boxwood)
Chamaecyparis species (False cypress)
Elaeagnus pungens (Silverberry)
Euonymus fortunei (Wintercreeper), shrub cultivars
Euonymus japonica (Evergreen euonymus)
Euonymus kiautschovica (Spreading euonymus)
Ilex cornuta (Chinese holly), small cultivars
Ilex crenata (Japanese holly)
Ilex glabra (Inkberry)
Ilex vomitoria (Yaupon)
Juniperus (Juniper), selected cultivars
Ligustrum species (Privet)
Lonicera nitida (Box honeysuckle)
Lonicera × *xylosteoides* 'Clavey's Dwarf' (Clavey's Dwarf honeysuckle)
Myrtus communis (Myrtle)
Osmanthus species (Devilweed)
Pittosporum crassifolium (Pittosporum)
Pittosporum eugenoides (Pittosporum)
Prunus laurocerasus (English laurel)
Prunus tomentosa (Nanking cherry; Manchu cherry)
Pyracantha coccinea (Scarlet firethorn)
Rhododendron maximum (Rosebay rhododendron)
Rosmarinus officinalis (Rosemary)
Taxus species (Yew)
Viburnum tinus (Laurustinus)
Xylosma congestum (Shiny xylosma)

Berberis darwinii

Boxwood hedges give interest to an open space while azaleas provide background color.

Above: *Syringa vulgaris*
Right: *Viburnum dilatatum*

Shrubs That Attract Birds

Nearly all shrubs, except for the low dwarfs, provide attractive habitats and protection for birds. The ones on this list provide an especially valuable nesting or hiding environment, or else tasty fruits in different seasons.

Arctostaphylos species (Manzanita)
Aronia arbutifolia (Red chokeberry)
Berberis species (Barberry)
Buddleia species (Butterfly bush)
Callistemon citrinus (Lemon bottlebrush)
Ceanothus species (Wild lilac)
Cornus species (Dogwood)
Cotoneaster species (Cotoneaster)
Elaeagnus species (Elaeagnus)
Escallonia species (Escallonia)
Fuchsia species (Fuchsia)
Ilex species (Holly)
Juniperus species (Juniper)
Ligustrum species (Privet)
Lonicera species (Honeysuckle)
Mahonia species (Oregon grape;
    Holly grape)
Malus sargentii (Sargent's crabapple)
Myrica pensylvanica (Northern bayberry)
Photinia species (Photinia)
Prunus species (Plum)
Pyracantha species (Firethorn)
Rhus species (Sumac)
Rosa species (Rose)
Rosmarinus species (Rosemary)
Salix species (Willow; Osier)
Symplocos paniculata (Sapphireberry;
    Asiatic sweetleaf)
Vaccinium species (Blueberry;
    Huckleberry)
Viburnum species (Viburnum)
Weigela florida (Old-fashioned weigela)

Shrubs with Fragrant Flowers

For those who love the beautiful fragrances that only flowers can bring, the following list should prove helpful. Many more shrubs in the Plant Selection Guide are fragrant, but these are the most powerful ones. One tip:

To experience most intensely the fragrance in your garden, take a stroll on days that are humid and mild. Early to mid-morning and evening hours can be especially delightful times for the nose.

Buddleia davidii (Butterfly bush)
Calycanthus floridus (Carolina allspice;
    Strawberry shrub)
Ceanothus (Wild lilac), western species
Choisya ternata (Mexican orange)
Clethra alnifolia (Summersweet; Sweet
    pepperbush)
Daphne species (Daphne)
Elaeagnus species (Elaeagnus)
Escallonia species (Escallonia)
Fothergilla major (Large fothergilla)
Gardenia jasminoides (Gardenia)
Hamamelis species (Witch hazel)
Leucothoe fontanesiana (Drooping
    leucothoe)
Lonicera species (Honeysuckle)
Magnolia stellata (Star magnolia)
Malus sargentii (Sargent's crabapple)
Osmanthus species (Devilweed)
Philadelphus species (Mock orange)
Pittosporum napaliense (Golden fragrance
    plant)
Pittosporum tobira (Tobira; Japanese
    pittosporum)
Prunus tomentosa (Nanking cherry;
    Manchu cherry)
Rhododendron arborescens (Sweet azalea)
Rhododendron × *loderi* (Loder hybrid
    rhododendron)
Rhododendron nudiflorum (Pinxterbloom
    azalea)
Rhododendron viscosum (Swamp azalea)
Rosa spinosissima (Scotch rose)
Rosa wichuraiana (Memorial rose)
Syringa vulgaris (Common lilac)
Viburnum × *burkwoodii* (Burkwood
    viburnum)
Viburnum × *carlcephalum* (Fragrant
    snowball viburnum)
Viburnum carlesii (Koreanspice viburnum)
Viburnum × *juddii* (Judd viburnum)
Viburnum tinus (Laurustinus)

Dwarf Shrubs

The trend toward increased urban dwelling and smaller property lots in the suburbs, coupled with a rising demand for plants that are easy to maintain, has resulted in the increasing importance of an unusual type of plant in the landscape: the dwarf shrub. The term *dwarf* is used in many different ways. Here we mean it to be a small, generally slow-growing shrub that matures to a height of 3 feet or less under normal growing conditions. This eliminates from our consideration the man-made dwarfs created by pruning and restricting root growth—such as container, bonsai, and topiary plants—or by grafting. Dwarf shrubs can have many origins. Some, like heather (*Calluna vulgaris*), are naturally low growing. Often these plants have evolved under harsh environmental conditions where survival favored those low dwarfs that could evade cold and drying winds by hiding under snow or behind hillocks or rocks. Many alpine plants fall into this category.

Some dwarfs occur as seedling mutations. These mutants can occur in nature—the dwarf Alberta spruce (*Picea glauca* 'Conica'), for example, was accidentally discovered on a walk through the woods. Others, and this is more common, are discovered in a nursery seedling bed. Dwarf shrubs can also originate as bud mutations, called sports, that are vegetatively propagated. A particular type of sport is called a *witches' broom*, in which a dense, compact, and slow-growing mass of twigs arises from a single bud mutation.

Some dwarf shrubs are actually the result of a virus disease that is carefully perpetuated by vegetative propagation. And some are produced by propagating a slow-growing side branch of a larger plant, resulting in a slow-growing dwarf with a prostrate habit. Many of the plants included in our list of dwarf shrubs, especially forms of the coniferous evergreens, are actually trees. Selections of juniper, false cypress, spruce, pine, arborvitae, and hemlock are examples.

Regardless of their origin, the usefulness of dwarf shrubs is virtually limitless. Where garden space is at a premium, they are ideal. Frequently, the unusual character of many varieties inspires the gardener to think of them only as specimens, but don't feel this is the only way dwarf shrubs can be used. Integrate and blend them as you would their larger forms. Dwarfs are excellent in foundation plantings, where their slow, restrained growth provides an easy-care answer to the transition from vertical walls to horizontal lawns and beds. Many dwarf shrubs stay low but spread wide, and are a good choice for a difficult, steep bank. Others have restrained growth in all directions that makes them a perfect choice for edging along drives, walks, borders, and beds—anywhere, in fact, that a neat, low, formal or informal hedge or demarcation is desired.

The generally slow-growing habit of dwarf shrubs can make them easier to care for in the landscape. Pruning and shearing need to be done much less frequently, and feeding requirements are usually fewer. For those dwarf shrubs that are propagated from side branches or juvenile growth parts, special care must be taken to ensure that they do not revert to their more vigorous, upright antecedents. Immediately remove any branches that exhibit a larger growth habit or foliage. This is particularly a problem with some forms of euonymus, false cypress, and juniper. Beware of overfeeding slow-growing dwarfs; they require much less fertilizer than their forbears. For the most part, however, the care of dwarf shrubs is the same as for their larger forms.

All species in the list on the following page have a complete description in this Plant Selection Guide, where you will find pertinent information on maintenance. The descriptions of the species are generally appropriate to the dwarf forms, except for the element of size. An asterisk (*) indicates wide-spreading and rapid-growing shrubs that are suitable for ground covers.

Viburnum opulus 'Nanum'

Calluna vulgaris

Raphiolepis indica

Xylosma congestum

Abelia × grandiflora 'Prostrata' (Glossy abelia)
Arctostaphylos uva-ursi (Bearberry manzanita; Kinnikinick)*
Berberis darwinii 'Corallina Compacta' (Darwin barberry)
Berberis thunbergii 'Crimson Pygmy' (Japanese barberry)
Buxus microphylla var. koreana 'Tide Hill' (Littleleaf boxwood)
Buxus sempervirens (Common boxwood) 'Bullata', 'Suffruticosa', 'Vardar Valley'
Calluna vulgaris (Scotch heather)
Caragana arborescens 'Nana' (Siberian peashrub)
Ceanothus gloriosus (Point Reyes ceanothus)*
Ceanothus griseus var. horizontalis (Yankee Point ceanothus)*
Chamaecyparis lawsoniana (Lawson false cypress) 'Minima Glauca', 'Nidiformis'
Chamaecyparis obtusa (Hinoki false cypress) 'Kosteri', 'Lycopioides', 'Nana'
Chamaecyparis pisifera 'Squarrosa Minima' (Japanese false cypress)
Coprosma × kirkii (Coprosma)*
Cornus sericea 'Isanti' (Red-osier dogwood)
Cotoneaster dammeri (Bearberry cotoneaster)*
Cotoneaster horizontalis (Rockspray cotoneaster) 'Little Gem', 'Perpusilla'
Daphne cneorum (Garland flower)
Erica carnea (Spring heath)
Erica vagans (Cornish heath)
Euonymus fortunei (Wintercreeper) 'Azusa', 'Emerald Cushion', 'Kewensis'
Euonymus fortunei var. coloratus (Wintercreeper)*
Euonymus japonica (Evergreen euonymus) 'Microphylla', 'Microphylla Variegata'
Forsythia 'Arnold Dwarf' (Forsythia)*
Fothergilla gardenii (Dwarf fothergilla)
Fuchsia × hybrida (Common fuchsia), selected cultivars
Gardenia jasminoides 'Radicans' (Gardenia)
Genista pilosa (Silky-leafed woadwaxen)
Genista sagittalis (Arrow broom)
Genista tinctoria (Common woadwaxen)
Hypericum calycinum (Aaronsbeard St. Johnswort)*
Hypericum frondosum 'Sunburst' (Golden St. Johnswort)
Iberis sempervirens (Evergreen candytuft)
Ilex cornuta (Chinese holly) 'Berries Jubilee', 'Carissa', 'Dazzler', 'Dwarf Burford'
Ilex crenata (Japanese holly) 'Border Gem', 'Golden Gem', 'Green Island', 'Kingsville Green Cushion', 'Mariesii'
Ilex glabra 'Compacta' (Inkberry)
Ilex vomitoria 'Nana' (Yaupon)
Juniperus chinensis (Chinese juniper) 'Alba', 'Armstrongii', 'Blue Vase', 'Fruitland', 'Mint Julep', 'Pfitzerana Arctic', 'Pfitzerana Kallay'
Juniperus chinensis var. procumbens 'Nana' (Creeping juniper)*
Juniperus chinensis var. sargentii (Sargent juniper)* 'Compacta', 'Glauca', 'Viridis'
Juniperus communis (Common juniper) 'Compressa', 'Depressa Aurea'*, 'Gold Beach', 'Hornibrookii'

Juniperus conferta (Shore juniper)* 'Blue Pacific', 'Emerald Sea'
Juniperus horizontalis (Creeping juniper)*
Juniperus sabina (Savin juniper) 'Arcadia', 'Broadmoor'*, 'Buffalo', 'Skandia', 'Tamariscifolia'
Juniperus virginiana 'Silver Spreader' (Eastern redcedar)
Lagerstroemia indica (Crape myrtle), petite series
Leptospermum scoparium (New Zealand tea tree) 'Horizontalis', 'Nanum', 'Snow White', 'Waeringi'
Leucothoe fontanesiana 'Nana' (Drooping leucothoe)
Lonicera tatarica (Tatarian honeysuckle) 'Nana', 'LeRoyana'
Lonicera × xylosteoides 'Clavey's Dwarf' (Clavey's Dwarf honeysuckle) 'Emerald Mound'
Myrtus communis (Myrtle) 'Compacta', 'Compacta Variegata', 'Microphylla'
Paxistima canbyi (Cliff-green; Mountain-lover)
Pieris japonica (Japanese pieris) 'Compacta', 'Crispa', 'Pygmaea'
Pinus mugo var. mugo (Dwarf mugo pine) 'Compacta', 'Gnome', 'Slavinii'
Pittosporum tobira 'Wheeler's Dwarf' (Tobira; Japanese pittosporum)
Platycladus orientalis (Oriental arborvitae) 'Aurea Nana', 'Bonita', 'Raffles'
Potentilla fruticosa (Bush cinquefoil)
Prunus laurocerasus (English laurel) 'Mt. Vernon', 'Nana', 'Otto Luyken'
Punica granatum (Pomegranate) 'Chico', 'Nana'
Pyracantha (Firethorn) 'Lodense', 'Red Elf', 'Tiny Tim'
Raphiolepis indica (India hawthorn)
Rhododendron canadense (Rhodora azalea)
Rhododendron impeditum (Cloudland rhododendron)
Rhododendron lapponicum (Lapland rhododendron)
Rosmarinus officinalis (Rosemary)* 'Collingwood Ingram', 'Prostratus'
Spiraea albiflora (Japanese white spirea)
Spiraea × bumalda (Bumalda spirea)
Spiraea japonica var. alpina (Japanese spirea, alpine variety)
Taxus baccata (English yew) 'Nana', 'Pygmaea', 'Repens'
Taxus cuspidata (Japanese yew) 'Aurescens', 'Densa', 'Intermedia', 'Nana'
Taxus × media 'Berryhilli' (Yew)
Thuja occidentalis (American arborvitae) 'Aurea', 'Boothii', 'Ericoides', 'Little Gem', 'Umbraculifera'
Viburnum davidii (David viburnum)
Viburnum opulus (European cranberry bush) 'Compactum', 'Nanum'
Viburnum trilobum 'Compactum' (American cranberry bush viburnum)
Weigela florida (Old-fashioned weigela) 'Foliis Purpuriis', 'Variegata Nana'
Xylosma congestum 'Compacta' (Shiny xylosma)

A Gallery of Shrubs

Banks of azaleas fill this Virginia garden with spectacular springtime color.

When you are selecting a shrub for your landscape, no description or photograph can really substitute for a live plant. But often it is difficult or impossible to locate a mature specimen of a shrub that interests you. So use this guide as a sort of tour through different regions of the country for a capsule introduction to a wide variety of shrubs.

Remember that any plant's requirements are flexible. Indeed, the challenge of proving the experts wrong is, for some, one of the greatest joys of gardening. When you run across a shrub that sounds particularly interesting, try to locate a mature, healthy example. Ask your gardening friends who have grown it how satisfied they are with its performance. Best of all, talk it over with a member of your nursery staff. Most likely, he or she has had direct experience with your choice, and has probably received considerable feedback over the years from satisfied (or dissatisfied) customers. Don't hesitate to take advantage of that knowledge to answer any question about local adaptation and usefulness that this guide does not answer.

Abelia × grandiflora

Abelia × grandiflora (Glossy abelia). Broadleaved evergreen (deciduous in the North). Zones 6–10.

The hardiest and most free-flowering of the abelias, this hybrid makes an effective specimen, informal hedge, grouping, or mass planting, combining particularly well with broadleaved evergreens. Showy, pinkish-white flowers cover the plant from July until frost. The finely textured, glossy, deep green summer foliage turns an attractive bronze in the fall. The glossy abelia is deciduous to semievergreen in the North and increasingly evergreen the farther south it is grown. The habit is graceful, rounded, and arching. Growing at a medium to fast rate, the plant reaches 4 to 8 feet high and wide. If you give it well-drained soil, half to full sun, and average watering, it will prove to be an easy-to-grow, pest-free shrub. While it can be sheared easily into formal shapes, doing so seriously reduces flowering. Instead, allow the glossy abelia to achieve its natural, graceful shape. Expect frequent winter dieback in northern Zone 6, although the new growth will come back quickly. Older, overgrown shrubs can be renewed by cutting back hard, almost to the ground, in late winter or early spring. Lower-growing cultivars, such as 'Prostrata' and 'Sherwoodii', make excellent, large-scale ground and bank covers.

Acer palmatum var. dissectum (Laceleaf Japanese maple). Deciduous. Zones 6–10.

For that refined, aristocratic touch, few shrubs can beat this dwarf tree. It is an outstanding specimen plant, with an open, picturesque form; soft, wispy foliage available in a variety of shades and variegations; and consistently showy fall color. It grows quite slowly 6 to 8 feet in height and width. The plant works well as a focal point for an entryway, near a patio, or naturalized in a woodland understory. Performing beautifully in containers, it makes an excellent bonsai subject.

In Zone 6 the roots of container plants need extra protection in the winter—mulch and add extra insulation to the container, or sink the container into the ground in a protected spot. Transplant from a container in winter or early spring into well-drained, acid soil (pH 5.5 to 6.5) that is rich in organic matter. Since this plant is susceptible to leaf scorch, filtered shade is preferable, especially in hot climates. It also needs protection from late frosts and drying winds (especially the cold, drying winds of spring).

Not all varieties of the Japanese maple are the lace-leafed dwarfs. Some are 15- to 25-foot trees with an extensive range of different foliage qualities. If you prefer a shrublike plant, always ask for the lace-leafed types. Some of the better cultivars are 'Crimson Queen', 'Garnet', 'Flavescens', 'Ornatum', 'Ozakazuki', 'Purpureum', and 'Reticulatum'. Native to Japan, China, and Korea.

Aesculus parviflora

Aesculus parviflora (Bottlebrush buckeye). Deciduous. Zones 5–8.

Spectacular late-season flowers, trouble-free foliage (unusual for the buckeyes), and adaptability to heavy shade make this shrub an excellent subject for a specimen; it also can be massed and clumped in problem shady areas, such as under large shade trees. Not for small areas, it has an open, wide-spreading (8 to 15 feet), suckering habit that can be troublesome if not given enough room to grow. The profuse flowers are large, erect clusters that grow 8 to 12 inches long, are white with red anthers, and bloom from early to late July. Aesculus parviflora thrives in moist, well-drained soil that is high in organic matter, but it tolerates full sun to heavy shade. It is native to rich, moist woods from South Carolina to Alabama.

'Roger's' is a superior cultivar that is worth seeking out: it produces huge flower clusters, 18 to 30 inches long, two weeks later than the species, and does not exhibit the suckering habit.

Aesculus pavia (Red buckeye; Zones 6–8). Though less hardy than bottle-brush buckeye, this is also relatively resistant to most of the leaf diseases that plague the buckeyes. Mildew can still be a problem; however, it will not affect this shrub's long-term vigor. In size and form much like bottlebrush buckeye, it differs by having bright red flowers in early spring. *A. pavia* 'Atrosanguinea' has darker red flowers, while 'Humilis' has a low, often prostrate form. Red buckeye is native to the coastal-plain woods, from southeast Virginia to Florida, west to Texas, and north to southern Illinois.

Arctostaphylos uva-ursi (Bearberry manzanita; Kinnikinick). Broadleaved evergreen. Zones 2–8A.

A low, mat-forming ground cover with evergreen foliage of fine, pleasing texture, bearberry manzanita is especially useful for poor, sandy soil. Drooping, tiny, bell-shaped flowers, attractive but not particularly showy, are followed by bright red berries. Since growth is relatively slow, set plants from containers or flats 2 feet apart for complete cover in about two seasons. Bearberry is salt tolerant and therefore makes an excellent beach plant. It is native to northern Europe and Asia, and to North America, where it is found from the Arctic south to Virginia, northern Mexico, and northern California.

Arctostaphylos uva-ursi

In addition to *Arctostaphylos uva-ursi*, over sixty species of *Arctostaphylos* are native to western North America, from southern California to British Columbia. Most are large (10 to 20 feet), open, picturesque shrubs with beautiful gnarled, smooth trunks; startlingly red or reddish bark; grayish-green to deep green, leathery evergreen foliage; and mildly to quite showy white to deep pink clusters of flowers. Useful as drought-tolerant natives in gardens west of the Rockies, all species are quite particular about soil and habitat. Check with your local nursery for the species and cultivar best suited to your garden.

Aronia arbutifolia

Aronia arbutifolia (Red chokeberry). Deciduous. Zones 5–8B.

The red chokeberry has spectacular bright red berries in profusion and consistently showy red to purple fall color. Naturalized at the edge of woodlands and around ponds and other wet areas, a large planting resembles an ocean of red in fall and winter. This distinctly leggy, upright shrub grows easily but slowly 6 to 10 feet high and 3 to 5 feet wide and is best used in masses and large groups that accentuate the fruit display and diminish the legginess. While tolerant of dry soils and prairie drought, it also makes an excellent choice for that problem wet area, and performs admirably in heavy soil. Fruiting is best in full sun, although possible in partial shade. Adaptable and little troubled by pests, *Aronia arbutifolia* is a carefree plant. Native to thickets in bogs, swamps, wet woods, and occasionally found in dry soils from Nova Scotia to Florida, and west to Michigan, Missouri, and Texas.

Aucuba japonica (Japanese aucuba). Broadleaved evergreen. Zones 7B–10.

The Japanese aucuba is valued for its ability to grow well in shade; its large and leathery evergreen leaves; and its adaptability to adverse growing conditions. It also makes an excellent container plant. Use it in problem shady areas, such as a dim, north-facing entryway, or under densely foliaged trees (it competes well with tree roots). Unpruned, the shrub becomes a leggy, open plant that grows 6 to 10 feet or more tall. To keep it a dense, rounded shrub, selectively cut back branches to a leaf node. Bright red berries make attractive accents in the fall and winter, but both male and female plants are required to set fruit. The Japanese aucuba performs well in any soil, and is drought tolerant once established; nevertheless, it still benefits from additional organic matter in the soil when it is planted. This is not a plant for hot, sunny, exposed locations. Numerous cultivars are avail-

Aucuba japonica

able with different leaf colors, variegations, and shapes. Native from the Himalayas to Japan.

Berberis darwinii (Darwin barberry). Broadleaved evergreen. Zones 8–10.

Literally covered with bright yellow-orange flowers in early March, this is undoubtedly the showiest barberry in flower. It will grow rapidly into an arching, loose shrub, 5 to 10 feet high and 4 to 7 feet wide, with small evergreen leaves. Its beautiful dark blue berries have the decided asset of attracting birds. The plant has a tendency to spread by underground stolons, and will become loose and open in old age unless pruned regularly. Like all barberries, it is not particular about soil and withstands drought well. 'Corallina Compacta' is an especially beautiful cultivar, valuable for its neat, dense, compact, and rounded shape. Native to Chile.

Berberis koreana

Berberis koreana (Korean barberry). Deciduous. Zones 5–8.

This is the showiest hardy barberry for flower and fruit, bearing spectacular, luminous yellow flowers in 3- to 4-inch-long drooping racemes from early to mid-May, followed by profuse bright red berries that persist well into winter. Like the Japanese barberry, it makes an excellent thorny barrier, and is extremely adaptable and trouble free. An individual plant is relatively small, growing into a dense oval, 4 to 6 feet high with slightly less spread. Unfortunately, Korean barberry suckers prolifically from the roots, occasionally outgrowing its bounds and forming large colonies. This flowering specimen's suckering habit can be overcome by pruning. Thus it is best reserved for large informal hedges, borders, and mass plantings. Native to Korea.

Berberis thunbergii (Japanese barberry). Deciduous. Zones 5–9.

As an extremely easy plant to grow, with impenetrable thorns and dense, shearable foliage, the Japanese barberry is one of the most popular hedge and barrier plants around. Outstanding fall color and mildly effective winter fruits are additional plus points, as are the numerous red-, yellow-, and variegated-leafed cultivars. Unfortunately, the plant tends to collect trash, which is particularly unsightly in the winter and irksome to remove due to the vicious thorns. Growing at a moderate rate to 3 to 6 feet high and 4 to 7 feet wide, this shrub has a natural outline that is upright, arching, and rounded, with a dense profusion of thorny stems and finely textured foliage. The Japanese barberry transplants easily, adapts well to nearly any soil, withstands drought well, and performs admirably in full sun or partial shade. Cultivars with colored foliage generally retain their color only if grown in full sun. The cultivar 'Crimson Pygmy' makes a good ground cover for a hot, sunny area, as well as a low hedge. Native from southern Europe across Asia to central China and the Himalayas.

Buddleia davidii (Butterfly bush). Deciduous. Zones 5–10.

An old-time favorite for pretty, fragrant midsummer flowers that attract multitudes of butterflies, this shrub is unfortunately wild and unruly in its growth habit. With extremely large leaves and coarse texture, it grows very rapidly to an open, rangy 6 to 10 feet high. The fragrant flowers are borne on 6- to 12-inch-long spikes that appear in July and August on the current season's growth. Treat this shrub as an herbaceous perennial in the rear of a perennial border, pruning it to within a few inches of the ground after it flowers each fall. This helps to keep it manageable and increases the number of flowering shoots. While *Buddleia davidii* is susceptible to many different pests, remember that spraying will also eliminate the visitation of any butterflies. Numerous cultivars are available for a choice of flower color, ranging from white through pinks and reds to blues. Native to China.

Buddleia alternifolia (Fountain buddleia) is hardy to Zone 6, where it does not exhibit the dieback of *Buddleia davidii*. It is also much more graceful and refined, its arching sprays of lilac-like flowers appearing in mid-May to June on the previous year's wood. Native to northwestern China.

Buxus sempervirens (Common boxwood). Broadleaved evergreen. Zones 6–10.

Used in formal gardens, this is the plant most commonly sheared into fantastic shapes—globes, cubes, teddy bears. Besides its use in topiary and trimmed hedges, the common boxwood also makes an uncommonly beautiful specimen in old age, growing quite slowly into a gnarled, spreading, and open treelike shrub 10 to 20 feet in height and width. It is most familiar as a young plant, however, when it is a dainty, rounded, compact shrub. Unfortunately, its usefulness is limited to warm, moist climates that do not exhibit extremes of heat and cold, and it is subject to a wide variety of insect and disease pests. Plant boxwood in a well-drained, moist soil that has been generously amended with organic matter, and mulch heavily to provide a cool, moist root run. Each year prune out the inner dead twigs and remove the fallen leaves that accumulate in the branch crotches; this will help to prevent twig canker disease, which is common in the East. Never cultivate around boxwoods—they root close to the surface. They will not tolerate drought. Protect them from drying winds and extreme temperatures; give them partial shade in hot climates, and full sun or partial shade elsewhere. Many cultivars are available for different forms and sizes, as well as for increased hardiness. 'Northern Find' and 'Vardar Valley' are two of the hardiest (Zone 5). Native to southern Europe, northern Africa, and western Asia.

Buxus microphylla (Littleleaf boxwood; Zones 6–10) is similar to the common boxwood, except that it is slightly hardier and more finely textured, and its foliage usually turns yellow-brown in cold weather. However, 'Tide

Buxus microphylla 'Compacta'

Callistemon citrinus

Calluna vulgaris

Hill', 'Wintergreen', and other cultivars of *Buxus microphylla* var. *koreana* (Korean boxwood) are hardy to Zone 5 and retain excellent green foliage all winter long. Cultural instructions and landscape uses are the same as for the common boxwood. Native to Japan.

Callistemon citrinus (Lemon bottlebrush). Broadleaved evergreen. Zones 9–10.

Common to the gardens of southern California and Florida, this long-blooming, drought-tolerant plant displays bright red, brushlike flowers that both enhance the landscape and attract hummingbirds. Its leaves are lemon scented. A massive shrub, growing 10 to 15 feet in height and width into a round-headed, open form, the lemon bottlebrush is best used as a screen, a tall, informal hedge, or possibly a specimen. It makes an excellent choice for the desert landscape, since it tolerates drought and a wide variety of soils, including those that are alkaline and saline. Both good drainage and full sun are preferred. Select named varieties from your nursery—this plant is quite undependable when grown from seed. Cultivars vary according to flower color, flower size, and compactness. Native to Australia.

Calluna vulgaris (Scotch heather). Narrow-leafed evergreen. Zones 5–7 (milder on coasts).

While its finely textured evergreen foliage, dainty, colorful flowers, and low, restrained habit make this one of the most treasured ground covers or rock garden plants, the famous Scotch heather can be finicky and difficult to grow. It *must* have perfectly drained soil that also retains moisture well. The best soil is acid (pH 6 or less), sandy or high in organic matter (most authorities recommend one-half coarse sand and one-half peat—volcanic sand is best, if you can get it), and infertile. If the soil is too rich, heather will grow taller but will decrease in flower production. The plant thrives best in full sun but will do well in partial shade (although again it will flower less). Mulch well and do not cultivate around the shallow roots. Heather will not tolerate drought. Prune or shear each fall after flowering to maintain compactness and encourage heavier blooming. Many cultivars—dense, many-stemmed, mat-forming shrubs with tiny, needlelike evergreen leaves—are available for size variation (4 to 24 inches high by 2 feet or more wide), flower color (whites, pinks, purples), time of bloom (midsummer to fall), and foliage color (deep green to yellow or bronze). Native to Europe and Asia Minor.

Calycanthus floridus (Carolina allspice; Strawberry shrub). Deciduous. Zones 5–9.

For fragrance in bloom and easy care, the Carolina allspice is hard to beat. Plant it wherever you can enjoy the fragrance—near outdoor living areas, under windows, beside screen doors, in a shrub border. The 2-inch, dull, reddish-brown flowers are merely "interesting" to look at, but they permeate the garden with a glorious, sweet strawberry scent in mid-May, and often sporadically into July. The shrub grows slowly to a neat, rounded outline, 6 to 9 feet high and 6 to 12 feet wide. It will grow in nearly any soil, but performs best in deep, moist loam. While adaptable to sun or shade, it will not grow as tall in full sun. The shrub transplants readily and is highly resistant to pests. Prune after flowering. Native to moist woods, from Virginia to Florida.

Calycanthus floridus

Calycanthus fertilis, another eastern native (occasionally mistaken for Carolina allspice), and *Calycanthus occidentalis*, a western native, are similar species, but do not have the pleasing floral fragrance of the Carolina allspice. Since fragrance is the chief reason for acquiring *Calycanthus floridus*, purchase it while it is in flower to ensure positive identification.

Camellia japonica (Common camellia). Broadleaved evergreen. Zones 8–10.

Beloved by southern gardeners for its large, beautiful flowers in winter and early spring and for its dense, polished, dark evergreen foliage, the camellia makes a fine specimen—whether standing alone or in a mixed shrub border. It is especially effective when massed or grouped in shady woodland gardens, and it blends nicely with other broadleaved evergreens.

Camellia japonica 'Pink Perfection'

While its size can vary according to cultivars, it usually grows to a height of 6 to 12 feet; occasionally, in great age, it can reach 20 feet or so. Often single trunked and branching well up from the ground, the camellia looks like a rounded, densely foliaged mass that is nearly as broad as it is tall.

The flowers are extremely variable—there are over three thousand named varieties—and normally last for about a month. The blooming season differs according to cultivar: from early (October to January) to mid-season (January to March) and late (March to May). The form of the flower varies from single to double, with various degrees of flutes and frills. The colors range from white to red, and the size from 2½ inches to 5 inches in diameter.

Camellias often tend to be lumped with rhododendrons in terms of cultural requirements, but this is not quite fair. Camellias are not nearly as touchy about soil as rhododendrons, and they withstand heavy soils better. Nevertheless, they still respond to plenty of organic matter and slight acidity (pH 6). Guard against overfertilization and salt buildup in the soil, and give them average watering. Avoid cultivating around their shallow roots.

When necessary, prune immediately after flowering. Many varieties set too many flower buds. If you prefer large blossoms, disbud these shrubs in midsummer: remove all but two flower buds on each branch end, and one for every 2 to 4 inches of branch along the stems (the flower buds are the fat, round ones; the slender ones are leaf buds). Petal blight is a serious, disfiguring disease that causes petals to turn an ugly brown. Sanitation is the best control. Remove all fallen petals immediately and dispose of them, and replace the mulch every year. Native to Taiwan, Korea, and Japan.

Camellia sasanqua (Sasanqua camellia; Zones 7B–10) is similar to the common camellia, except that it blooms earlier—from autumn to early winter. Again, this shrub comes in a tremendous variety of flowers and forms. Some are low-growing, sprawling shrubs that are useful for ground covers and espaliers; others make good hedges or screens. All make good specimens. Native to Japan.

Caragana arborescens (Siberian peashrub). Deciduous. Zones 2–7.

Valuable as a hedge, screen, or windbreak where growing conditions are difficult—especially in the Northern Plains States—the Siberian peashrub contributes bright yellow flowers from early to mid-May. A large shrub, growing rapidly into a sparse, angular, open structure 15 feet high and 12 feet wide, it often is trained as a small tree. Shearing encourages denser growth, but if you prefer a neat, formal hedge, choose another plant. The Siberian peashrub resists most pests, although leafhoppers can be damaging. Because it grows well in dry, rocky soils and exposed, windy sites, it is an effective shrub in a difficult spot. Variety *nana*, a dwarf form with contorted branches, and variety *pendula*, with angular, weeping branches grafted to a standard, are two interesting varieties. Native to Siberia, Manchuria, and Mongolia.

Caryopteris × *clandonensis* 'Azure'

Caryopteris × *clandonensis* (Blue spirea; Bluebeard). Deciduous. Zones 6–8.

Noteworthy for its subtle, unusual blue haze of flowers from mid-August to frost, the blue spirea is most striking when contrasted with white or yellow flowers or massed in large groups. Otherwise, its gray-blue, misty effect can easily get lost in the landscape. The blue spirea, usually dying to the ground in winter, grows each year to a loose, open, and airy 2- to 3-foot shrub. In milder climates where it does not die back, it will become gangly, floppy, and unattractive. Whatever the climate, plant blue spirea as a perennial in a border. Cut it back to the ground each winter to keep it compact and increase the flowering, and give it average water and good garden soil. 'Azure' has bright blue flowers; so does 'Heavenly Blue', although it is slightly more tender. 'Blue Mist' has light blue flowers.

Caryopteris incana, although inferior to *Caryopteris* × *clandonensis*, is still commonly sold. It is more tender (Zone 7) and has less effective flowers.

Ceanothus species (Wild lilac). Some broadleaved evergreen; some deciduous species. Zones 8–10 in the West.

This genus of shrubs generally thrives in West Coast gardens, where over forty species can be grown. Two deciduous species, *Ceanothus americanus* and *C. ovatus*, are native to eastern North America, but the western evergreen natives are the ones with the most ornamental interest. Their hallmarks are beautiful, fragrant blue or white flowers and usually glossy, dark evergreen leaves.

Ceanothus griseus var. *horizontalis*
'Yankee Point'

Many species and varieties are available, from 8-inch ground covers to 30-foot small trees. The evergreen varieties will not tolerate heavy soils or too much water. Plant them in very rocky, sandy soil and away from sprinklers. Except for the initial season or two of establishment, do not overwater. Plant wild lilac only in full sun. To avoid transmitting a deadly canker disease, prune only during the dry summer months. These shrubs are most effective in large masses, either as ground or bank covers on large, rocky slopes, or as higher, billowing masses. Occasionally they are used as specimens because of the striking blue flowers of some cultivars. However, *Ceanothus* tends to become rangy with age, and most species live only for a relatively short time. Check with your nursery for the species or cultivar most useful to you.

Chaenomeles speciosa (Common flowering quince). Deciduous. Zones 5–9.

While this shrub is the most ornamental of the quinces, it still remains a single-season plant with only two assets: a thorniness that is good for barriers, and early spring flowers that are quite showy for about ten days. For the other fifty weeks of the year it is mediocre at best. Variable in habit, it is usually a rounded, dense shrub 6 to 10 feet high and wide, but cultivars are available from prostrate to open to erect forms, some of which are thornless. Like the Japanese barberry, this plant has the annoying habit of collecting trash, which is painful to extract from the thorny twigs and which is particularly unsightly in exposed winter branches.

The flowers are effective in late March (late February in the South), especially when massed, and are available in a confusing array of very similar cultivars, from red and scarlet to pink and white. The fruits make good jams and jellies. Common flowering quince is easy to grow and adaptable to a wide variety of soils and conditions, including dry soils and prairie drought. This quince flowers most prolifically when placed in full sun and when pruned annually to about 6 inches from the ground immediately after spring bloom. Potential problems include leaf spot (particularly in wet climates), scale, and chlorosis in alkaline soils. Quince will not flower as prolifically in warm winter climates. Native to China.

Chamaecyparis species (False cypress). Conifer. Zones 4–8, according to the species.

Chamaecyparis lawsoniana 'Minima Aurea'

Although many of the species grow as large trees, a huge variety of dwarf cultivars that work well as coniferous evergreen shrubs is also available. Many false cypresses are well adapted to moderate and moist coastal climates, but there are also many cultivars that perform well in the harsher conditions of the Midwest. Take care to match the selection to the climate. The evergreen foliage is similar to the juvenile leaves of junipers, and cultivars vary in foliage color (bright yellows, deep greens, grays, and blues) and habit (from tiny, inches-high tufts to open, picturesque small trees). Transplant false cypress into rich, well-drained soil in the spring; give it full sun in moist, mild climates, and partial shade elsewhere. Prune to control form just before the new foliage emerges in the spring. Most forms have a tendency to die out in the center and lose lower branches with age. Remove this foliage with a strong jet of water. Protect all *Chamaecyparis* from hot, drying winds.

Chamaecyparis lawsoniana (Lawson false cypress; Zones 6–8). This false cypress is most adapted to moist coastal climates, and is not suitable for midwestern conditions. On the West Coast, root rot causes a significant problem in this species. Yellow-leafed varieties are particularly susceptible to burn from hot sun and drying winds. Native to southwestern Oregon and northwestern California.

Chamaecyparis obtusa (Hinoki false cypress; Zones 5–8). Tolerating neutral soils somewhat better than other false cypresses, this is probably the best choice for midwestern conditions. It is available in a wide variety of dwarf forms. Native to Japan and Taiwan.

Chamaecyparis pisifera (Japanese false cypress; Zones 4–8). The hardiest of the false cypresses, this one is notorious for losing its inner and lower foliage with age, and distinctly prefers acid soil. Native to Japan.

Choisya ternata

Cistus 'Elma'

Clethra alnifolia 'Rosea'

Choisya ternata (Mexican orange). Broadleaved evergreen. Zones 8B–10.

The early, deliciously scented white flowers of this shrub are a delight near entryways, outdoor living areas, windows, walkways, and paths— wherever fragrance can be enjoyed. The fan-shaped evergreen foliage grows densely at the ends of branches, creating an interesting layered, sculptured texture that is effective as an informal hedge or screen. The Mexican orange is touchy about soil conditions: it needs well-drained, acid soil that is rich in organic matter, and is intolerant of alkaline or saline soils. It will tolerate full sun on the coast, but needs partial shade in hot summer climates. In deep shade it will become leggy and straggly and be particularly prone to insect attacks. Water infrequently but deeply, and prune yearly to maintain a compact, dense form about 4 to 5 feet high and wide. Native to Mexico.

Cistus species (Rockrose). Broadleaved evergreen. Zones 8–10.

Useful in the Mediterranean climates of the West, the rockroses make an excellent large-scale bank and ground cover that requires little maintenance and offers much spring color. An added asset is its fragrant foliage, especially on hot days. Drought resistant and adaptable to salt spray, ocean winds, and desert heat, rockroses are bushy, dense, rounded shrubs that generally grow 3 to 4 feet tall and 4 to 5 feet wide. When massed they look like a billowing dark or gray-green sea of foliage. Give them fast-draining soil, and pinch the tips of young plants to encourage denser growth. Don't try to move them once they're established—they won't transplant well. Native to the Mediterranean region.

Clethra alnifolia (Summersweet; Sweet pepperbush). Deciduous. Zones 3–9.

In addition to extremely fragrant, cool white spikes of flowers that appear in July and August, when flowers are scarce, summersweet is particularly useful in difficult wet, shady areas of the garden, although it will thrive in nearly any acid to neutral soil. Once established, it will grow slowly to a broad, oval mass 3 to 8 feet high and 4 to 8 feet wide. Its handsome dark green foliage, which is pest free, turns a clear yellow in the fall before dropping.

Summersweet tolerates salty, sandy coastal conditions, but it performs best in moist, acid soil that is heavily supplemented with organic matter. It has the reputation of being difficult to establish, so try planting balled-and-burlapped or container-grown plants in early spring. Water them profusely until established. Though native to swamps, clethras are usually grown in well-drained soils in nurseries; thus the roots are no longer adapted to swampy soil conditions. When transplanting into wet soils, ease the transition by planting 3 to 4 inches higher than the soil level and mulching heavily.

Pruning is rarely necessary, but if you must, do it in early spring. This shrub is best left to grow naturally into its clean, dense, oval shape. *Clethra* is intolerant of drought. While in flower it will attract great quantities of bees.

'Paniculata', a cultivar with longer-flowered spikes, is superior to the typical species. 'Rosea' has clear pink buds that open into flowers of white tinged with pink. Native to swamps and moist, sandy soils from Maine to Florida.

Coprosma repens (Mirror plant). Broadleaved evergreen. Zones 9–10.

When this plant is pruned to restrain its rapid, sometimes awkward upright growth to 10 feet high and 6 feet wide, its extremely shiny, glossy leaves make it an excellent quickly forming hedge, screen, foundation plant, or espalier. Since the flowers and fruits are inconspicuous, and its habit is rangy and open when neglected, use this shrub for its attractive evergreen foliage where you don't mind occasionally having to train it. It adapts particularly well to seashore conditions and is drought tolerant once established. Give it full sun on the coast or partial shade in hot inland areas. It will perform well in nearly any soil. Because it grows rapidly, *Coprosma repens* will need regular pruning to stay dense and neat. Several forms have yellow- or white-variegated leaves. *Coprosma* × *kirkii* is a wide-spreading, 2- to 3-foot-high shrub that makes a tough evergreen ground cover, particularly on banks where erosion may be a problem. Native to New Zealand.

Coprosma repens 'Coppershine'

Cornus alba 'Sibirica' (Siberian dogwood). Deciduous. Zones 2–8.

The flaming-red winter stems of this dogwood distinguish it from all other landscape plants—none other is as bright, nor, some think, as difficult to integrate into the garden. Its loose, open, and very erect branches grow rapidly to a height of 8 to 10 feet, with lateral branching occurring only in the upper third of the shrub. The spread is quite variable, usually ranging from 5 to 10 feet. Extremely vigorous and apt to overgrow neighboring shrubs, the Siberian dogwood is also difficult to use as a single specimen. It can be effective in a shrub border, however, and is especially beautiful when massed on a large scale, such as along drives, on banks, or naturalized around a pond. Siberian dogwood transplants easily and adapts to nearly any soil when it has sun or light shade. Like most dogwoods, it is beset by a host of insect and disease pests; maintaining a vigorous plant is the best protection. In order to encourage vigorous new growth each year, on which the winter stem color is most evident, prune hard every spring by removing at least one-third of the old wood—more if you want a compact plant. Don't be afraid to cut it completely back to the ground each spring. Native from Siberia to Manchuria and North Korea.

Cornus sericea 'Flaviramea'

Cornus sericea, also listed as *C. stolonifera* (Red-osier dogwood; Zones 2–8). This is the North American counterpart of *Cornus alba*. The difference lies chiefly in its more muted (some think more effective) dark red winter stem color and its preference for moist, water-logged soils. *Cornus sericea* 'Flaviramea' has an unusual bright yellow winter stem color, but is notoriously susceptible to cankers and twig blights. However, if you prune the shrub heavily each spring, these generally don't pose a problem. Dwarf forms, such as 'Isanti', have recently appeared on the market. Native to wet places from Newfoundland to Manitoba and south to Virginia and Nebraska.

Corylus avellana 'Contorta' (Harry Lauder's walking stick). Deciduous. Zone 5.

A thoroughly distinctive shrub with uniquely curled and twisted stems, twigs, and leaves—it has a decidedly oriental flavor—Harry Lauder's walking stick is a definite loner in the landscape. Use it as an accent or focal point in an entryway or courtyard. Because of its interesting winter silhouette, it is especially effective against a light-colored wall. A rapid grower, the shrub will form a rounded mass of contorted, twisted branches 8 to 10 feet in height and width (usually larger than anticipated), and can even become a 20-foot small tree. The flowers are borne in pendulous yellowish or tan catkins that are quite unusual and showy in March before the leaves appear. Adaptable to a wide range of soils, acidity, and sunlight, it is an easy plant to grow. In the nursery, choose plants that are propagated by cuttings, and thus are growing on their own roots. If you happen to get a grafted plant, immediately prune out any suckers that arise from below the graft union— the more vigorous understock has a tendency to overtake the contorted top growth. Give it average water.

Cotinus coggygria 'Purpureus'

Cotinus coggygria (Smoke tree). Deciduous. Zones 6–8 (can be grown in Zones 4 and 5 with winter dieback).

A long-lasting, cloudlike pink or white display in midsummer, along with several good purple-leafed cultivars, has made this plant a long-time favorite in the low-maintenance garden. It is quite large—often a small tree growing 25 feet high. Usually, however, the smoke tree is a loose, open shrub with many upright stems 10 to 15 feet in height and greater in width, creating a rounded, irregular appearance. It has proved most useful for shrub borders as a textural and color accent, and in massings and groups. The foliage on the species is an attractive blue-green, with occasionally outstanding fall color in the reds, yellows, and purples.

Many of the purple-leafed cultivars fade to green as the season progresses. But 'Velvet Cloak', one of the best selections, retains its purple color throughout the season. The floral display varies on individual plants, so stick with the named varieties. 'Daydream' is an especially floriferous form with pink pedicels.

The smoke tree transplants easily and adapts to a wide variety of soils, including dry, rocky ones. Give it full sun. It must have frequent and deep watering when young, but is drought tolerant once it is established. Resist the temptation to prune this plant (except to remove dead branches): each pruning cut will stimulate the growth of several long, slender shoots, ultimately creating a ragged, unkempt-looking plant. Native from southern Europe to central China.

Cotoneaster dammeri (Bearberry cotoneaster). Broadleaved evergreen. Zones 6–9.

The glossy, dense leaves, good fruiting color, rapid growth rate, and low, prostrate habit make this one of the best hardy, broadleaved evergreens for ground covering. It can be used on banks and slopes, in masses, in a shrub border, or as a low foreground plant in front of tall, leggy shrubs. The bearberry cotoneaster will spread rapidly to 6 feet wide or more (its branches root where they touch the ground), and will remain under 1½ feet high. The finely textured, lustrous, dark green leaves are speckled with white flowers in late May, followed in late summer by bright red berrylike pomes that resemble tiny apples. Some cultivars, such as 'Coral Beauty', flower and fruit more freely than the species. 'Lowfast' is hardier to southern Zone 5. *Cotoneaster dammeri* transplants easily from containers and adapts to many soils, although it prefers fast drainage. It is an excellent choice for dry, rocky soil in an exposed, sunny location. Fireblight and aphids can be problems. Native to central China.

Cotoneaster divaricatus

Cotoneaster divaricatus (Spreading cotoneaster). Deciduous. Zones 5B–9.

This is one of the most handsome cotoneasters for summer and fall foliage, fruit, and graceful form. Use it in a shrub border where it will blend well with other shrubs, and consider it as a refined textural asset for formal hedges, mass plantings, and groupings. It will grow rapidly 5 to 6 feet high and 6 to 8 feet wide. While the rose-colored flowers that bloom in May are unexciting, the bright- to dark-red fruits that nearly cover the plant from September through November are spectacular. The finely textured foliage is a beautiful dark, glossy green in summer, changing in the fall to brilliant fluorescent yellow and red combinations that last a long time (this is one of the last shrubs to defoliate). Spreading cotoneaster prefers well-drained, moist, fertile soils, but it performs well in dry, rocky ones. It tolerates wind, adapts to various pH levels, and is a good choice for seashore conditions. Give it full sun or light shade. *C. divaricatus* is one of the most trouble free of the cotoneasters. Native to western and central China.

Cotoneaster horizontalis (Rockspray cotoneaster). Deciduous (semi-evergreen in mild climates). Zones 5B–9.

Spilling over walls, down slopes, and over rocks, the angular, layered form and herringbone branches of the rockspray cotoneaster add an unusual texture to the garden. Often used as a largescale bank or ground cover (excellent for erosion control), this 2- to 3-foot-high shrub will spread 5 to 8 feet or more. The attractive but not overwhelming pink flowers often abound from late May to early June, attracting prodigious numbers of bees; red berries dot the plants from late August through November and are frequently quite showy. The plant's glossy semievergreen foliage is deciduous in northern areas, where it turns orange and red before dropping. In mild climates the leaves usually remain a glossy green all winter. Many cultivars are available for differences in form and foliage color. See *C. dammeri* for cultural suggestions. Native to China.

Cotoneaster horizontalis

Cotoneaster multiflorus (Many-flowered cotoneaster). Deciduous. Zones 6–9.

This shrub is not only one of the most trouble free of the cotoneasters but also one of the most beautiful. Its white flowers, blooming from early to mid-May, are quite spectacular, and these are followed by abundant bright red berries that last from late August into October. In habit it is a graceful, arching, mounded, or fountainlike shrub that grows 8 to 12 feet or more high and 12 to 15 feet wide. In flower and form it is similar to, and a good substitute for, a large Vanhoutte spirea. It is definitely not for the small landscape—use it in a shrub border and for massing in spacious areas where it has plenty of room to grow. The foliage, an interesting blue-green with a medium-fine texture, has little or no change of color before dropping in the fall. Plant container-grown shrubs in well-drained soil in a sunny, airy location. It is best to root-prune the plants as you set them out to help develop a strong, fibrous root system. Native to China.

Cotoneaster multiflorus

Cytisus × praecox (Warminster broom). Deciduous. Zones 6–10.

While not strictly evergreen, the Warminster broom looks that way—its dense, vertical stems remain green all winter long. Even in summer, foliage is sparse or nonexistent; nearly all the photosynthesis takes place in the green stems, which are the plant's main textural asset in all seasons. In May the profuse pale yellow flowers create an extremely showy display. Use this plant as a specimen in a shrub border; in large rock gardens; where dry, poor soil presents a problem; or where an interesting textural evergreen accent in winter and a showy spring display are desired. Under most conditions this shrub will grow 4 to 6 feet high with an equal or greater spread, forming a rounded mass of many parallel (mostly vertical) stems.

Cytisus × praecox

In spring, move only young, container-grown plants into perfectly drained soil. Bacteria on the roots of this plant fix nitrogen from the atmosphere, and Warminster broom actually prefers infertile and poor soil. Young plants can be tip pinched, but older plants do not respond well to pruning of any kind—it is best to let them develop their natural form.

Many other *Cytisus* species are available, but most become rampant, naturalizing, self-sowing pests. Particularly notorious is Scotch broom (*Cytisus scoparius*), which has become an invasive weed on the West Coast and in parts of the Northeast. Unfortunately, it is one of the most commonly available brooms. Some cultivars, such as *Cytisus scoparius* 'Carla', and most hybrids, such as *C. × praecox*, are generally not a weed problem. Native to the Mediterranean region.

Daphne cneorum (Garland flower). Broadleaved evergreen. Zones 5–7.

Few can forget the penetrating, delicious fragrance of daphne once they

Daphne cneorum

Daphne odora

have experienced it. The plant has finely textured evergreen foliage with rosy-pink clusters of flowers at the ends of the branches in April and May. It will grow slowly 6 to 12 inches high and 2 feet or more in spread, forming a loose, low trailing mass. Use it as a small-scale ground cover, in a rock garden, in shady spots, or in groupings where its fragrance can be most appreciated. Always plant *Daphne* from containers into moist, well-drained soil. While there are different opinions about the proper pH levels, most experts agree that neutral soil is best. Protect the plant from hot sun and drying winds, mulch to keep the roots cool and moist, and don't disturb it after it is established by cultivating or trying to move it. Plant *Daphne* fairly high to reduce the chances of crown rot. Native to Central and Southern Europe.

Daphne × *burkwoodii* (Burkwood daphne; Zones 6–8) is a larger *Daphne* with extremely fragrant May flowers that open white and fade to pink. It grows to a compact 3 to 4 feet high and wide. 'Somerset', a larger cultivar that grows 4 to 5 feet wide, is reputed to be the easiest daphne to grow.

Daphne odora (Winter daphne; Zones 8–10), more than any other, is responsible for daphne's reputation as unpredictable and frustrating—full-grown plants often die suddenly for no discernible reason. Despite this, it is the most popular *Daphne* in mild regions. Rosy-pink flowers that bloom in February and March adorn the 3-inch-long, lustrous, dark green leaves. The fragrance is legendary. This *Daphne* must have perfect drainage and be planted high. Water infrequently during the summer months to increase flowering and prevent root rot. 'Aureomarginata' is a popular variegated form that is said to be hardier and easier to grow. Native to Japan and China.

Deutzia gracilis (Slender deutzia). Deciduous. Zones 5–8.

Deutzia is another of the old-fashioned, popular favorites that are briefly showy in the spring, but have little to offer the rest of the year. There are many *Deutzia* species and cultivars, but this one is probably the most graceful in form and the most dependable for flowering. This low, broad-mounded shrub grows 2 to 6 feet high and 3 to 6 feet wide, with graceful upright-arching branches and a dull green foliage. It is best used in a shrub border, where its nondescript appearance when not in flower can blend with other shrubs. In mid- to late May, pure white flowers literally cover the shrub like a bank of new snow. Easy to grow, *Deutzia gracilis* transplants readily in the spring into any reasonably good garden soil, and will take full sun to light shade. Severe winter dieback is frequently annoying, and dead wood should be pruned out annually. *Deutzia* flowers on old wood, so prune immediately after flowering. Native to Japan.

Deutzia × *malifloria* is a twiggy, erect shrub 5 to 7 feet tall, with white flowers that appear after those of slender deutzia. 'Avalanche' is a more compact form that grows 4 feet high and wide.

Elaeagnus pungens 'Maculata'

Deutzia × *rosea* **'Carminea'** is more dwarf in habit, with a great abundance of rosy-pink flowers.

Elaeagnus pungens (Silverberry). Broadleaved evergreen. Zones 7–10.

The inconspicuous but powerfully fragrant flowers that bloom in October and the olive-colored evergreen foliage are this tough shrub's hallmarks, along with adaptability, thorny branches, and edible red fruit in the spring. Good in problem areas of heat, wind, and drought, silverberry actually prefers poor, infertile soil. It responds well to shearing, which increases its density. This is an excellent hedge plant, and its thorny branches will form an impenetrable barrier. Without pruning, it will rapidly become a rigid, sprawling, angular shrub growing anywhere from 6 to 15 feet tall. Cultivars are available with variegated foliage. Native to Japan.

Enkianthus campanulatus (Redvein enkianthus). Deciduous. Zones 5–9.

Redvein enkianthus is treasured for its many ornamental features, including delicate yellowish clusters of bell-like May flowers veined with red, spectacular orange and red fall color, and an interesting horizontal branching structure. It is an excellent specimen plant and combines well with rhododendrons. Use it where it can be appreciated up close, such as around entryways or in outdoor living areas. A narrow, upright shrub or small tree with stratified branches and tufted foliage, it grows slowly to 6 to 8 feet high in northern climates, and can reach 20 to 30 feet in mild ones. Culture is similar to that of rhododendrons: plant in moist, well-drained, acid soil that is rich in organic matter, in a location that has full sun to partial shade (shade is preferable in hot summer climates). *Enkianthus* will not tolerate drought or alkaline soils. Native to Japan.

Erica **species** (Heath). Narrow-leafed evergreen. Zones 4–8, varying according to species.

Quite similar to *Calluna* (heather), these evergreen shrubs offer more variation in size, are generally more tender, and bloom earlier in the spring. The smaller forms make outstanding ground covers and mass plantings, foreground plants for a shrub border, and rock garden specimens; the larger forms make striking textural and color accents in the spring. All are most effective when grown in large masses or beds. Like heather, *Erica* is a culturally finicky plant—refer back to the description of *Calluna vulgaris* (page 96) for its growing requirements. Many of the species listed below have a large number of cultivars.

Erica veitchii

Heaths native to northern Europe

- [ ] *Erica carnea* (Spring heath; Zones 6–8). A dwarf, spreading form growing 6 to 16 inches high and 2 to 6 feet wide, this shrub tolerates more alkaline soils than do most heaths. It will look best if pruned or sheared annually, just after flowering.
- [ ] *Erica vagans* (Cornish heath; Zones 6–8). This bushy shrub grows 2 to 3 feet tall and 3 to 4 feet wide, and its flowers bloom latest of all heaths—from July until September.

Heaths native to southern Europe

- [ ] *Erica arborea* (Tree heath; Zones 9–10). A rather awkward shrub or small tree that grows 10 to 20 feet high, *Erica arborea* has fragrant white flowers that bloom from March to May.
- [ ] *Erica mediterranea* (Mediterranean or Irish heath; Zones 8–10). With upright growth 4 to 7 feet high, this finely textured shrub is good strictly for background foliage. Its flowers are inconsequential.

Escallonia rubra (Red escallonia). Broadleaved evergreen. Zones 8–10.

Escallonia grows quickly, produces attractive red, fragrant flowers in the summer and fall (year-round in milder climates), and tolerates the wind and salt spray of coastal gardens. It makes an excellent screen or windbreak, and is useful for massing and integrating into the shrub border. Pruning encourages its dark, evergreen foliage, although it causes a corresponding reduction in flowering. A light annual pruning will maintain a compact form; left to itself, however, the shrub will quickly grow 6 to 15 feet tall with a dense, rounded, upright habit. Escallonia will not tolerate highly alkaline soils, and needs partial shade in hot inland gardens. It can tolerate short periods of drought, but performs best with adequate water. Native to South America, principally Chile.

Escallonia × *exoniensis* '**Balfouri**' (Zones 9–10) will grow as high as 10 feet, with graceful, drooping branchlets and pink blossoms.

Escallonia × exoniensis 'Frades'

Euonymus alatus 'Compactus'

Escallonia × *exoniensis* **'Frades'** (Zones 9–10) produces more abundant pink flowers and retains a more compact 5- to 6-foot habit.

Euonymus alatus (Burning bush; Winged euonymus). Deciduous. Zones 4–7.

Popular especially for its brilliant scarlet fall color, *Euonymus alatus* displays a neat, vase-shaped habit and clean, pest-free foliage. However, it will eventually get quite large and open—8 to 10 feet high and as wide—so consider this before planting. Use it as an unclipped hedge or screen, in groups, in the shrub border, or as a specimen. Pruning will destroy the naturally neat outline of the plant, causing "witches' brooms" and uneven growth. Burning bush transplants easily and adapts to many growing conditions and soils, except to very wet ones. It does equally well in full sun or heavy shade, where it still develops good fall color; however, its brightest hues come in full sun. The cultivar 'Compactus' is a slightly smaller form. It is often sold as a cute little dwarf, which it most certainly is not. Native from Northeastern Asia to central China.

Euonymus fortunei (Wintercreeper). Broadleaved evergreen. Zones 5–8.

While popular among the hardiest broadleaved evergreens, the shrub forms of wintercreeper are susceptible to several serious diseases and insects. Many of the *Euonymus fortunei* cultivars are spreading, semiprostrate ground covers. The shrub forms are quite variable in habit and ultimate size, so check at your nursery when in doubt. Some cultivars, propagated from "juvenile" growth, do not fruit; others bear heavy crops of bright orange fruits in fall and winter. *Euonymus* transplants easily, tolerates all but the wettest soils, and withstands full sun to heavy shade. In harsh, exposed locations the foliage is prone to yellowing and browning in winter. In moist, humid climates and sites with poor air circulation, mildew is a serious problem. Anthracnose, crown gall, and leaf spot are even more serious diseases, often decimating entire plantings. Scale, aphids, and thrips cause problems, too. Native to China.

Euonymus japonica (Evergreen euonymus; Zones 8–10). A shrub or small tree that grows to a 15-foot height and an 8-foot spread, this popular low-maintenance, tough plant tolerates harsh situations and poor soils. However, *Euonymus japonica* is notoriously susceptible to mildew and a range of sucking insects—especially scale, aphids, mites, and thrips—and it needs a location where air circulation is good and water does not stand. Many cultivars are available; the strongly variegated golden and white forms are most popular.

Euonymus kiautschovica (Spreading euonymus; Zones 6–9). While this is generally an 8- to 10-foot-high evergreen shrub, in cold-winter areas the foliage often turns a ghastly yellow-brown and hangs on interminably. It has the same pest problems as *Euonymus fortunei*. 'Dupont' is a hardier, more compact form; 'Manhattan' is similar to 'Dupont'; and *E. hamiltonia* has cleaner foliage and is more resistant to scale.

Exochorda racemosa (Pearlbush). Deciduous. Zones 5–8.

Popular from time immemorial for its white, pearl-like buds, which open into showy blooms in mid-May, this is another single-season plant with little value the rest of the year. Pearlbush will grow 9 to 15 feet in height and spread. This upright, irregular shrub becomes quite unruly as it gets older—prune it annually just after flowering to help it maintain a more compact habit. Plant it in well-drained, acid soil, give it full sun to partial shade and average watering, and it will attract no serious pests. Native to eastern China.

Exochorda racemosa

Exochorda × macrantha 'The Bride' is a superior hybrid cultivar; it is lower growing and more compact, reaching 3 to 4 feet in height and spread.

Forsythia × intermedia (Border forsythia). Deciduous. Zones 5–9.

Few have witnessed the bright yellow burst of forsythia at the close of a harsh winter and not been heartened by this harbinger of spring. Unfortunately, this shrub's only attribute is spectacular pale to deep yellows in late March or early April (February to March in mild climates). An upright, arching, vigorous shrub that constantly needs grooming, if unchecked it will rapidly grow 8 to 10 feet high and 10 to 12 feet wide. Prune forsythia annually, right after it completes flowering, by removing one-third of the oldest canes. Give it plenty of room and let it grow in its natural form; it is usually not sheared. Renew older, overgrown plants by cutting them almost entirely to the ground. Although forsythia grows in nearly any soil, it needs plenty of water and fertilizer. A location in full sun will maximize flowering. The roots are reasonably hardy, but the flower buds are often killed by late freezes as far south as mid-Zone 6. If you live in northern zones, select hardy varieties, like 'Karl Sax' and 'Beatrix Farrand', and plant in protected areas. Many cultivars are available with a choice of growth habit, and for quantity, color (from pale to deep yellow), and size of bloom.

Forsythia × intermedia 'Spectabilis'

Forsythia ovata (Zone 4B). This forsythia is ornamentally inferior, but it is useful in those northern, borderline areas where the flower buds of *Forsythia × intermedia* are often killed. Native to the mountains of Korea.

Forsythia suspensa (Zones 5–8). While not as free-flowering as *Forsythia × intermedia*, it displays a graceful, pendulous form excellent for cascading over banks and sides of streams. Native to China.

Fothergilla major (Large fothergilla). Deciduous. Zones 6–8.

Fothergilla is one of the most attractive and desirable of the southeastern native shrubs. Its profuse honey-scented white inflorescences resemble small, round bottlebrushes, and flower in late April to early May. Its clean, dark green, pest-free foliage consistently provides an extremely showy fall display of bright yellow, orange, and scarlet. An extremely neat, rounded shrub that grows 6 to 10 feet high with a slightly narrower spread, *Fothergilla* shows to advantage in groups, mass plantings, and foundation plantings. It is especially attractive as a specimen or integrated into a shrub border.

Fothergilla major

Fuchsia magellanica 'Alba'

Although well-drained, acid soil is a must, *Fothergilla* is a relatively adaptable, entirely pest-free plant. It will grow well in partial shade and dry, rocky soils, but full sun and soils rich in organic matter will improve flowers and fall color. Native to dry, sunny ridges in the southern Appalachians from Virginia to South Carolina.

Fothergilla gardenii (Dwarf fothergilla; Zones 6–8). Differing from the large fothergilla by its smaller size (to 3 feet) and by flowers that bear *before* the leaves, this shrub is excellent for small spaces. Unfortunately, it is rarely available in nurseries.

Fuchsia × hybrida (Common fuchsia). Deciduous to evergreen. Zone 10.

Fuchsias are common evergreen shrubs in frost-free areas and are often seen as houseplants elsewhere. In intermediate climates they are commonly perennial but deciduous. A widely variable group of plants, they display bright, multicolored flowers and have a trailing to upright habit. Blooming from early summer until frost, the flowers attract hummingbirds. Some forms make excellent trailing cascades for hanging baskets or moist banks; others are used as upright specimens or integrated into a shrub border. Fuchsias definitely perform best in areas with cool summers, high atmospheric moisture, filtered shade, and rich, moist soil that is high in organic matter. In dry climates they need heavy mulching, frequent misting and watering, and protection from hot, searing winds. Give them light applications of liquid fertilizer every 10 to 14 days throughout the growing season, spray regularly to control sucking insects, and pinch them back frequently to encourage dense growth. Prune annually in the early spring, before new growth starts, by removing about as much wood as was formed the previous season. Always leave at least two healthy buds on each branch.

Fuchsia magellanica (Hardy fuchsia; Zones 6–10). In northern areas this shrub is treated as a perennial, dying to the ground and growing to a rounded 3-foot shrub each year. In the deep South, it is a shrub commonly reaching 4 to 8 feet in height. The flowers are bright red with blue inner petals, and are smaller than those of the common fuchsia. It blooms profusely from late June until frost. A graceful shrub with attractive foliage, the hardy fuchsia performs best in partial shade and rich, moist, well-drained soil (although it is not as particular as *Fuchsia × hybrida*). Native to Chile, where it forms thickets in low, moist areas near water.

Gardenia jasminoides (Gardenia). Broadleaved evergreen. Zones 8–10.

Gardenia jasminoides

The legendary fragrance of gardenia flowers is a treasured asset to any garden, but don't discount the superb glossy evergreen leaves. Use gardenias as specimens in containers and raised beds, as hedges and low screens, or as espaliers. Most varieties will grow 3 to 6 feet high and wide. Lower-growing forms, such as 'Radicans', make effective ground covers on a limited scale. Unfortunately, gardenias are quite fussy in their growing requirements: they will not tolerate alkaline soil, saline water, poor drainage, or drought. Plant their crowns high in an acid soil rich in organic matter. Gardenias prefer a protected location in partial shade—full sun only in foggy areas. Late frosts can be quite damaging, especially at the northern limits of their range. Mist the foliage regularly in the early mornings when the plant is not in bloom, and feed every three to four weeks during the growing season with an acid plant food. Spray regularly to control sucking insects. Gardenias will not bloom well in cool summer areas. Native to China.

Genista tinctoria (Common woadwaxen). Deciduous. Zones 2–9.

This is the hardiest of the *Genista* species, and features spectacular yellow flowers in June. It has a small, neat, rounded habit and is 2 to 3 feet high, composed of strongly vertical, nearly leafless evergreen stems. All genistas require full sun and sharp drainage, but otherwise they are easy to grow and adaptable, actually preferring poor, dry, infertile soil. They tolerate drought and coastal conditions well. Leave genistas alone after they become established—they do not transplant easily. All genistas are native to the Mediterranean regions.

Genista hispanica (Spanish gorse or Spanish broom; Zones 6B–9) has bright yellow flowers in early June. It grows only 1 to 2 feet high but has a wide spread.

Genista monosperma (Bridal veil broom; Zones 9–10) has fragrant white flowers in both winter and spring. It is a large, upright shrub, growing 20 feet high and 10 feet wide.

Genista pilosa (Silky-leafed woadwaxen; Zones 6–10) has yellow flowers in late May and grows 1 to 1½ feet tall and 7 feet wide. It has silvery leaves.

Genista sagittalis (Arrow broom; Zones 5–10) is a rapidly growing prostrate shrub that has outstanding yellow flowers in May and June. It grows 6 to 12 inches high and 7 feet wide.

Genista tinctoria 'Plena'

Hamamelis × intermedia (Hybrid witch hazel). Deciduous. Zones 6–8.

All witch hazels are delightful for their spicy fragrance and delicate showy winter flowers. (During periods of extreme cold, the flower petals curl into a tight ball, which enables them to withstand prolonged icy periods in freezing weather.) While this hybrid is not as fragrant or restrained in size as others, it is the showiest of all the witch hazels available in the United States. As early as February, the leafless branches are covered with deep yellow blossoms that last about a month. The red-flowered cultivars, such as 'Jelena' (which is actually a coppery-orange), while interesting, are not as outstanding from a distance as those with yellow flowers. This is not a shrub for small gardens—it will eventually reach 15 to 20 feet in height with a comparable spread. Expect an outstanding display of fall color in reds, oranges, and yellows before the leaves drop.

Hamamelis × intermedia 'Primavera'

Plant witch hazels in deep, rich soils that have an abundant supply of moisture. They will not tolerate drought, but they need little pampering—they are virtually pest free. Use them as screens, backgrounds, or large focal points, or train them into small trees. They are excellent as a naturalized woodland understory. Consider planting them near windows, where they can be seen from indoors on a cold, wintry day.

Hamamelis vernalis (Vernal witch hazel; Zones 6–9). With small, powerfully fragrant yellow flowers in January and February, this witch hazel has a neater, smaller habit (6 to 10 feet high and usually much wider) that is round and dense. The leaves turn a clear yellow in the fall. Native to gravelly, often-flooded stream banks in the Ozark Mountains.

Hamamelis virginiana (Common witch hazel; Zones 5–9). This is the hardiest and also the largest and rangiest of the witch hazels, growing 20 to 30 feet high and wide. Its yellow flowers in November and December often coincide with clear yellow fall foliage, reducing their effectiveness; however, they are quite fragrant. Native to forest understories from Canada to Georgia and west to Nebraska.

Hibiscus syriacus (Shrub althea; Rose of Sharon). Deciduous. Zones 6–9.

An old-fashioned favorite for its late-summer-to-frost flowers, the shrub althea has traditionally been used as a focal specimen; however, it has little to offer when not in flower and is much more effective when grouped or massed in a shrub border. It is a large, very erect, round-topped shrub or small tree that grows at a moderate rate 8 to 12 feet tall and 6 to 10 feet wide. A great many cultivars are available for flower color—whites, reds, purples, violets, and combinations in between. *Hibiscus syriacus* is extremely tolerant of the salt and wind of coastal gardens, and prefers a hot summer. Wet weather will tend to rot the flower buds. Although this shrub is not particular about soils, it will not do well in wet or dry ones. It does best in full sun, but will tolerate partial shade.

If left unpruned, it will produce profuse but small blooms. For larger flowers, prune hard each spring to two to three buds per stem (this plant flowers on the current year's growth). Its leaves are among the last to appear in the spring, which frequently (but needlessly) worries gardeners unfamiliar with this shrub. The leaves are also among the first to drop in the fall. Spray regularly for Japanese beetles, scale, aphids, and whiteflies. This shrub is also susceptible to a wide range of diseases in humid climates. Native to China and India.

Hibiscus rosa-sinensis (Chinese hibiscus; Zones 9–10). Popular in Florida, California, Texas, and Hawaii, this shrub will grow rapidly to 30 feet in height. Literally thousands of cultivars are available, with large single or double flowers in whites, pinks, reds, and yellows. Hibiscus has distinct requirements: good drainage; abundant moisture, sun, and heat; and protection from wind and frost. It will seldom bloom in cool-summer areas. Feed it monthly during the growing season, and protect it from aphids. Prune out about one-third of the old wood each spring to keep older plants vigorous, and tip pinch to increase bloom. Native to China.

Hydrangea macrophylla (Bigleaf hydrangea). Deciduous. Zones 7–10.

This hydrangea has an excellent late-summer floral display (July and August) and lustrous, neat foliage in mild-winter areas. It is also the hydrangea commonly grown in pots by florists; as a rule, however, cultivars suitable as container plants don't do as well in the garden. Outside, it is a round shrub with many erect, slightly branched stems reaching 4 to 8 feet in height (sometimes 12 feet). It spreads indefinitely, due to its tendency to sucker vigorously.

The bigleaf hydrangea seems to *prefer*, not just tolerate, seashore conditions, where it can be planted in full sun. Otherwise, plant it in partial shade and in rich, moist, well-drained soil that's high in organic matter. Soil acidity affects the plant's uptake of aluminum, which in turn determines whether the flowers will be pink or blue. Blue flowers result from a pH of 5 to 5.5, pink flowers from a pH of 6 to 6.5 or higher. To increase acidity and provide aluminum for blue flowers, apply aluminum sulfate to the soil; to decrease the acidity for pink flowers, apply lime. To achieve either color, make the application well before flowering time. Bigleaf hydrangeas flower on old wood, so prune just after the shrub flowers. If the plant dies back from a hard winter, it will not produce flowers that season.

The many cultivars available are generally divided between the Hortensias and the Lace-caps: the Hortensias have all sterile flowers forming large globular heads; the Lace-caps have a delicate ring of large, sterile flowers surrounding a cluster of tiny, fertile ones. Flowers can be single or double; are available in white, pinks, and blues; and are generally clustered in heads that are 5 to 10 inches in diameter. Native to Japan.

Hydrangea quercifolia (Oakleaf hydrangea). Deciduous. Zones 6–9.

While its delicate white flowers and deep red or purplish fall leaves make this shrub a pleasing one, its foliage often predominates in the garden. The leaves are attractively large and coarse, with a characteristic oak leaf shape. This shrub is useful in the border for an accent in large masses, in difficult shady places, or as a specimen. It is an upright and irregular shrub that

Hibiscus syriacus

Hydrangea macrophylla

Hydrangea quercifolia

slowly grows 6 to 8 feet high and 4 to 6 feet wide, with a tendency to sucker from the roots and form large colonies. The lacy, conical flower clusters appear in late June through July; the large, sterile flowers surround the tiny, fertile ones in a ring. They persist on the shrub for a long time, fading to pink, then to purplish-pink, and finally to brown. Plant this shrub in moist, well-drained, fertile, somewhat acid soil, in sun or half shade. If necessary, it will tolerate dense shade quite well, although there will be less fall leaf color and fewer flowers. Mulch well in dry climates to maintain a cool, moist soil around the roots. Because this shrub flowers on old wood, it is strictly a foliage plant in areas where winters reach 0°F. or colder; severe weather causes serious dieback. Native to Georgia and Florida, west to Mississippi.

Hypericum prolificum (Shrubby St. Johnswort). Deciduous. Zones 5–9.

The pert, bright yellow flowers of this hardiest *Hypericum* are a welcome addition to any garden. They last over a long season from mid-June through August. Fresh, clean, blue-green foliage covers this dense, rounded shrub, which grows 1 to 4 feet high and wide. If you plant it in light, well-drained soil that receives bright sun, *Hypericum* will prove to be tough, durable, easy to maintain, and pest free. It tolerates poor, dry, sterile soil, city air pollution, and partial shade beautifully. Pruning is seldom necessary; if you do prune, however, the best time is in the late spring, after new growth hardens off. Use shrubby St. Johnswort in a border, for large-scale masses or small groupings, as foundation planting, or as a low informal hedge. Native from New Jersey to Iowa and Georgia.

Hypericum calycinum (Aaronsbeard St. Johnswort; Zones 6–10) is a deciduous, low-growing, spreading shrub suitable for a ground cover. It tends to become a weedy pest that is difficult to control. To maintain a dense growth, mow to the ground every few years, when appearance warrants it.

Hypericum frondosum (Golden St. Johnswort; Zones 6–9) grows 3 to 4 feet high and wide. It has very handsome blue-green foliage and large bright yellow flowers. 'Sunburst' is a lower-growing form (2 to 4 feet high and wide) that is excellent for a low border shrub.

Hypericum × moseranum (Goldflower St. Johnswort; Zones 8–10). This low evergreen shrub is one of the few plants that will do well under eucalyptus trees.

Hypericum patulum (Goldencup St. Johnswort; Zones 7–10) is a semievergreen or evergreen species growing as high and wide as 3 feet. Variety *henryi* is more vigorous and has larger flowers. 'Hidcote' is a smaller, 18-inch shrub with large, fragrant yellow flowers that bloom from June to October. 'Sungold' is supposedly more hardy.

Hypericum patulum 'Hidcote'

Iberis sempervirens (Evergreen candytuft). Broadleaved evergreen. Zones 5–10.

A handsome mat-forming evergreen shrub that produces generous drifts of pure white flowers in April or May, *Iberis* can be used as a ground cover among woody shrubs or in a combination with spring bulbs. Extremely showy in bloom, the neat 6- to 12-inch-high shrub will spread at a medium-to-rapid rate, and is covered in all seasons by dark green, finely textured foliage. It transplants easily, either from containers or as seedlings, into light soil of average fertility. Do not overfertilize, or the shrub will become loose and rangy. Prune hard each year after flowering. It's important to remove spent flowers to increase next year's bloom and keep plants dense. Unless drainage is excellent, don't overwater; excessive moisture encourages several disease problems. 'Christmas Snow' repeats its bloom in the fall. 'Little Gem' is more of a dwarf and hardier than the species. 'Purity' is similar, but has larger flower clusters. Native to southern Europe and western Asia.

Iberis sempervirens 'Pygmaea'

Ilex cornuta 'Rotunda'

Ilex crenata 'Helleri Gold'

Ilex glabra

Ilex cornuta (Chinese holly). Broadleaved evergreen. Zones 7–10.

While the species is a large, upright shrub 10 to 15 feet tall, many smaller, denser cultivars of this shrub are available. The leaves are an extremely handsome, dark, polished green in all seasons, and are larger and coarser than those of the Japanese holly. The profuse fruits are normally a brilliant red. Unlike those of other hollies, they will develop without fertilization, so you don't need both male and female plants. 'Dwarf Burford', 'Carissa', and 'Dazzler' are heavy-fruiting forms that have a slow-growing, dwarf habit; 'Rotunda' is especially dense and low growing; and 'Burfordii' is a reputedly hardier cultivar said to perform well in Zone 6. See Japanese holly (following) for cultural recommendations. Native to eastern China and Korea.

Ilex crenata (Japanese holly). Broadleaved evergreen. Zones 6B–10.

The Japanese holly is commonly mistaken for boxwood, due to its neat, rounded shape and its dark green, dense, lustrous, finely textured foliage. This slow-growing shrub responds well to pruning, and will eventually reach 5 to 10 feet in height with a usually greater spread (however, old specimens in arboreta often reach 20 feet or more). It makes an excellent selection for hedges, foundation planting, and massing, and for a soft evergreen texture in a shrub border. It transplants easily into moist, well-drained, slightly acid soils, does well in sun or shade, and appears to tolerate pollution. Often sheared into formal shapes, the Japanese holly should be pruned after the new growth has matured in the spring. Its fruits are black and inconspicuous. A wide range of cultivars is available for size, form, and hardiness. 'Black Beauty', 'Hetzii', and 'Helleri' are three of the hardiest compact types; 'Microphylla' and 'Convexa' are larger hardier forms. Native to Japan.

Ilex glabra (Inkberry). Broadleaved evergreen. Zones 3–10.

The inkberry is the hardiest broadleaved evergreen available to northern gardeners. The handsome dark green foliage grows densely on younger plants in all seasons; older plants often reach 6 to 8 feet in height by 8 to 10 feet in spread, and develop a leggy openness (although this is quite variable). The fruits are black and not particularly showy. *Ilex glabra* is native to swamps from Nova Scotia to Florida and west to Mississippi. In the wild it suckers profusely, forming large clumps. When planted in moist, acid soil, it is easy to grow and pest free. It responds well to pruning; in fact, heavy pruning is an excellent way to renew leggy old plants. This shrub, and especially its cultivar 'Compacta'—a dense, dwarf clone—are excellent for massing, hedges, and foundation planting.

Ilex verticillata (Common winterberry). Deciduous. Zones 4–8.

This deciduous holly is unusual for its adaptability to wet, swampy soils, to which it is native. A popular plant in the eastern United States, it is an outstanding fruiting shrub, bearing great quantities of bright red berries on bare branches far into the winter. Birds find the berries tasty, so the effective season often depends on the birds' appetite. Winterberry can grow 20 feet high in the wild, but usually reaches only 6 to 9 feet in the garden, with a similar spread. It is particularly effective when planted in large masses, such as in the shrub border and near water. Be sure to plant at least one male within a few hundred feet of any females to ensure fruiting. The shrub will tolerate dry soil, but prefers moist, acid ones high in organic matter. It will not grow in alkaline soils. Plant it in full sun to partial shade. 'Winter Red' is a new cultivar that is superior for its neat, dense growth, 8 to 10 feet high and wide, and for its unbelievably abundant bright red fruits. Native from Newfoundland and Minnesota to Georgia, Tennessee, and Missouri.

Ilex vomitoria (Yaupon). Broadleaved evergreen. Zones 7B–10.

While the species is a small evergreen tree, several compact dwarf cultivars are available, such as 'Nana' and 'Stokes'. Popular in the southeastern United States, this holly is more tolerant of alkaline soils and drought than are other hollies. Its finely textured foliage can easily be sheared into formal shapes. While the species is considered one of the heaviest fruiting of the hollies, the dwarf forms are generally sterile. Native to the southeastern United States.

Juniperus **species** (Juniper). Conifer. Hardiness varies with variety.

Few gardens in North America are without a juniper somewhere on the property. *Juniperus* is extremely versatile, available in a perplexing array of forms and sizes, adaptable to nearly any growing conditions, and one of the original low-maintenance plants—in short, it is an immensely popular plant genus. "If you can't grow junipers, then don't bother planting anything else," says one authority.

Junipers are commonly used, but also commonly misused. Their low-maintenance reputation masks their susceptibility to a wide range of pests, including twig blight, bagworms, white juniper scale, spider mites, spruce mites, twig borers, root rot, and water molds. When planted in shade, they quickly become spindly and loose. In wet soils they are especially susceptible to disease. And gardeners tend to forget about their eventual size, which often makes removal and replacement difficult.

Even though they offer gardeners a finely textured evergreen shrub (particularly in the northern garden, where such plants are usually in short supply), junipers are often disappointing: many varieties turn dull purple, gray, or dirty green in cold weather. Some gardeners, however, consider this winter color-change an attractive asset.

Nevertheless, when properly located and well established, there is a juniper to solve nearly any landscape problem. These plants prefer sandy, well-drained soil and a sunny, open exposure, but they will grow well in just about any location (and in any soil) provided it isn't waterlogged or in deep shade. Guard against overwatering junipers or planting them in the path of the lawn sprinkler system.

Most of the species whose descriptions follow are large trees with a confusing variety of shrubby, prostrate, or columnar cultivars. While it is impossible to list all the cultivars in this book, a few of the most recommended ones follow each species description. When in doubt, ask someone at your local nursery which cultivar is best for your area. When inquiring, stress your desire for pest resistance and for an accurate estimate of the plant's ultimate size.

Juniperus chinensis (Chinese juniper; Zones 4–10, although cultivars may vary in hardiness). Included under this extremely diverse species, whose hybrids and cultivars range from prostrate ground covers to 75-foot-high trees, are many of the most popular shrublike forms. Most (especially the cultivar 'San Jose') are quite susceptible to Phomopsis twig blight, which can be devastating in wet years. Beware of the eventual size of many selections—the extremely common 'Pfitzerana' and 'Hetzii' will grow 15 feet high and 30 feet wide or more. These plants prefer alkaline soils. The species is native to China, Mongolia, and Japan.

Some of the better varieties include:

'Armstrongii', a dwarf form, 4 feet high and wide, with soft, gray-green needles.

'Iowa', a spreading, relatively open shrub that is 6 feet high and wide and has bluish-green needles. It is blight resistant.

'Mint Julep', a 2- to 3½-foot-high, 6-foot-wide dwarf with bright green foliage and blue fruit.

Juniperus chinensis var. *procumbens* 'Nana'

Var. *procumbens* (Creeping juniper; Zones 6–10), another low, spreading juniper frequently used as a ground cover that extends over banks and hillsides and tumbles over rocks and walls. A single plant will grow 1 to 2 feet high and 10 to 15 feet wide, at a slow to medium rate. Like *J. horizontalis*, this juniper can be wiped out by Phomopsis blight. 'Nana' is a dwarf, compact form that grows about half the size of the species.

Var. *sargentii* (Sargent juniper), growing 1½ to 2 feet high and spreading 9 to 10 feet wide, with blue-green foliage. This juniper and its cultivars are resistant to Phomopsis blight.

'Sea Spray' (hardy to Zone 5), a new cultivar that is reportedly resistant to Phomopsis blight, water molds, and root rot. Growing 1 to 2 feet high and wide spreading, with good, intense blue-gray foliage, it has been recommended as a substitute for the more disease-plagued *Juniperus horizontalis* cultivars.

Juniperus communis (Common juniper; Zones 2–10). A typical plant of this species is 5 to 10 feet high, spreading 8 to 12 feet, with spiny needles that are gray or blue-green in the summer, turning to a yellowish- or brownish-green in winter. Although all forms of this plant are tremendously susceptible to Phomopsis blight, extreme hardiness and adaptability to the poorest, driest soils make it a worthwhile choice for difficult sites.

This species is native to more places than is any other tree or shrub in the world—northern and central Europe, the Mediterranean region, Asia Minor, Iran, Afghanistan, the western Himalayas, Canada, and the United States from New England to North Carolina, and west to California.

'Compressa' is a dwarf form growing to an erect, relatively narrow 2 to 3 feet, with silvery-green needles.

Variety *depressa* (Canadian juniper) rarely grows over 4 feet high, but often ranges as much as 15 feet wide. This is not a plant for the small garden.

'Depressa Aurea' is similar to variety *depressa*, but has yellow foliage.

'Gold Beach' is an interesting choice for a rock garden, growing only 6 inches tall and 2 feet wide. In the spring the yellow new growth changes to green.

Juniperus conferta (Shore juniper; Zones 6–10). Marked by intense bluish-green, softly textured foliage, this prostrate shrub makes an excellent ground cover for coastal gardens. Growing 1 to 2 feet high, it will slowly spread 6 to 8 feet, forming a dense, handsome mat. It is extremely tolerant of poor, sandy soils and coastal salt-spray conditions, but will not grow well in wet, heavy soil. 'Blue Pacific' and 'Emerald Sea' are two cultivars worth considering, due to their extra-low habit and clean, blue-green foliage. Native to Japan.

Juniperus horizontalis (Creeping juniper; Zones 3–10). Almost all the many cultivars of this low, spreading ground cover plant turn an unattractive grayish-purple in winter. All forms are extremely susceptible to Phomopsis blight, which, under conditions of high humidity, can devastate entire plantings. Nevertheless, this is a popular species because of several of its intensely blue, extremely prostrate cultivars. Native from Nova Scotia to British Columbia, south to Massachusetts and Montana.

'Bar Harbor' and 'Wiltonii' (also known as 'Blue Rug') are two of the favorites, and 'Blue Chip' is one of the best. When selecting these plants, consider their grayish-purple winter effects. 'Emerson', a slow-growing form that grows 1 foot high and 9 to 15 feet wide, has intense blue-green foliage that holds its color throughout the winter.

Juniperus sabina (Savin juniper; Zones 5–10). The stiff, distinctly vase-shaped branches of this shrub can spread 10 to 15 feet at maturity, with a height of 4 to 6 feet. It is particularly tolerant of urban pollution, and a few of its cultivars are resistant to Phomopsis blight. The lower-growing forms of

Juniperus communis 'Echiniformis'

this plant are excellent for massing, foundation planting, and bank coverings. The foliage is dark green in summer, often turning brownish-green in cold weather. This juniper is native to the mountains of central and southern Europe.

'Arcadia', an excellent dwarf form, grows 1 foot high by 4 feet wide and exhibits good resistance to Phomopsis blight.

'Broadmoor' grows 18 inches tall and 10 to 15 feet across after a time, building up more height in the center with age. It, too, is blight resistant.

'Skandia' is another blight-resistant shrub, similar to 'Arcadia', with bluish-green foliage.

'Tamariscifolia', although very popular on the market, is susceptible to several pests.

'Von Ehron', a vase-shaped form, grows 5 feet high by 5 feet wide. It is resistant to Phomopsis blight.

Juniperus scopulorum (Rocky Mountain juniper; Zones 4–10). This is normally a narrow, erect tree that grows 30 to 40 feet high naturally. Its smaller cultivars are valued as hedges, screens, and windbreaks because of their generally upright habit, slow rate of growth, and bluish cast to the foliage. The species is native to dry ridges of the higher elevations of the Rocky Mountains, from Alberta to Texas.

Some of the more compact cultivars include:

'Lakewood Globe'. This becomes a round 4 to 6 feet after ten years of growth; it has blue-green foliage.

'Silver Star'. A wide-spreading form, it grows 3 feet high and 6 to 8 feet wide, and has silvery-gray foliage.

'Table Top Blue'. This silvery-blue form grows 5 to 6 feet high and 8 feet wide in ten years, and has a distinctly flat-topped appearance.

'Welchi'. A very narrow, compact column that grows up to 8 feet high. Its gray-green new growth turns a distinctly blue-green in the summer.

Juniperus virginiana (Eastern redcedar; Zones 2–10). This species is most valued for its many cultivars, all of which are resistant to Phomopsis blight, but which are more susceptible to cedar apple rust and bagworms than are most other junipers. The foliage ranges from deep green to gray-green, and often assumes a brownish, dull cast in the winter. The eastern redcedar grows wild throughout eastern and central North America.

Some of the better compact forms include:

'Kosteri'. An extremely wide-spreading, low-growing form, it reaches 3 to 4 feet high and 25 to 30 feet wide after many years. The foliage turns purplish in the winter and is grayish-blue in all other seasons.

'Nana'. This extremely hardy, narrow, upright form grows 10 to 20 feet high.

'Skyrocket'. The narrowest blue-gray columnar form available, it grows 10 to 15 feet tall in old age.

'Tripartita'. Very similar to a small Pfitzer juniper, it grows only 4 feet tall and 7 feet wide, and has pale green or slightly gray leaves.

Kalmia latifolia (Mountain laurel). Broadleaved evergreen. Zones 5–8. For spectacular white to deep pink flowers and excellent evergreen foliage, this eastern native is an undisputed treasure in any garden where it can be grown. Use it as a specimen and as a companion for azaleas and rhododendrons. Slow growing, it is dense, rounded, and neat when young, becoming gnarled, picturesque, and open in old age. In the wild it can reach 30 to 35 feet high, but under cultivation 7 to 15 feet is a more reasonable figure. In the harsher climate of the Midwest, mountain laurel rarely grows over 3 to 7 feet high. Plant it from a container into cool, moist, well-drained, acid soil that is high in organic matter, and give it full sun for optimum flowering. In hot-summer areas, however, it prefers partial shade. Mulch, rather than

Kalmia latifolia 'Clementine Churchill'

Kerria japonica 'Pleniflora'

cultivate, around its shallow roots. This is not a good choice for dry, Mediterranean climates or areas without frost (Zones 9–10). Cultivars are available with flower color from white to deep, bright pink. Native from New Brunswick to Indiana and south to Florida and Louisiana.

Kerria japonica (Japanese kerria). Deciduous. Zones 5–9.

The Japanese kerria is valued for its bright yellow flowers in the spring and bright green winter stems. This deciduous shrub performs well in practically the densest shade—use it where shade is a problem. Plants are better grouped; a single plant tends to appear rather disorganized. It will grow slowly 3 to 6 feet high and eventually spread 6 to 9 feet. Keep this shrub away from rich, fertile soils—it will become rank and weedy and produce fewer flowers. A tough, carefree shrub, it should be planted in deep to partial shade; its flowers fade quickly in full sun. A protected location with good drainage will reduce the chance of winter damage. Prune directly after flowering, since it flowers on last year's wood. 'Pleniflora', the most popular cultivar, is double flowered and extremely showy—some gardeners even consider it too gaudy. Several rare cultivars have white or yellow foliage or stems. Native to China and Japan.

Kolkwitzia amabilis (Beautybush). Deciduous. Zones 5–8.

This old-time, low-maintenance shrub, of limited value when not in bloom, is nevertheless quite a spectacle in season. Flowers are produced in late May in great profusion, and are a good, bright pink. A large shrub with medium texture in the summer and coarse texture in the winter, the beautybush grows rapidly to 6 to 10 feet high (sometimes 12 feet) and has a slightly lesser spread. The upright-arching form usually becomes quite leggy, but the reddish peeling bark of the lower trunks and branches can be quite attractive. Still, the beautybush looks best in the rear of a shrub border in large gardens. Easily transplanted, it is indifferent to soil type or pH. Give it a sunny location and plenty of room to grow, and prune out older stems every year. Renew old, overgrown shrubs by cutting them completely to the ground. Prune after flowering, since beautybush blooms on old wood. Native to western China.

Kolkwitzia amabilis

Lagerstroemia indica

Lagerstroemia indica (Crape myrtle). Deciduous. Zones 7B–10.

Brilliant floral displays in late summer and early fall, spectacular fall foliage color, and intriguing mottled bark in the winter make this truly an all-season plant. It is actually a small tree, but most forms can be grown as a large, upright-rounded shrub, 15 to 25 feet high and as wide. Several dwarf cultivars 5 to 12 feet tall are available as well. Crape myrtle makes a beautiful specimen or focal grouping, particularly with a ground cover planted underneath it. This shrub can also be effectively integrated into a foundation planting, or used as a hedge or screen. New foliage is bronze, maturing to a medium green, then turning into bright reds, yellows, or oranges in the fall. Flowers are produced in great profusion from July to September. A wide variety of cultivars are available with white, pink, deep red, and lavender flowers.

Crape myrtle flowers on the current season's growth, so it can be pruned as late as early spring and still produce flowers the same season. Plant it in moist, well-drained soil that is rich in organic matter, and choose a hot, sunny location. Spray to control aphids. Try to find the newer dwarf cultivars developed by the National Arboretum for resistance to powdery mildew. Otherwise, you will need to spray annually just prior to flowering to control this disease. Prune regularly to increase new flowering wood by removing small twiggy growth on small shrubs, or 12 to 18 inches of each branch on large ones. Older, overgrown plants can be cut clear to the ground to renew or contain them. Native to China and Korea.

Leptospermum scoparium (New Zealand tea tree). Narrow-leafed evergreen. Zones 9–10.

For an outstanding floral display from late winter to spring and an interesting accent of finely textured, fragrant evergreen foliage, consider the New Zealand tea tree. It can be an effective choice in gardens with a mild climate, particularly the Mediterranean climates of the West Coast. New Zealand tea requires excellent drainage and prefers full sun. Once established, it is drought tolerant and pest free. If you must shear or prune for a formal appearance, do so lightly. Never prune back to bare wood, since it does not produce buds that break into new growth (adventitious buds). New Zealand tea tree is an excellent choice in seacoast gardens as a specimen, accent, or focal point in the shrub border. The prostrate forms make interesting and colorful ground covers, but don't expect their fairly open habit to suppress weeds. Extremely variable from seed. A wide range of cultivars is available for flower color (in reds, pinks, and white) and habit (from 6 to 10 feet high, to prostrate ground covers 8 to 12 inches high and 2 to 3 feet wide). The profuse colorful flowers appear from late winter to midsummer, depending on the cultivar, and are effective for about two to four weeks. Native to Australia, Tasmania, and New Zealand.

Leptospermum scoparium 'Red Damask'

Leucothoe fontanesiana

Leucothoe fontanesiana (Drooping leucothoe). Broadleaved evergreen. Zones 5–7.

Most commonly planted in the East in moist, acid gardens, the drooping leucothoe makes a wonderful companion to rhododendrons, azaleas, and mountain laurel because of its lustrous, dark evergreen foliage, and its graceful form. The bright green or bronze new foliage in spring and the purplish color in winter are important assets; so are the delicate, subtle, fragrant white flowers in spring. Use *Leucothoe* as a foreground planting for leggy shrubs; a graceful high ground cover for shady slopes; or for grouping in a shrub border. It is a perfect shrub to naturalize in a shady woodland wildflower garden.

    L. fontanesiana transplants easily from a container in early spring, but is fastidious about its requirements. It will be basically trouble free if it gets moist, well-drained, acid soil high in organic matter, as well as full shade, ample moisture, and protection from drought and drying winds. Leaf spot, though, can be a problem. Prune right after flowering; however, this plant's natural graceful, fountainlike form (3 to 5 feet high and often wider) makes pruning generally unnecessary. To rejuvenate older plants, cut them clear to the ground. 'Rainbow' has yellow, green, and copper-variegated foliage. 'Nana' is a dwarf form that is 2 feet high and 6 feet wide. Native to streamsides in the mountains of Virginia to North Carolina and Tennessee.

Ligustrum **species** (Privet). Some evergreen, some deciduous species. Hardiness varies according to the species.

Highly adaptable, pest free, and low in maintenance requirements, the shrubby privets are most often used as formal and informal hedges, backgrounds, and screens. In early summer most have spikelike white clusters of flowers, whose strong scent is variously described as ranging from offensive to pleasant. All privets transplant easily bare root, are adaptable to nearly any soil except a wet one, and take full sun to partial shade. They perform well under adverse conditions of pollution and drought. If flowers are desired, prune just after blooming; otherwise, prune any time. All privets grow rapidly and respond well to pruning and shaping.

Deciduous types

☐ *Ligustrum amurense* (Amur privet; Zones 4–10). A hardy privet that is excellent for hedges, this species has good, clean, medium- to finely textured foliage. Native to northern China.

Ligustrum species

☐ *Ligustrum × ibolium* (Ibolium privet; Zones 5–10). This shrub is similar to the excellent California privet, but it is hardier.

☐ *Ligustrum obtusifolium* (Border privet; Zones 4–10). The border privet is not only one of the hardiest privets, but also one of the most attractive because of its broad, horizontal growth habit and good dark green foliage. It will grow 10 to 12 feet tall and 12 to 15 feet wide, although it can easily be kept much smaller. Var. *regelianum* is a low, 4- to 5-foot-high shrub with unusual, horizontally spreading branches that look best when allowed to grow naturally. Native to Japan.

☐ *Ligustrum ovalifolium* (California or oval-leaf privet; Zones 6–10). Excellent glossy, semievergreen leaves often tempt gardeners to grow this plant north of its range, where it dies to the ground every winter. Where hardy, it is a deservedly popular hedge plant. Native to Japan.

☐ *Ligustrum* 'Vicaryi' (Golden privet; Zones 6–10). In full sun the leaves of this popular plant are a glaring yellow; in shade they are yellow-green to light green. Clipped hedges will remain yellow-green, since the shaded inner leaves are constantly exposed from clipping. 'Hillside Strain' is a hardier variety that is useful in Zone 5, although it is a gaudy plant difficult to integrate into the landscape.

☐ *Ligustrum ovalifolium* (California or oval-leaf privet; Zones 6–10). Excellent glossy, semievergreen leaves often tempt gardeners to grow this is an annoyance, to say the least.

Evergreen types

☐ *Ligustrum japonicum* (Japanese privet; Zones 7B–10). This privet makes an excellent hedge or screen in southern or western gardens. It has excellent lustrous evergreen leaves. Its habit is dense and compact (it grows rapidly 6 to 12 feet high), and it responds well to pruning. It is also commonly used for training into topiary. An excellent container plant, it looks best when given plenty of water and protected from the hot sun. Many forms are available. This plant is frequently labeled incorrectly in nurseries as *L. texanum*. Native to Japan and Korea.

☐ *Ligustrum lucidum* (Glossy privet; Zones 7B–10). Often confused with the Japanese privet, this privet is more treelike (it grows 35 to 40 feet high). To distinguish it from *L. japonicum* among young nursery plants, feel the undersides of the leaves. If the veins are raised, it is *L. japonicum*; if they are recessed, it is *L. lucidum*. Native to China.

☐ *Ligustrum* 'Suwanee River'. This evergreen hybrid eventually grows 4 to 6 feet high, with a compact, tight habit. Its dark green, wavy leaves are useful as a low hedge or in a foundation planting.

Lonicera tatarica (Tatarian honeysuckle). Deciduous. Zones 3B–9.
The chief attributes of this shrub are intensely fragrant early May flowers that are available in the widest color range of any honeysuckle (whites, pinks, and reds), and showy bright red berries in June. The dense, bluish-green foliage has a medium texture. Unfortunately, this shrub becomes quite leggy, requiring a foreground planting and like nearly all honeysuckles displays an impossible winter appearance. It is best used in a shrub border, where these features can be hidden. This is an upright, arching shrub, 10 to 12 feet high and wide. Its berries are favored by birds, which will deposit the seeds all over the garden, establishing seedlings everywhere. Easily transplanted and adaptable to many soils, *L. tatarica* prefers full sun. Prune just after flowering. Renew overgrown plants by cutting them clear to the ground. 'Arnold Red' has good pink flowers and grows only 3 feet high. Native to central Asia.

Lonicera nitida (Box honeysuckle; Zones 7B–10). This finely textured evergreen with fragrant white flowers blooms in June. Tolerant of coastal condi-

Lonicera 'Zabellii'

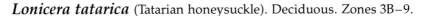

tions, it responds well to pruning and makes an excellent hedge. Unlike other honeysuckles, which can have rampant growth habits, it presents a neat, refined appearance.

***Lonicera × xylosteoides* 'Clavey's Dwarf'** (Zones 5–10) is an excellent choice for a low hedge, forming a neat 3- to 6-foot mound with clean, fresh green foliage. 'Emerald Mound' is a beautiful low-growing cultivar with wonderful bluish-green leaves, becoming 3 feet high and 4 to 6 feet wide.

Magnolia quinquepeta 'Nigra'

Magnolia quinquepeta, formerly *M. liliflora* (Lily magnolia). Deciduous. Zones 6–10.

The large, showy flowers of the lily magnolia are purple on the outside and white on the inside, and bloom from late April to early May (earlier in mild climates). A smaller, more open shrub than the star magnolia, it will grow slowly to 8 to 12 feet in height, with a similar spread. Treat it like the star magnolia in terms of culture and landscape use. Several cultivars are available; the most popular is 'Nigra', which has larger, deeper purple flowers and a more restrained habit. Native to China.

Magnolia stellata (Star magnolia). Deciduous. Zones 5–10.

Especially when displayed against the dark background of evergreens or a brick wall, the large, fragrant white flowers of the star magnolia are a glorious sensory experience in early to mid-April (March in the South). Actually a large shrub or small tree that grows slowly to 15 or 20 feet tall and 10 to 15 feet wide, it is often planted without due consideration for its ultimate size. Use it as a specimen, in groups, or focused in a shrub border or foundation planting. The flowers are delicate and often damaged by wind and rain, but late frosts present the most danger because of the early blooming period. Put this plant in a protected location, and avoid southern exposures, which would force the flowers out even earlier. Plant magnolias in spring, in deep, rich, moist, well-drained soil. Never cultivate around the roots—they are fleshy and close to the surface, and are easily damaged— and do not plant the crown below the soil level. Give magnolias full sun to partial shade. Pruning, although rarely necessary, should be done immediately after flowering. Native to Japan.

Magnolia stellata 'Pink Stardust'

'Rosea' has pink buds that open into white flowers, while 'Pink Star' has flowers that remain clear pink. 'Ann' is a new hybrid cultivar worth considering for its fragrant, lilylike, deep pink buds and clear pink flowers, which open later and last longer than the species. It also displays a superior, uniform 8- to 12-foot, upright habit. While better form and flower are important considerations, its chief advantage is a later flowering period, and hence decreased susceptibility to late frosts.

Mahonia aquifolium (Oregon grape). Broadleaved evergreen. Zones 5–9.

Mahonia aquifolium is an open, loose shrub with upright, heavy stems and very showy, bright yellow flowers that bloom in late April. It is popularly used as an evergreen ground cover in shady areas, but its irregular spreading habit and mature height (3 to 6 feet and sometimes 9 feet tall) look best when integrated into a shrub border or foundation planting, or as a specimen. While its spiny, hollylike leaves are evergreen, the leaves often turn a purplish-bronze at the onset of cold weather. In locations that are exposed to wind and sun, the leaves scorch and turn brown. The shrub is inclined to spread by underground stems, but this tendency to openness and straggliness can be somewhat controlled by an annual pruning, just after flowering, to maintain a 3-foot height. Plant *Mahonia* in a moist, acid soil and protect it from hot sun and wind. Several cultivars are available with better form, winter leaf colors, and profuse flowering. Native to damp forests from British Columbia to Oregon.

Mahonia aquifolium

Mahonia bealei (Leatherleaf mahonia). Broadleaved evergreen. Zones 6B–10.

Striking structural interest is the chief attribute of this plant: it often grows 10 to 12 feet high and has strongly vertical, little-branched stems and large, compound leaves that are held horizontally. The effect is exotic and tropical, especially when displayed against a wall or dramatically lit at night. In addition, the shrub produces large, showy clusters of yellow flowers, followed by powdery blue, grapelike fruit. This mahonia will not tolerate drought, hot sun, or winter sun and wind, and should be planted in a rich, moist soil and given plenty of water. Consider the ultimate size of *Mahonia bealei* before planting, since it is difficult to alter the shrub's growth by pruning.

Mahonia lomariifolia (Zones 8B–10). This shrub is more tender than *Mahonia bealei*, but it also is more dramatic, with larger, coarser foliage. Both these mahonias make excellent container plants. Avoid planting where the spiny foliage can scratch people. Both are native to China.

Malus sargentii (Sargent's crabapple). Deciduous. Zones 5–9.

Most crabapples are thought of as trees; this one is small enough to be used as a shrub. A superb, easy-to-grow plant, it has a strongly horizontal shape, growing 6 to 8 feet tall and usually spreading twice as wide. It is graced with spectacular clouds of fragrant white flowers in mid-May (most effective in alternate years); good dark green foliage in summer; and profuse bright red, pea-sized crabapples, attractive to birds, in fall and early winter. It adapts to a wide variety of soils, preferring full sun and average watering. Although it is seldom necessary, pruning should be done directly after flowering and before next year's buds set in mid-June. *M. sargentii* is highly resistant to many of the diseases that commonly plague crabapples. For the curious collector, 'Tina' is an extremely dwarf form, 18 to 24 inches high and 2 to 3 feet wide. 'Rosea' has clear pink buds. Native to Japan.

Myrica pensylvanica (Northern bayberry). Deciduous. Zones 2–7.

Bayberry is a plant that actually prefers infertile, dry, sandy soils. Excellent for large-scale massing in poor soil and coastal areas, it also adapts well to difficult urban sites, where it will form rolling, billowing masses of clean, deep, lustrous green foliage, ranging 5 to 12 feet in height. Bayberry tends to sucker and form large colonies, but is also good for a shrub border or an informal hedge, and in combination with broadleaved evergreens. Its grayish-white, waxy berries grow in great quantities along the stems of female plants, and persist all winter long. All parts of the plant are aromatic—the berries have been used since Colonial times to make fragrant candles. Transplant bayberry from a container into any soil, ranging from sand to clay, and give it full sun to partial shade. It tolerates salt spray and wind, and attracts no serious pests. Renew older, leggy plants by pruning them down to the ground. Native to coastal areas from Newfoundland to North Carolina, and along the Great Lakes.

Myrtus communis (Myrtle). Broadleaved evergreen. Zones 9–10.

With its glossy, bright green foliage, which is delightfully fragrant when bruised, myrtle is commonly used in the hot, dry areas and coastal gardens of Arizona and California for formal or informal hedges, screens, mass plantings, or backgrounds. It takes shearing extremely well and is easily trained; unpruned, it is usually seen as a 5- to 6-foot-high and 4- to 5-foot wide, round, bushy shrub. However, when very old it can attain treelike dimensions—up to 15 feet tall and 20 feet wide. Sweet-scented, mildly attractive flowers are produced in the summer. The smooth, rusty-tan bark is showy on older specimens. Other than requiring fast drainage, myrtle is

Malus sargentii

Myrica pensylvanica

not particular about soil. Many cultivars are available, mostly for form and foliage color. Native to the Mediterranean region.

Nandina domestica (Nandina; Heavenly bamboo). Broadleaved evergreen (semideciduous in the North). Zones 6B–10.

Not even remotely related to true bamboo, *Nandina* is a deservedly popular shrub in southern gardens. A strongly vertical form contrasts nicely with delicate, wispy foliage that is evergreen in mild climates. Creamy white, erect flower spikes borne on the ends of the vertical branches in June are followed by bright red clusters of berries. Even if it receives only a few hours of sun a day, *Nandina* has brilliant crimson to purple foliage in fall and winter. Often reaching 8 feet in height and 2½ to 3 feet in width, this shrub is effective as a hedge or screen, in a mass or grouping, and as a solitary specimen in an entryway or container. It is particularly effective when backlit. *Nandina* will lose its leaves at 10°F., and will die back to the ground at 0°F., although it recovers quickly the following season. In the northern limits of its range, it is best used as an herbaceous perennial. Since cross-fertilization seems to improve fruiting, try to plant *Nandina* in groups. It performs well in nearly any soil, in sun or shade (although some protection is required in particularly hot climates), and established plants tolerate drought well. Prune out old, leggy canes annually to encourage dense growth. *Nandina* competes well with tree roots, and is little troubled by pests, although it will develop chlorosis in alkaline soils. Several cultivars are offered for form, dwarf size, foliage color, and improved hardiness. Native to central China and Japan.

Nandina domestica

Nerium oleander (Oleander). Broadleaved evergreen. Zones 8–10.

This is a commonly used shrub in the South and west of the Rockies. It has coarse evergreen foliage; attractive red, pink, white, or yellow flowers in summer; and low maintenance requirements, especially in hot, dry climates. A broad, rounded, and bulky shrub, oleander grows very rapidly to 8 to 12 feet tall and 6 to 10 feet wide, sometimes becoming open and leggy. Plant oleander in full sun, in any soil from dry sand to wet clay. Tolerating heat, salt, and drought, it is an excellent choice for desert gardens. Prune the shrub in early spring to control size and form; remove old wood that has flowered each year. Tip pinch to encourage density, or pull off suckers from the base to encourage a more open growth habit. Oleander is plagued by many insects and diseases, particularly in shady or humid environments. Mildew, scale, and aphids are among the most severe pests.

Nerium oleander

Since all parts of the plant are extremely poisonous to humans and animals, be very cautious when disposing of clippings from pruning. Smoke from burning plant parts, whether green or dried, can cause severe skin and respiratory irritations; contact with leaves can give some people dermatitis; and ingesting even small portions of oleander can cause severe illness, even death. Many cultivars are available for flower color, fragrance, and dwarf habit. Native to the Mediterranean region.

Osmanthus fragrans (Sweet olive). Broadleaved evergreen. Zones 8–10.

While the powerfully fragrant, nearly year-round flowers are an attraction, the glossy evergreen foliage and compact form of sweet olive make this shrub an outstanding hedge, screen, background, espalier, or container plant. It is very easy to care for and quite adaptable. Plant *O. fragrans* in any soil, from sand to clay, give it partial shade, and it will grow at a moderate rate to a 10-foot-wide, 10-foot-high shrub with a rounded outline. It can easily be kept smaller by pruning and responds well to shearing. Prune any time of year; pinch the growing tips to encourage dense growth. 'Auriantiacus', with orange flowers in October, will astound you with its powerful fragrance. Native to eastern Asia.

Osmanthus heterophyllus 'Variegata'

Osmanthus delavayi (Delavay osmanthus; Zones 8–10). Small, finely textured leaves and a graceful, arching habit distinguish this *Osmanthus*. It also boasts the largest flowers of the genus, which are white, profuse, and fragrant from late March to May. Particularly handsome on banks and walls where branches can cascade, *O. delavayi* also responds well to being pruned as a hedge or foundation plant.

Osmanthus heterophyllus (Holly olive; Zones 7–10). This is perhaps the handsomest of the *Osmanthus* species, often confused with English holly. Holly has alternate leaves, while *Osmanthus* has opposite leaves. Possessing spiny, lustrous dark green leaves and hidden fragrant yellow flowers in the fall, this *Osmanthus* is unusually shade tolerant. A number of cultivars are available with variegated foliage.

Paeonia suffruticosa (Tree peony). Deciduous. Zones 5–9.

Although the attractive large leaves of this deciduous, woody shrub are a decided asset, the tree peony is grown chiefly for its flowers. And what flowers they are! They're huge—6 to 10 inches or more in diameter—with exquisite colors and a delicate texture, like crepe paper. An astounding array of cultivars and hybrids are available, from white, yellow, pink, and red, to maroon, violet, and purple. Usually growing into a rather open, leggy shrub, 4 feet high and wide and sometimes larger, the tree peony has leaves that are in proportion to the flowers—equally huge, often 18 inches long. Their deeply cut lobes, however, give the plant a curious mixture of coarse and fine texture. The flowers, unfortunately, are short lived: they last ten days at the most, much less in hot or moist weather. Single or semidouble forms are preferable; the fully double blossoms are so heavy they require individual staking.

Plant tree peonies in early fall in rich, moist, well-drained soil. These plants live a long time, so choose their positions in the garden carefully—they are difficult to transplant. Grafted forms must be planted with the graft union at least 4 inches below the ground, so that the grafts may eventually form their own roots. During the first year, protect tree peonies from rabbits by covering the plants with wire cages, and mulch well. Carpenter bees are a serious pest in the East; control them by plugging their entry holes or cutting the plant back to the ground and destroying the refuse. Don't mulch after the first year, and remove fading blossoms immediately to help control Botrytis fungus. Native from Bhutan to Tibet and China.

Paeonia 'Golden Isles'

Paxistima canbyi (Cliff-green or Mountain-lover). Broadleaved evergreen. Zones 5B–8.

Cliff-green is most popular in the gardens of the Northeast and Pacific Northwest as an excellent evergreen ground cover. It grows only 12 to 24 inches high and spreads slowly to 3 to 5 feet. Its lustrous, dark green leaves change to an attractive bronze in the winter. *Paxistima* is a finely textured, neat, compact shrub that works well as a foreground for taller shrubs, as an edging plant, or as a low hedge. The flowers and fruit are inconspicuous. Best bought in a container, it transplants easily into moist, well-drained, acid soil. Although found on rocky soil in the wild, under cultivation it seems to appreciate soils that are high in organic matter. It grows denser and more compact in full sun, but it tolerates partial shade well. This is a shrub to leave alone once established—it rarely requires feeding or pruning, and has no severe pests. *Paxistima* grows best in regions with moist air. Native to rocky woods and slopes in the mountains of West Virginia, Ohio, and Kentucky.

Paxistima canbyi

Philadelphus coronarius (Sweet mock orange). Deciduous. Zones 5–8.

The white, late-May flowers of this shrub are legendary for their powerful fragrance, and have been popular for ages. Unfortunately, the sweet mock-orange has little else to offer: usually it is a coarse, leggy, straggly shrub that grows rapidly to an upright and irregular 10 to 12 feet high and wide. Even the smaller cultivars are irregular and unattractive when not in flower. The plant is easy to grow, not particular about soil, and will perform well in sun or partial shade. Free from serious pests, it has a wide-ranging root system that is highly competitive and indicative of its tolerance to adverse conditions. It requires annual pruning to maintain a semblance of presentability. Do so right after flowering; remove all older wood, or even cut it to the ground. Use *Philadelphus* where its fragrance can be appreciated—in a border, or near outdoor living areas, entryways, and windows. Since many of the mockoranges offered by nurseries vary widely in fragrance, select for fragrance when the plants are in flower. Native to Europe and southwestern Asia.

Philadelphus **'Frosty Morn',** a new hybrid hardy to Zone 4, has double flowers that rival *P.* × *lemoinei* for fragrance.

Philadelphus × *lemoinei* (Zones 6–8). Among the cultivars of this hybrid are some of the best choices for fragrance, including 'Avalanche' (4 feet tall with single white flowers) and 'Innocence' (8 feet tall with single flowers).

Philadelphus × *virginalis* also has many cultivars, which are generally less fragrant than *P. coronarius* or *P.* × *lemoinei*, but many of which are hardier (to Zone 4 or 5). 'Minnesota Snowflake' is a fragrant one, 6 feet high and hardy to Zone 4. 'Girandole' is 4 feet tall with double flowers.

Photinia × *fraseri*. Broadleaved evergreen. Zones 7B–10.

Best known for its bright, bronzy-red new foliage in the spring, this evergreen shrub is showier than many flowers. Photinia also produces attractive ivory-colored flowers in many 4-inch clusters in late March and April. If left unpruned, it will grow at a moderate rate to a rounded 10-foot-tall and somewhat wider shrub, but it is easily restrained. Use it as a screen, formal or informal hedge, or espalier, or train it into a single-stemmed small tree. Its lustrous, dark green foliage makes an excellent background. Although it does not fruit as profusely as other photinias, its red berries are quite attractive to birds. Plant this shrub in well-drained soil that has been amply amended with organic matter. Even though it is heat resistant in the desert, water it generously. Take care not to splash water onto the leaves—they are susceptible to fireblight. If fireblight does occur, the ends of branches will blacken, as if burned. Carefully prune them out, sterilizing the shears in alcohol or chlorine bleach after each cut, and destroy or dispose of the refuse. Spray regularly for aphids and scale.

Photinia × *fraseri*

Photinia serrulata (Chinese photinia; Zones 7B–10). This is an extremely large shrub or small tree that grows 36 feet high. Its large, coarsely textured leaves make a good screen. It blooms profusely in the spring. The dull white flowers change to a brownish-pink, are quite showy, and are followed by red berries.

Picea abies **'Nidiformis'** (Bird's nest Norway spruce). Conifer. Zones 2–4.

This is a popular dwarf spruce that makes a dense, low, flat-topped evergreen cushion, 3 to 6 feet high and 4 to 8 feet wide. It is useful as a specimen or curiosity in rock gardens, entryways, or other focal spots. Preferring moderately moist, well-drained, sandy soil, it will tolerate other kinds as long as they have sufficient moisture. The farther south below Zone 5 it is planted, the weaker it becomes: it prefers the moist climates of deep-winter cold and summer coolness. This spruce does not perform well in hot, dry, windy locations or in heat reflected from walks and pavements. Like all spruces, it is best in full sun or light shade. It is also a poor choice for polluted urban environments. Many other choice dwarf forms of the Norway spruce are available, from low- and wide-spreading to erect or pendulous, but this one is most common. Native to northern and central Europe.

Picea glauca **'Conica'** (Dwarf Alberta spruce; Zones 2–7) is a stiffly conical and extremely slow-growing (about 1 to 2 inches per year) dwarf, often described as an upside-down ice cream cone. It may eventually reach 6 to 8 feet in extreme old age. Its finely textured, light green needles and its unusual form make this an interesting specimen or oddity—probably best used in a focal grouping. In hot, dry areas, it is very susceptible to red spider mites. A heavy shower with a strong stream of water will help to control this problem. For severe infestations, use a miticide. Native to northern North America.

Pieris japonica (Japanese pieris). Broadleaved evergreen. Zones 6–9.

A beautiful broadleaved evergreen related to rhododendrons and kalmias, the Japanese pieris is grown for its delicate pendulous panicles of white or pinkish-white flowers that bloom in early spring (mid- to late March) and last for two to three weeks. It is also favored for its beautiful deep green foliage, with bronzy-red new growth in spring. Growing slowly to a 9- to 12-foot height and 6- to 8-foot spread, with an irregular, upright but rounded outline, pieris can be used as a specimen, in a shrub border, or in group plantings. It is especially nice in combination with other acid-loving broadleaved evergreens, and it integrates well into a foundation planting. Preferring moist, acid soil, it is not quite as particular as other members of the heath family. Protect it from wind and winter sun, especially in cold-winter areas. When pruning is necessary (which is seldom, if ever), do it just after flowering. Leaf spot, a dieback fungus, lace bugs, scale, and mites can be severe problems. In the northern limits of the shrub's range and in exposed situations, the flower buds, which are already developed by winter, often die. Several cultivars are available with more compact form, pink flowers, and unusual foliage color and texture. Native to Japan.

Pieris floribunda (Mountain pieris; Zones 5–8). Hardier, lower, and bushier than *Pieris japonica* (growing 2 to 6 feet high with a similar spread), this *Pieris* has upright panicles of fragrant white flowers that remain throughout the month of April. Additional advantages are greater resistance to lace bugs and tolerance to more alkaline soils. Unfortunately, the plant rarely is available. Native to cool, damp mountain slopes from Virginia to Georgia.

Pieris forrestii (Chinese pieris; Zones 8B–10). This shrub is more tender than *Pieris japonica*. It has extremely showy scarlet foliage, larger leaves, and a denser, larger habit. Native to China.

Pieris japonica

Pinus mugo (Dwarf mugo pine). Conifer. Zones 2–8, but not in the desert.

Since this plant is often sold as a cute little cushion that will grow only 2 to 4 feet high, many homeowners are surprised to find a 10-foot-tall, 15-foot-wide haystack monster on their doorsteps 15 or so years later. If you want a *reliably* small plant, seek out the harder-to-find cultivars, such as 'Compacta', 'Gnome', or 'Slavinii'. The mugo pine, however, can be controlled by annual pruning: remove approximately two-thirds of each young, expanding candle in the spring to maintain a compact, dense form. Use the mugo pine for textural evergreen interest in a foundation or a low mass planting or in groups. Plant it in moist, deep loam in full sun or partial shade. Many other dwarf pines are becoming increasingly available, although they are less common than the mugo pine. Such dwarf pines include specially selected cultivars of *Pinus strobus* (white pine) and *Pinus sylvestris* (Scotch pine). *Pinus mugo* is native to the mountains of Europe, from Spain to the Balkans.

Pinus mugo

Pittosporum tobira (Tobira; Japanese pittosporum). Broadleaved evergreen. Zones 8B–10.

Clean, dark, leathery evergreen foliage; early, creamy-yellow spring flowers with a scent like orange blossoms; and a broad, dense habit—all have made this a popular plant in southern and western gardens for screens and mass plantings, in a shrub border, or as foundation planting. It is particularly effective in containers or trained as a small, crooked-stemmed tree. Smaller cultivars, some with variegated foliage, are available for foreground plantings and ground covers. However, if you prefer a formal hedge, you would do well to avoid this plant. This pittosporum does not respond well to hard pruning or shearing, although frequent light pinching can help to maintain a compact habit. If allowed to grow naturally, it reaches 6 to 15 feet in height and is usually slightly wider. Fairly drought resistant, it nevertheless appreciates adequate water and an annual light fertilization. Aphids and scale can be a problem. Full sun to partial shade is best, although the plant tolerates dense shade well.

Pittosporum tobira 'Variegata'

Pittosporum crassifolium (Zones 9–10) is a large shrub that will grow up to 25 feet high, although it can easily be held to a 6-foot hedge. The finely textured, gray-green foliage responds well to shearing, and tolerates wind and coastal salts. 'Nana' is a 3-foot dwarf.

Pittosporum eugenoides (Zones 9–10) is an excellent, popular hedge plant, with wavy-edged, glossy, light green leaves that respond well to shearing. Fragrant yellow flowers, however, are produced only on unpruned plants.

Pittosporum napaliense (Golden fragrance plant; Zones 9–10) is a 12-foot-high, 8-foot-wide, coarsely textured shrub. Grow this one for its excellent spring display of profuse golden-yellow flowers and its powerful fragrance.

Platycladus orientalis (Oriental arborvitae). Conifer. Zones 7–10.

Like the American arborvitae, this species is a 50-foot tree from which many dwarf, shrublike cultivars have been developed. Northern gardeners should beware—it is frequently offered in bargain sales far north of where it is hardy. Many of the dwarf cultivars are extremely popular in the South, especially the bright yellow- or blue-foliaged forms. 'Aurea Nana' is a rounded yellow dwarf, while 'Blue Spire' is a pyramidal form with blue leaves. The Oriental arborvitae, besides being more tender, differs from the American arborvitae in the distinctly vertical, fan-shaped planes of its branches. While it is tolerant of drier soils and less atmospheric moisture, it still needs protection from harsh, dry winds. Native to northern China and Korea.

Potentilla fruticosa (Bush cinquefoil). Deciduous. Zones 2–8.

Few shrubs can earn as many plus points as the bush cinquefoil for suitability in a shrub border, as a foundation planting, for massing and edging, and as a low informal hedge or foreground plant. Its bright yellow, 1-inch flowers are abundant from June until frost on dense, upright stems which grow slowly to a neat, rounded plant, 1 to 4 feet high and 2 to 4 feet wide. Its dainty, finely textured, deciduous foliage is a handsome bright green. Bush cinquefoil will grow well in any soil, from wet to dry, heavy to light. It tolerates extreme cold and drought, is virtually free from pests (although occasionally susceptible to mites during dry spells), and requires no pruning. It will flower most abundantly in full sun, but tolerates partial shade nicely. In short, it is one of the most care-free plants around. Many cultivars are available in a range of sizes, flower colors (white, yellow, orange, or red), and foliage colors (bright green to gray-green). Orange- and red-flowering varieties fade quickly in full sun, so they are best planted in partial shade. Native to meadows and bogs of the Northern Hemisphere.

Potentilla 'Abbotswood'

Prunus laurocerasus (English laurel). Broadleaved evergreen. Zones 7–10.

Grown for its large, dark evergreen leaves, this sizable shrub (or small tree) is most commonly seen in southern gardens as a formal hedge, screen, or background plant. Give it partial shade (except on the coast) and protect it from scale and fungal leaf spot with regular spraying. It is not particular about soil. Left unpruned, in southern climates it has been known to grow 25 or 30 feet tall. In more northerly climates 4 to 6 feet is more likely. Because of its extremely rapid growth rate, expect it to demand a high level of maintenance as a clipped hedge. Shearing will mutilate the large leaves; instead, prune selectively. Beware of its greedy, far-reaching roots. Native to southeastern Europe and Asia Minor.

'Schipkaensis', if given protection, is hardy to Zone 6. It has smaller leaves and grows only 9 feet tall. 'Otto Luyken' is another excellent low-growing form, hardy to Zone 6B.

Prunus tomentosa (Nanking cherry; Manchu cherry). Deciduous. Zones 2–8.

One of the handsomest of the deciduous shrubby cherries, this broad shrub will eventually reach a picturesque, open, 6- to 10-foot height and 15-foot spread. It accepts shearing well, making a beautiful, dense hedge, although in that case the fruits are sacrificed. The handsome bark is a shiny, exfoliating reddish-brown, and a distinct attraction in the winter. But its chief beauty lies in its pink buds, which open into white, fragrant flowers in early to mid-April (March in mild climates), followed by edible scarlet fruits. Use this plant as a specimen or a hedge, in groups and masses, or in a shrub border. Native to northern and western China, Korea, and the Himalayas.

Prunus 'Cistena' (Purple-leafed sand cherry; Zones 2–7). This shrub is valuable for extreme hardiness and for intensely reddish-purple foliage that holds its color all summer long; the pink, fragrant May flowers and black fruits are of secondary importance. This small shrub grows rapidly to an upright and irregular 8 to 10 feet.

Prunus glandulosa (Dwarf flowering almond; Zones 5–8). Undistinguished when not in flower, this straggly, 4- to 5-foot-high, upright shrub is widely grown due to its ease of propagation.

Prunus maritima (Beach plum; Zones 4–7), a rounded, dense, 6-foot-high bush, is generally inferior but useful for its tolerance of the salt sprays and sandy soils of the seacoast. The fruits are edible, and follow white, early May flowers. Varieties have been selected for larger fruits.

Prunus triloba (Flowering almond; Zones 6–9) is a large, treelike shrub, growing 12 to 15 feet high. Its chief attraction is its bloom. The abundant flowers in late April (earlier in the South) are small, pink, and double, and are borne in large quantities. Unfortunately, they are frequently killed by a late freeze just as they are opening.

Punica granatum (Pomegranate). Deciduous. Zones 8–10.

This deciduous shrub is valuable for its showy, waxy orange or scarlet flowers in July and August and its brilliant yellow autumn foliage. A few varieties will also produce delicious fruits. It makes an excellent desert shrub, quite tolerant of heat and alkaline soils, and withstands considerable drought if the quality of the fruit is unimportant. *Punica granatum* will grow into a fountainlike arching plant with a height of 12 to 15 feet and form a dense, twiggy mass. Several cultivars are available with flower variation, from a single or double scarlet to white, yellow, and red. Selections are also available for fruit quality ('Wonderful' is the most popular), and for size, ranging from 18-inch pot or edging plants ('Nana') to 15-foot border shrubs.

Prunus tomentosa

Punica granatum

Plant pomegranates in full sun for best flowering and fruit; for quality fruit, water regularly and deeply. Native from southeastern Europe across Asia to the Himalayas.

Pyracantha coccinea (Scarlet firethorn). Broadleaved evergreen (semideciduous in the North). Zones 6B–10.

Showy white flowers in spring, excellent evergreen or semievergreen foliage, and spectacular red or orange fruit in fall and winter distinguish this all-season shrub. The form can always be called irregular, although varieties range from upright to prostrate; several dwarf cultivars are available as well. Growing at a medium to fast rate to 6 to 18 feet in height and spread, pyracantha has vicious thorns that make an excellent impenetrable barrier. Useful as a specimen, screen, or barrier hedge, it is especially popular espaliered against walls and along fences. Espaliering is easy, as long as you keep up with it. Be aware of the plant's ultimate size and thorniness and resist the temptation to plant it next to doors, drives, walks, or patios, where it will eventually attack people, clothes, cars, whatever. A nasty plant to prune, it needs plenty of room to grow. It responds well to full sun and well-drained soil, but don't try to move it after it is established. Guard against standing water on its foliage at flowering time, because this encourages fireblight, which is a serious problem. Scale, aphids, spider mites, apple scab, and lace bugs can also be damaging. Many varieties are available, most of them hardy only to Zone 7. 'Kasan', 'Lalandi', 'Thornless', 'Wyatti', and 'Chadwicki' are all hardy to Zone 6. 'Teton' is a new, strongly vertical form (12 feet high by 4 feet wide), also hardy to Zone 6. 'Fiery Cascade' is the hardiest (Zone 6) red-fruiting form. 'Mohave' has beautiful heavy crops of fruit that are scab resistant. Native from Italy to western Asia.

Pyracantha coccinea 'Mohave'

Raphiolepis indica (India hawthorn). Broadleaved evergreen. Zones 8B–10.

Raphiolepis is one of those easy-to-care-for garden workhorses that is both spectacularly showy and extremely serviceable for a multitude of purposes. Its leathery evergreen foliage and neat, dense, restrained habit (3 to 5 feet high and wide) make it an excellent low background, mass planting, informal hedge, or large-scale ground cover. Consider it as a foreground plant in a shrub border, or as a trouble-free container plant. The flowers bloom in midwinter or spring, and usually again in the fall. They vary from white to red, according to the cultivar. Dark-flowered cultivars are generally lighter in color the farther south they are grown. India hawthorn prefers full sun, but tolerates partial shade well, in addition to a variety of soils. While reasonably tolerant of drought, it looks best when frequently watered. Minimize splashing water onto foliage, since fireblight and leaf spot can be problems, as can aphids. Native to southern China.

Raphiolepis 'Springtime'

Rhododendron species (Rhododendrons and azaleas). Some evergreen, some deciduous species. Hardiness varies according to the variety.

Probably no other group of plants elicits such devoted praise or causes such helpless frustration as the genus *Rhododendron*. In areas where they grow, you can choose from a bewildering variety of striking, often brilliant flowers borne in legendary profusion. Besides these famous flowers, rhododendrons and azaleas frequently have outstanding form and foliage, along with more subtle qualities apparent on close inspection. Unfortunately, there are many areas in the United States where these plants do not adapt well—in the desert or the Plains States you will probably find rhododendrons difficult, if not impossible, to grow. Fortunately, vigorous and diverse breeding efforts in this genus are expanding the range somewhat.

Rhododendron is an extremely complicated genus containing over nine hundred species, with over ten thousand named cultivars listed in the

Rhododendron species

International Register. The genus is divided into several series, one of which is Azalea. Botanists and horticulturists are still arguing over exactly what anatomical characteristics separate Azalea within the genus *Rhododendron*. While many azaleas are deciduous and most rhododendrons are evergreen, there are important exceptions in each case. A common misconception is that azaleas are always smaller in form and leaf than rhododendrons; in fact, several rhododendrons are tiny, rock-garden dwarfs with leaves smaller than those of any azalea. And whether or not a plant is evergreen has little bearing on the matter—both azaleas *and* rhododendrons have deciduous and evergreen species. For most people it is enough to understand that while all azaleas are rhododendrons, not all rhododendrons are azaleas—leave it at that.

The reputation of rhododendrons as difficult and frustrating is actually misleading. *If planted in a favorable location and given the proper growing conditions, azaleas and rhododendrons are easy, care-free, and long-lived plants.* The trick is in having, creating, or finding those favorable growing conditions. Look for the following points:

Acid soil (pH 4.5 to 6.5) that is well drained and retains moisture well. If you have to amend your soil to provide these conditions, try a mixture of one-fourth soil, one-half organic matter (peat, composted oak leaves, ground cedar, or composted pine chips are excellent for their acid reaction), and one-fourth coarse sand. Volcanic sand, if available, is a good choice because of its porous and moisture-retaining properties. But guard against using seashore sand; it can contain deadly salts. Adding some slow-release fertilizer is also beneficial. If you have serious heavy-soil problems, raised beds may be the best answer. Since rhododendrons are shallow rooted, even mounding the soil and planting high can improve drainage enough to make the difference between death and survival. If you have neutral or alkaline soil, you *can* acidify it, but it is a tricky operation, and you will have to maintain its acidity on a regular basis. Rhododendrons will let you know when the soil has reverted to its alkaline state by declining in vigor and developing chlorosis (the leaves turn yellow while the veins remain green)—actually an iron deficiency caused either by alkalinity (which makes the iron in the soil unusable) or by an actual lack of iron. The best way to acidify the soil is with ferrous sulfate, or sulfur (commonly sold as flowers of sulfur). A soil test report will tell you exactly how much to apply. Some commercial growers have even used dilute sulfuric acid with great success. Ammonium sulfate can also be used, but with great caution—its powerful, quick-acting nitrogen can burn tender roots.

Protection from winter sun and wind and excessive summer heat. This point is especially important for the evergreen varieties. Due to their shallow root systems, rhododendrons cannot reach below the frost line and transmit water to their leaves when the soil is frozen. Yet their evergreen leaves constantly transpire water, even in the coldest winter. At this vulnerable time, sun and wind can be deadly as well as rapid freezing and thawing. You can protect your plants by shading them from the winter sun with a temporary barrier. A 3-inch organic mulch in fall will moderate winter soil temperatures and add needed organic matter to the soil. Contrary to popular opinion, the evergreen leaves are quite tolerant of sun during the growing season. Most deciduous types can be grown in full sun if summers are not too hot. The fact remains, however, that the optimum condition for nearly all rhododendrons and azaleas is the filtered shade of high tree branches in both summer and winter. The eastern side of a sheltering structure also makes a good planting location.

Adequate atmospheric and soil moisture. Most rhododendrons in cultivation are native to the Northeast and Pacific Northwest of the United States, and eastern Asia and Japan, regions where rain is both plentiful and evenly distributed the year round. They will not tolerate drought for any length of time. Water them regularly during dry periods, but don't let them get soggy. Beware of water that is alkaline or high in salts. The very best water is rainwater, and if you want to grow rhododendrons successfully you'd do well to capture rainwater to help them through the dry periods.

A mulch is very helpful for retaining moisture and keeping the roots cool. For best results, use organic matter that breaks down with an acid reaction, such as oak leaves, pine needles and bark, or cedar chips. Don't use peat as a mulch; it forms a crust and actually repels water when dry. Also avoid maple and elm leaves because of their heavy matting properties and alkaline reactions. Mulch to a settled depth of 2 to 3 inches—no deeper. Where plants have problems with flower spot or petal blight, replace the mulch each year.

Benign neglect. One of the most common mistakes with rhododendrons and azaleas is overfeeding. They are extremely sensitive to excessive levels of nitrogen around their fibrous roots. They do benefit, however, from occasional light feeding with a fertilizer formulated for acid plants. In good garden soils, little fertilizing should be necessary. If you are using organic mulches such as wood chips, sawdust, or shredded oak leaves, you will need additional nitrogen. Avoid manure; it is usually high in salts, to which rhododendrons are extremely sensitive.

Never cultivate around the roots of rhododendrons and azaleas. Use mulch or gentle pulling for weed control. To encourage the adequate hardening off of any new growth before the onset of winter, stop any fertilizing two months before the first frost. Try to anticipate weather conditions in the fall, and just prior to the first hard freeze, give your rhododendrons a good, deep watering to send them into winter with plenty of moisture.

Pruning should seldom be necessary; remember that most rhododendrons will naturally achieve an open, picturesque form. If you want greater density, prune lightly back to the nearest growth bud in the spring just after flowering (later pruning will remove next year's flower buds). Or prune more heavily to rejuvenate old plants, always leaving at least two visible growth buds. Unlike forsythia or privet, not all rhododendrons break new buds on old wood. If you want to test your rhododendron's ability to sprout, cut back one or two inconspicuous branches in late winter. If they sprout, the rest of the plant can be cut back the following year. (See page 65 for more pruning details.)

The descriptions that follow are only a sampling of this complex genus. In general, dependable results are most likely if you purchase named varieties. Plants grown from seed can be extremely variable and often disappointing. For particular cultivars adapted to your area, consult with the staff at your local nursery. And for further information, refer to *Rhododendrons of the World* by David G. Leach (New York: Charles Scribner's Sons, 1961) and *Azaleas* by Fred C. Galle (Birmingham, AL: Oxmoor House, 1974).

Rhododendron arborescens (Sweet azalea; Zones 5–7). Producing white flowers in early June and July with a delightful fragrance similar to that of heliotrope, this deciduous shrub will grow 8 to 20 feet high and wide. In the summer it is covered with bright green leaves that turn dark red in the fall. Native from New York to Georgia and Alabama, along mountain streams and in cool mountain meadows.

Rhododendron calendulaceum (Flame azalea; Zones 5–8). The long-lasting June flowers of this deciduous eastern native range from yellow through orange and scarlet. And the fiery colors of fall are echoed in its foliage as it changes from green to yellow to bronze. This shrub is quite variable both in color and fragrance, so make your purchase when it is in bloom. Most

Rhododendron aborescens

Rhododendron canadense

Rhododendron catawbiense

selections will reach 6 to 8 feet in height. Native from Pennsylvania through Georgia and west to Tennessee.

Rhododendron canadense (Rhodora azalea; Zones 2–6). Found wild in bogs and in moist, very acid soils, this small, rounded, 3- to 4-foot shrub has small deciduous leaves and light purple flowers in mid-May. It is most useful in a low, wet spot in a garden with cool summers. Native from Newfoundland and Labrador to New York and Pennsylvania.

Rhododendron carolinianum (Carolina rhododendron; Zones 5–8A). This restrained, rounded, 3- to 6-foot shrub bears white or pink flowers against dark, medium-sized evergreen leaves. It is native to the Blue Ridge Mountains of Carolina and Tennessee.

Rhododendron catawbiense (Catawba rhododendron; Zones 5–7). This is one of the hardiest large evergreen rhododendrons, growing to an open 6- to 10-foot height and width in the garden, although it often reaches 15 to 20 feet in the wild. Trusses of reddish-purple flowers are borne in great quantities in mid- to late May. Many beautiful cultivars are available, from bright red to purple or white, some of which are among the hardiest rhododendrons for harsh climates. Native to the Appalachian Mountains from West Virginia to Georgia and Alabama.

Rhododendron **Gable Hybrids** (Gable hybrid azalea; Zones 6–8). Actually quite a variable group of these hybrids have been bred for supposedly increased hardiness; however, don't consider them for use north of Zone 6. Their evergreen foliage tends to redden and fall in the northern part of their range. The flowers are borne abundantly in May and are predominately in the red-to-purple hues, with some light violets, orange-reds, and pinks.

Rhododendron × *gandavense* (Ghent hybrid azalea; Zones 5–7). Many of the cultivars of this deciduous group are hardy to −20°F., and some are being grown successfully as far north as Zone 4. A diverse parentage has produced many cultivars; the flowers range from white and yellow to pink, orange, and red and may be single or double. Usually growing 6 to 10 feet high with a comparable spread, the Ghent hybrids seem to perform best in light shade.

Rhododendron impeditum (Cloudland rhododendron; Zones 5–8). The hardiness rating of this rhododendron is based largely on the availability of snow cover or similar protection during the winter (as with most other dwarf rhododendrons). Growing only 18 inches high and wide, with tiny, dense, gray-green leaves, it makes an attractive plant for a sheltered spot in a rock garden. It is one of the many garden plants that has flowers usually listed as blue, although they are actually more of a mauve or lavender. This shrub is even more sensitive than most rhododendrons to hot, dry summers.

Rhododendron **Indica Hybrids** (Indian hybrid azalea; Zones 8–10). This group of tender evergreen azaleas was originally developed for greenhouse forcing, but many cultivars have since been selected as outstanding landscape plants for mild climates. They are a common sight in gardens of the deep South and California. They generally fall into two groups. The Belgian Indica hybrids are the most tender and should not be grown where temperatures fall below 15°F. The southern Indica hybrids have been selected from the Belgian hybrids for greater sun tolerance and more vigorous growth. Most are hardy to 10°F., although damage to flower buds can occur below 15°F. Flower colors for both groups range from white through violet, pink, red, and salmon.

Rhododendron kaempferi (Kaempfer azalea; Zones 6–8). In May this azalea and its hybrid forms are covered with flowers that range from white to rose to red-orange and salmon. The plants can reach 5 to 6 feet high in five years or so, and may eventually grow 10 feet tall. The leaves are semievergreen in the North and evergreen in the South, often turning red at the onset of cold weather. These shrubs should not be planted where winter temperatures drop below −10°F. In their native Japan they are frequently found growing on sunny hillsides and by the sea, but their flower colors last longest when they are grown in light shade. *Rhododendron kaempferi* is one of the few deciduous azaleas that will flower well in the deepest shade.

Rhododendron keiskei (Kieske rhododendron; Zones 6B–8). This shrub is unusual—one of the few evergreen rhododendrons to bear yellow flowers. Extremely variable in size, cultivars range from a tiny 6-inch, rock-garden plant to an 8-foot, open shrub. Whatever their size, however, all cultivars have small, finely textured leaves.

Rhododendron **Knapp Hill-Exbury Hybrids** (Zones 6–8, although some newer cultivars are hardy to Zone 4). Spectacular, brightly colored flowers literally cover these shrubs in late May and early June. They are available in hundreds of different shades of white, pink, rose, red, salmon, yellow, and orange. The flowers are large, and borne in many huge trusses. The medium green deciduous foliage turns into a brilliant yellow, orange, and red in fall. Like most of the deciduous azaleas, these are somewhat less choosey about soil acidity and winter shade, but are relatively intolerant of hot summer conditions. They will generally reach 4 to 8 feet in height, with a comparable spread.

Rhododendron × *kosteranum* (Mollis hybrid azaleas; Zones 5B–7). Quite similar to the Ghent hybrids, these deciduous azaleas are not quite as hardy or long lived. Cultivars are available with yellow and gold flowers through salmon and orange-red. They bloom in late May. Unfortunately, many nurseries offer "Mollis hybrids" that are grown from seed. Thus it is always best to select plants when they are in bloom. Mollis hybrid azaleas will perform well in full sun and neutral soil, and grow to a restrained, rounded, 3- to 8-foot form.

Rhododendron lapponicum (Lapland rhododendron; Zones 3–7). Grow this unusually hardy evergreen shrub in rock or alpine gardens where summers remain cool. Small purple flowers appear in June on a 1½-foot, low, prostrate form against tiny dark green leaves.

Rhododendron × *loderi* (Loder hybrid rhododendrons; Zones 8–10). Famous for their powerful fragrance and showy flower clusters in shades of white to pink, these evergreen rhododendrons should not be planted where winter temperatures fall below 0°F. Although the growth rate is slow, these shrubs eventually get too large for most gardens, developing into open plants 8 feet or more in height and width.

Rhododendron maximum (Rosebay rhododendron; Zones 4–8). This North American native is the tallest evergreen rhododendron that's hardy in the North. In the wild it can reach as tall as 30 feet, but a height of 4 to 15 feet is more likely in most northern gardens. With its loose and open habit, this plant looks best in large masses; it can make a splendid hedge. The flowers—pink in bud and white or rosy-purple when open—are borne late in the season, in June or July; unfortunately, they are partially hidden by the large, 4- to 8-inch leaves. This rhododendron must be grown in at least partial shade in order to thrive.

Rhododendron mucronulatum (Korean rhododendron; Zones 5–8). This deciduous shrub is an example of a rhododendron that is not evergreen. It is the first of all hardy rhododendrons and azaleas to flower—the bright, rosy-purple blossoms can appear as early as mid- to late March. For this

A seedling Exbury azalea.

Rhododendron keiskei

Rhododendron maximum

Rhododendron mucronulatum

reason, it is extremely susceptible to premature warm spells and late freezes, which can kill the flower buds overnight. Always remember to plant this shrub where it is sheltered from southern or southwestern sun in February and March. The early flowers and compact habit make it a good choice for planting on the northeastern side of the house or in a sheltered shrub border. 'Cornell Pink' is a particularly beautiful pink cultivar.

Rhododendron nudiflorum (Pinxterbloom azalea; Zones 4–9). A hardy, deciduous azalea with fragrant pinkish-white flowers that bloom in late April or early May, this one features a low, neat habit, usually 4 to 6 feet wide and high. The foliage is bright green in the summer, turning to a dull yellowish-brown in fall. This shrub will grow well in full sun and dry, sandy, rocky soils—a rare exception for the genus.

Rhododendron obtusum (Hiryu azalea; Kirishima azalea; Zones 7–9). A few cultivars of this evergreen azalea are hardy to $-10°F$. Unfortunately, many of the more tender varieties are commonly sold as far north as Zone 5B, with disappointing results. In milder gardens where hardiness is not a problem, the Hiryu azalea has proved itself a spectacular, reliable, and popular shrub. Several of its brilliant red cultivars have become familiar sights in the landscape—'Hinodegiri', 'Hino-Crimson', and 'Hershey's Red', for example. The form is broad, low, and spreading, reaching 3 to 6 feet high and perhaps twice as wide at maturity. The small leaves give it a fine texture. The flowers appear in March and April in great quantities, and range from white to pink, to lavender, to scarlet.

Rhododendron **P.J.M. (P. J. Mezzit) Hybrids** (Zones 5–8). This group of evergreen rhododendrons grows 3 to 6 feet high into a rounded, relatively dense mass. The dark green foliage turns a deep purple in cold weather, and the plants are sometimes deciduous in the northern extremes of their range. However, the P.J.M. hybrids are some of the most cold-hardy of the small-leafed rhododendrons. The flowers vary in the intensity of their bright, lavender-pink color, so it is best to buy one of these plants when they are in bloom.

Rhododendron schlippenbachii (Royal azalea; Zone 5). The royal azalea is an upright and rounded deciduous shrub, growing 6 to 8 feet high and wide. In summer the foliage is a dark green; in fall it presents a thrilling kaleidoscope of yellows, oranges, and brilliant reds. The fragrant pale pink to white flowers are borne in early to mid-May, but vary in intensity when grown from seed; so select your plant when it is in bloom. Unlike most other rhododendrons and azaleas, this one does not require very acidic soil, being comfortable with a pH range of 6.7 to 7.

Rhododendron vaseyi (Pinkshell azalea; Zones 5–9). The deciduous foliage of this hardy North American azalea is a medium green in summer, changing to a light red in fall. The delightfully fragrant flowers are a clear, pale

Rhododendron nudiflorum

Rhododendron obtusum (background)

Left: *Rhododendron* 'P.J.M.'
Right: *Rhododendron schlippenbachii*

pink, and appear from early to mid-May. The graceful, delicate effect of this shrub is enhanced by its pleasantly irregular habit: 5 to 10 feet high and usually slightly less wide.

Rhododendron viscosum (Swamp azalea; Zones 4–8). Unlike nearly all other rhododendrons and azaleas, this shrub actually thrives in damp, soggy soil, and is a perfect answer to that problem wet spot in the acid garden. In addition, it features small white or pink blossoms that have a powerful, clovelike fragrance. The growth habit is loose and open, ranging from 3 to 8 feet high and 3 to 8 feet wide; consequently, this shrub does best in mass plantings where an informal, naturalized look is desired.

Rhododendron viscosum

Rhus copallina (Flameleaf sumac; Shining sumac). Deciduous. Zones 5–8.

For some strange reason, nurseries seldom offer this plant, preferring its larger, weedier, and shorter lived cousin, the staghorn sumac. Yet this open, picturesque shrub or small tree is the best sumac for ornamental use. While occasionally reaching a height of 30 feet in the wild, it rarely exceeds 8 feet in cultivation. It will spread into clumps through suckering, but in a much more restrained and controllable manner than the staghorn sumac. Its shiny green foliage is darker than that of any other sumac, and the large compound, almost tropical leaves turn a brilliant red-orange in fall. Unlike other sumacs, the flameleaf sumac thrives in containers. It transplants easily and adapts to many soils, but it prefers well-drained soils and will not tolerate standing water. A relatively long-lived plant, it can be used as a specimen for fall color and interesting silhouettes. It is also beautiful when naturalized in large groups.

Rhus copallina (fall color)

Rhus typhina (Staghorn sumac; Zones 4–8). Individual plants live for a relatively short time, but it is hard to suppress the profuse weedy suckers with which this large, 25-foot shrub or small tree forms massive colonies. Staghorn sumac is a beautiful, picturesque plant with finely textured foliage and downy stems and fruit. It also has the gorgeous fall color and structural interest of the flameleaf sumac. The common temptation to use it as a focal specimen usually ends in disaster: the specimen plant itself dies after a few years but lives on through its suckers. It is best to reserve this plant for naturalizing in large waste areas.

Rosa species (Rose). Mostly deciduous, some evergreen species. Hardiness varies according to the species.

Volumes have been written extolling the virtues of this most venerable, popular, and complex genus. The hybrid teas, floribundas, grandifloras, and climbers are represented by an incredible profusion of cultivars that has placed the rose at the pinnacle of horticultural breeding. While these plants are usually grown for the beauty of their individual flowers, to call them "hobby" roses would diminish their popularity and significance. Words like "passion" or "obsession" are closer to fact.

Some of the species roses may not be as well known, but they are infinitely more useful to the landscape gardener. Unlike the hybrid roses mentioned above, species roses are generally much easier to grow, are relatively pest free, and require little special pruning or feeding. Most species have more seasonal and short-lived (but effective) flowers, excellent foliage qualities, larger size, increased hardiness, and, occasionally, attractive fall fruit and foliage color.

Rosa banksiae (Banks rose; Zones 8–10). This tender, large semievergreen or evergreen rose will climb on trellises and fences as high as 18 feet. Grown without support, it will form a sprawling, rambling mass 6 to 8 feet high and nearly twice as wide. The flowers are yellow fading to white, and are borne

Rosa rugosa flowers (left) and hips (right).

in unbelievable profusion in May and June. White and double-flowered forms are available. Native to China.

Rosa foetida (Austrian briar; Zones 4–9). The single deep yellow flowers of this 10-foot-high and equally wide shrub have been popular for centuries. 'Bicolor' has coppery-red flowers tinged with yellow. 'Persiana' has smaller, double yellow flowers. Native to western Asia.

Rosa hugonis (Father Hugo rose; Zones 5–10). This is one of the best and most popular of the yellow-blooming species roses. The single canary-yellow blossoms appear in May, along with the late tulips, and are thought by many to be the most exquisitely beautiful rose blossoms in bud. The plant grows rapidly 6 to 8 feet high and often wider, with an upright, arching habit. Despite its nice, finely cut foliage, this plant tends toward raggedness when not in bloom. Prune the oldest wood to the ground each year after blooming to encourage more flowering and to keep the plant neater. Use Father Hugo roses as a screen or informal hedge, in the shrub border, or trained on a trellis. Native to central China.

Rosa rubrifolia (Redleaf rose; Zones 2–8). Especially valuable in the harsh climate of the northern prairie states, this rose features clean, reddish-tinged foliage. The single pink flowers in the spring are not particularly overwhelming. Native to central Europe.

Rosa rugosa (Rugosa rose, Saltspray rose; Zones 2–10). Well adapted to the sandy soils and saline environment of coastal gardens, the rugosa rose is probably the easiest rose to grow. The flowers range from rose-purple to white, single or double, according to the cultivar selected. After a heavy late-spring bloom, they continue to blossom lightly all summer. Forming a dense, brambly mat 4 to 6 feet high and wide, the stout, upright, and prickly canes withstand pruning well and make an effective barrier hedge. The leaves are an outstanding deep, lustrous green, changing to yellow in the fall; they make an effective backdrop for the brick-red hips. This is an excellent choice for difficult, rocky, or sandy soils. Native to northern China, Korea, and Japan.

Rosa spinosissima (Scotch rose; Zones 4–10). The free-spreading, suckering habit of this 3- to 4-foot-high shrub makes it a useful, rapidly growing bank or ground cover, especially where erosion is a problem. It is available in a variety of flower colors, from pink to white to yellow, single or double. The generally fragrant blossoms appear in late May and early June in prodigious quantities. The low habit, profuse bloom, variety of cultivars, and ease of culture all contribute to the Scotch rose's popularity. Native to Europe, Western Asia, and now naturalized in the northeastern United States, this is the only rose native to Ireland.

Rosa virginiana (Virginia rose; Zones 4–10). This is another rose that does well by the sea, but it is extremely easy to grow anyplace there is well-

Rosa hugonis

Rosa spinosissima 'Altaica'

drained soil. In addition, it is our most beautiful native rose, attractive in all seasons. The single pink flowers open in June. The foliage is a crisp, glossy dark green, and unusually free from pests. In the fall the plant develops brilliant foliage coloration, starting with purple, then changing to orange, red, crimson, and finally yellow. The bright red hips, borne in great quantities, are effective into the winter. The canes add to the winter interest because of their reddish hue. This rose can grow 6 feet high and spread indefinitely by underground stems, but it is easily restrained as a 3-foot hedge. Where as a result of its vigorous habit it spreads a bit too far, simply cut the whole shrub back to the ground. It will rapidly recover. Native from Newfoundland to Virginia, Alabama, and Missouri.

Rosa wichuraiana (Memorial rose; Zones 6–10). Especially in milder climates where its foliage is semievergreen or evergreen, this trailing rose makes an excellent ground cover. Spreading 8 to 16 feet or more, and achieving a maximum height of 1½ feet, it forms a dense mat of glossy, deep green foliage that few weeds can penetrate. The small, fragrant white flowers appear in late June through July, making it one of the last rose species to bloom. Native to China, Korea, and Japan.

Rosmarinus officinalis (Rosemary). Narrow-leafed evergreen. Zones 7–10.

Best suited to mild, Mediterranean climates with dry summers and wet winters, this is the rosemary familiar to good cooks. Its fragrant evergreen foliage clips and shears well. With their fine, grayish-green texture, trailing types make excellent cascades over walls, and lower types make excellent erosion-controlling bank or ground covers. Use larger types as a clipped hedge or in a dry shrub border. Size varies according to cultivar—from 2 to 6 feet high and often twice as wide. The showy light blue flowers appear in late winter or very early spring; certain cultivars, such as 'Collingwood Ingram' and 'Lockwood de Forest', have been selected for their bright blue flowers. The shrub is attractive to birds and bees. Rosemary must have sharp drainage; overwatering and overfertilizing will produce rank, stretchy growth. It tolerates heat, sun, infertile soil, and drought. Set ground cover varieties 2 feet apart for a quick cover. Native to southern Europe and Asia Minor.

Rosmarinus officinalis 'Collingwood Ingram'

Salix gracilistyla (Rosegold pussy willow). Deciduous. Zones 5–10.

If you are determined to grow pussy willows, this one is distinctly the best. Its rapid growth to a 6- to 10-foot height and width is quite restrained and neat compared to that of other willows. And its catkins are the largest, earliest (March), and most beautiful. The stamens on male catkins are a shimmering gold, while underneath there is a distinct rosy fuzziness. Use this willow to naturalize in damp or wet, difficult soil, or possibly to accent a shrub border with its bluish-gray foliage. The branches are wonderful to cut and force indoors in earliest spring. Preferring moist, even water-logged soil, the rosegold pussy willow will also tolerate dry soils. Like all willows, it is plagued by many pests and is a weak-wooded, somewhat messy, and short-lived plant. Prune heavily to keep it vigorous and healthy. Native to Japan, Korea, and Manchuria.

Salix caprea (Goat willow; Zones 5–10). Often sold as a cute little pussy willow, this plant will quickly become a messy, awkward giant, growing 25 to 30 feet tall and spreading 15 to 20 feet wide. Avoid this plant.

Salix discolor (Pussy willow; Zones 4–10). Grown for its fuzzy gray catkins in poor, wet soils, this huge, wild, and unruly shrub grows 20 feet high and as wide, and forms a mass of upright stems. It is a messy plant, constantly dropping twigs, leaves, and branches. Native from Labrador to South Dakota and south to Missouri.

Salix gracilistyla

Spiraea **species** (Spirea). Deciduous. Zones 5–10.

To most people the word spirea implies bridalwreath or Vanhoutte spirea, two old-fashioned favorites that seem to be as awkward, large, and cumbersome as they are popular. While many superior, more dwarf cultivars are available to the diligent gardener, no spirea is particularly inspiring when out of bloom. Use spireas as an inexpensive, rapidly growing, easy-to-maintain filler in a shrub border, where their dull appearance when not in bloom can be masked. The lower-growing types make passable coarse ground covers. Easily transplanted, they are not particular about soil. They are subject to many pests, including fireblight, leaf spot, powdery mildew, and a host of insects, but none of these appears to be fatal as long as the plant has full sun and good air circulation. Spireas differ as to pruning requirements: summer-flowering types should be pruned in late winter or early spring, since they bloom on the current year's wood; spring-flowering types should be pruned directly after blooming. Renew older, leggy plants of either type by cutting them to the ground in early spring.

Spiraea albiflora (Japanese white spirea) is a low (1½ foot), rounded, dense shrub with white flowers that produce in late June and July on the current year's growth. The relatively neat, compact habit of this plant makes it superior to many other spireas. Native to Japan.

Spiraea × bumalda (Bumalda spirea) is a low, spreading shrub growing 2 to 3 feet high and 3 to 5 feet wide, with white to deep pink flowers blooming from mid-June to August on the current year's growth. 'Anthony Waterer' is an extremely popular deep rose cultivar, but several other superior cultivars are available. They include 'Crispa' (growing 2 feet high with twisted leaves), 'Gold Flame' (low growing with brightly colored red, copper, and orange foliage in early spring and fall), and 'Nyeswood' (especially dense and compact with good, pink flowers).

Spiraea japonica (Japanese spirea) is similar to *S. × bumalda*, except for a larger, coarser growth habit 4 to 5 feet high. 'Atrosanguinea', a superior deep rose-red cultivar that grows from 2½ to 4 feet high, is hardier (Zone 4B). The Japanese spirea blooms on new wood from early June through July. Native to Japan.

Spiraea nipponica **'Snowmound'** (Snowmound spirea) is a delightful white-flowered, dwarf spirea that grows 3 to 5 feet high and as wide. It is superior to the Vanhoutte spirea because of its denser, neater, more compact form. Native to Japan.

Spiraea prunifolia (Bridalwreath spirea) is a rangy, coarse, open shrub, growing 4 to 9 feet tall and 6 to 8 feet wide. The dull white flowers appear in April on old wood. Native to China.

Spiraea × vanhouttei (Vanhoutte spirea) grows rapidly to become an 8- to 10-foot-high, arching, fountainlike shrub, spreading 10 to 12 feet. This extremely tough shrub is popular for use in the border and for mass planting. Its size definitely limits it to large gardens. It blooms from early April to May and the white flowers appear on old wood.

Symplocos paniculata (Sapphireberry; Asiatic sweetleaf). Deciduous. Zones 5–8.

Brilliant azure-blue fruits practically cover this shrub in the fall, and are a tremendous eye-catcher in the garden. Unfortunately, they are equally as attractive to birds as to people. The profuse powder-puff, creamy white flowers that bloom in May and June are actually more showy than those of many old-time favorites, such as deutzia, honeysuckle, and mock orange. Curiously, sapphireberry is seldom offered by nurseries. This large shrub

Spiraea × bumalda 'Anthony Waterer'

Symplocos paniculata

grows 10 to 20 feet tall and wide, and fruit production seems to vary from plant to plant. For more dependable fruiting, plant two or more of these shrubs together for cross-fertilization, and in full sun if possible. Sapphireberry transplants easily into any well-drained soil. Long lived and pest free, this shrub is a dependable bloomer whose flower buds are hardy to −25°F. Native to rocky slopes, edges of woods, and forest glades in full sun, from the Himalayas to Japan.

Syringa vulgaris

Syringa vulgaris (Common lilac). Deciduous. Zones 3B–7, somewhat successful farther south.

Beloved by gardeners since time immemorial for its mid- to late-May, powerfully fragrant flowers, the common lilac is a wonderful plant for the rear of a shrub border or for any out-of-the-way place where its delightful scent can be appreciated. Resist the temptation to plant it as a specimen or in highly visible spots: it has little to offer when not in flower, which is about 50 weeks out of the year. It is a large, upright, often irregular shrub growing 20 feet in height and 12 to 15 feet in spread, and its gray to dark green or bluish-green leaves are often covered with powdery mildew by midsummer. An incredible profusion of cultivars is available for flower color: pinks, blues, violets and purples, white.

The plants live a long time, and seem to survive the most adverse calamities. However, it isn't easy to keep lilacs looking attractive, and they normally produce good flowers only every other year. Plant them in full sun in neutral, rich soil that is high in organic matter. While they respond well to a light annual fertilizing, too much fertilizer will decrease flowering. Remove spent flowers immediately to increase next year's bloom, and prune out 50 to 75 percent of the basal suckers each year. Renew old plants by cutting them back severely, almost to the ground. Besides mildew, lilacs are plagued by many irritating (although usually not fatal) diseases and insects. Most lilacs do not perform well in mild climates. Exceptions are cultivars selected for this purpose, including 'Lavender Lady', 'Blue Boy', 'Chiffon', 'Mrs. Forrest K. Smith', and 'Sylvan Beauty'. Native to southern Europe.

Tamarix hispida (Kashgar tamarix). Deciduous. Zones 5–10.

For a bright pink, August to September display under the harshest seashore conditions, try this slender, wispy, 4- to 6-foot shrub. Like every tamarix, its winter appearance is impossible; hide it well in the shrub border. However, this is the neatest and most restrained of the tamarixes for the small garden. The foliage is needlelike (similar to that of junipers) but deciduous, creating a feathery, light green effect. Tamarix requires well-drained soil and is touchy about transplanting, so always purchase young, container-grown plants. However, it is extremely tolerant of salty, sandy soil; harsh, dry winds; and considerable drought. While it makes an excellent choice for desert gardens, it will need periodic watering. If the soil is too fertile, the shrub will become quite leggy and rangy. All tamarix plants grow very rapidly. Prune when dormant in early spring. Native to central Asia.

Tamarix parviflora (Small-flowered tamarix; Zones 5–10). Similar in form and flower to *T. ramosissima*, this tamarix flowers on old wood, so prune it hard each year just after flowering. Native to southeastern Europe.

Tamarix ramosissima, also called *T. pentandra* (Odessa tamarix; Zones 2–10). This is the hardiest tamarix of all—larger, leggier, and more awkward than *T. hispida*—growing 10 to 15 feet high, and 20 to 30 feet in mild climates. Since it flowers on new growth, it should be cut back hard or even leveled to the ground each year after the leaves drop in the fall. Its root system can become quite invasive. It performs beautifully in coastal gardens and the arid Southwest. In mild areas it naturalizes readily, often becoming difficult to handle. Native from southeastern Europe to central Asia.

Tamarix hispida

Taxus species (Yew). Conifer. Zones 5 and 6B–8.

While the species are large, 40- to 50-foot-high trees, the many cultivars available are among the most useful coniferous evergreen shrubs for the landscape. Hardy and trouble free, with handsome dark green foliage and a wide variety of dense, refined forms, they have only one drawback: they are overused. Like junipers, yews are often planted without consideration for their ultimate size. Your nursery will help you select the appropriate cultivar, but be sure to ask how big it will grow. Yews accept formal pruning well and are often clipped into hedges or other shapes. Consider them also for mass planting, as an evergreen touch for a shrub border, and as a foundation plant. When they are allowed to develop their natural forms, the effect is usually graceful and appealing. Give yews soil with excellent drainage and they will be generally easy to grow and pest free, in sun or shade. In heavy, wet soils they will be stunted and sickly, if they survive at all. Give them adequate moisture and protect them from sweeping wind. In hot, dry climates, give them a northern exposure and hose the foliage frequently during the driest periods. The foliage is poisonous if eaten, as are the seeds of their colorful, red fruits.

Taxus baccata (English yew; Zones 6B–10). This least hardy yew has several cultivars that are excellent for southern or other warm climate gardens. Native throughout Europe.

Taxus cuspidata (Japanese yew; Zones 5–10). Many excellent cultivars of this species are available, ranging from a low, 1-foot-high and 3-foot-wide form with yellow new growth ('Aurescens') to a 40- to 50-foot pyramidal form ('Capitata'). Native to Japan and Korea.

Taxus × media (Zones 5–10). A hybrid between the above two species, this yew has an extremely wide variety of cultivars, from low, spreading types to tall, narrow ones.

Taxus baccata

Thuja occidentalis (American arborvitae). Conifer. Zones 2–10.

While this is actually a large, upright coniferous tree growing 40 to 60 feet tall, many slow-growing cultivars are often used in foundation plantings, as hedges, or as screens. Varieties range from inches-high rock-garden plants to 20-foot, columnar small trees that are useful as screens. Most cultivars turn an ugly yellow-brown in cold weather—'Nigra' and 'Techny' are two that retain good dark green foliage all winter long. Plant arbovitae in moist, well-drained soil in full sun. It tolerates highly alkaline soils, and will perform best in areas of high atmospheric moisture. The branches and foliage are quite susceptible to damage from winter winds, snow, and ice. While many pests are listed as potential problems, these plants are generally easy to care for and trouble free. Native from Nova Scotia and Manitoba south to the Carolinas and Tennessee.

Thuja occidentalis 'Globosa'

Tsuga canadensis 'Pendula' (Sargent's weeping hemlock). Conifer. Zones 4–8B.

This is the most commonly grown dwarf hemlock. It displays a graceful, pendulous habit and refined evergreen foliage. While it can reach 5 to 6 feet in height and two or three times that in spread in extreme old age, a size of 3 to 4 feet high by 8 to 9 feet wide is a more reasonable expectation in one lifetime. This plant makes an outstanding focal specimen in a border, by an entryway, in a raised bed, or in a container. Plant it in moist, well-drained, acid soil. Unlike most conifers it tolerates shade well; in fact, it prefers partial shade. If drainage is good, the soil is moist, and there are no drying winds, hemlock will tolerate full sun. It will not tolerate wind, drought, or waterlogged soils, however, and in areas where summer temperatures exceed 95°F., it is likely to develop leaf scorch. This is not a plant for heavily polluted areas. With the right location, hemlock is usually a trouble-free and long-lived plant. Native from Nova Scotia to Minnesota, and south through the Appalachian mountains to Alabama and Georgia.

Vaccinium corymbosum (Highbush blueberry). Deciduous. Zones 4–8A.

Although grown primarily for its delicious fruit, both in home and commercial gardens, the highbush blueberry makes an outstanding ornamental plant when given the right growing conditions. It is a fairly large shrub, often reaching 6 to 12 feet high and 8 to 12 feet wide, but grows slowly and is easily restrained. Its dark, lustrous, almost blue-green foliage consistently turns into bright yellow, bronze, orange, or red combinations in the fall, and densely covers a rounded, compact form. Just as the leaves emerge in May, small white flowers are borne in great quantities, followed by the popular fruits that ripen in late July through August. Even without a spraying program, a single bush will usually provide enough berries for a few pies, some jam, and the birds.

If given moist, acid (pH 4.5 to 5.5), well-drained soil that is high in organic matter, the highbush blueberry is generally easy to grow. While it is native to swampy soils, in the garden it performs best in sandy, acid ones. Mulch it well to promote cool, moist soil around the roots, and give it full sun to partial shade and regular, adequate moisture. When grown commercially for fruit, blueberries usually require a regular spraying program and protection from hungry birds. When grown in the landscape for ornamental purposes, however, the fruit yield is generally sufficient for both humans and birds without requiring any elaborate netting or other protective devices. Use highbush blueberries as a tasty and attractive addition to a shrub border, in a foundation planting, or massed naturally in large areas. Check with your local extension agent for the cultivars that grow best in your region. Native from Maine to Minnesota and south to Florida and Louisiana.

Viburnum **species.** Some evergreen, some deciduous species. Hardiness varies according to the species.

Viburnum is a particularly diverse genus that contains a wide range of valuable shrubs for the garden. Some are grown for their moderately attractive and powerfully fragrant blossoms; others display extremely showy combinations of flower, fruit, and fall color. Most perform best in a moist, well-drained, slightly acid soil, although they are generally quite adaptable to other soils. Many insects and diseases can attack viburnums; however, these shrubs are usually trouble free if kept vigorous.

Viburnum × *burkwoodii* (Burkwood viburnum; Zones 6–10) is an upright, somewhat straggly shrub, 8 to 10 feet high and 5 to 7 feet wide. It is grown primarily for its powerfully fragrant flowers that open pink and then turn to white. Flowers appear in early to late April, before the leaves. Use this fine plant for a shrub border, where its fragrance will perfume an entire garden. In southern gardens the foliage is evergreen.

Viburnum × *carlcephalum* (Fragrant snowball viburnum; Zones 6–9) is another delightfully fragrant shrub that produces white flowers in late April or May. Its loose, open growth, 6 to 10 feet high and wide, blends well into the shrub border.

Viburnum carlesii (Koreanspice viburnum; Zones 5–8) is a popular fragrance shrub for northern gardens. In late April to early May it produces pinkish-white flowers that have a spicy, sweet scent. It will grow to a rounded, dense 4 to 5 feet high and 4 to 8 feet wide, occasionally reaching a height of 8 feet. Native to Korea.

Vaccinium corymbosum (fall color)

Viburnum × *carlcephalum*

Viburnum dilatatum

Viburnum davidii (David viburnum; Zones 8–10). This small (1 to 3 feet high and 3 to 4 feet wide), dense, large-leafed evergreen shrub does well in southern gardens. Its dark, metallic-blue fruits are especially appealing. Native to China.

Viburnum dilatatum (Linden viburnum; Zones 5B–8) is an upright, open shrub that grows 8 to 10 feet high and 5 to 8 feet wide. Although the white flowers in May and June are a welcome attraction, this shrub's most outstanding season comes in September and October, when the fruits ripen. The profuse bright red fruits often remain on the branches into December. Linden viburnum is best used in a shrub border, where its tendency to become leggy can be minimized. Be sure to plant several together—cross-fertilization improves fruiting. Native to eastern Asia.

Viburnum × *juddii* (Judd viburnum; Zones 5–10) is a relatively new hybrid similar to *Viburnum carlesii*, except that it is more reliably hardy in northern Zone 5.

Viburnum macrocephalum (Chinese snowball viburnum; Zones 7–10) bears white, round balls of sterile flowers in late May to early June—the largest flower clusters of any viburnum, often 8 inches in diameter. In the northern part of its range it needs protection from winter winds, and it is one *Viburnum* that must have well-drained soil. It is a dense, rounded shrub, 6 to 10 feet high and wide, and in southern areas it is semievergreen.

Viburnum opulus (European cranberry bush; Zones 4–10) is a popular and very effective shrub because of its delicate, pinwheel, white flowerheads, which put on a beautiful show in mid-May. The sterile, showy flowers are on the outside of the cluster, while the fertile, less conspicuous ones are at the center. Bright red fruits appear from September to November, and are usually accompanied by good fall foliage color. This large shrub grows 8 to 12 feet high (possibly 15 feet) and spreads 10 to 15 feet. It is best used in large gardens—in a border, as a screen, or for mass planting. 'Compactum' is an excellent dense, dwarf cultivar that is about half the size of the species. 'Nanum' is another dwarf that bears no flowers or fruits. Unfortunately, *V. opulus* (especially the cultivar 'Roseum') is very susceptible to aphids, which disfigure young leaves. For this reason, *V. trilobum*, a nearly identical American native, makes a good substitute.

Viburnum plicatum **var.** *tomentosum* (Doublefile viburnum; Zones 5–9). Many experts consider this the most beautiful of all flowering deciduous shrubs. The profuse flowers—lacy, pinwheel, and pure white—bloom in May, and are gracefully arranged along the horizontally tiered, stratified branches. In summer the foliage is a good dark green, and in fall it displays possibly the best autumn color of any *Viburnum*—tints of rust-red to purplish-red. It is one of the earliest viburnums to show good fruit color; the bright red fruits ripen in July and August, and are attractive to birds. Growing 8 to 10 feet high and slightly wider, this shrub makes an excellent specimen, and is a perfect horizontal complement to the usually upright-oriented shrub border. It combines well with broadleaved evergreens, and is particularly stunning against dark-red brick backgrounds or with red-blooming flowers, such as some azaleas. Foundation plantings, masses, and screens are also good uses for this shrub. Doublefile viburnum will not tolerate heavy, wet soils. When planted in fertile, moist, well-drained soil, it is generally an easily maintained, trouble-free plant. Native to China and Japan. Many superior cultivars have been selected for their form, flowers, and fruits, such as 'Mariesii' (largest flowers and best fruits), and 'Pink Beauty' (smaller flowers and leaves with outstanding deep pink blossoms).

Viburnum × *rhytidophylloides* (Zones 6–10) is best known for the selection 'Willowwood'. This is a large shrub, 8 to 10 feet tall and wide, with large,

Viburnum plicatum var. tomentosum

Viburnum trilobum flowers (left) and fruit (right).

coarse, leathery leaves that remain a dark green throughout the winter. It is slightly hardier than its parent, *V. rhytidophyllum*, performing well under harsh midwestern prairie conditions. The coarse texture of the foliage is accentuated in the winter, when the leaves hang limply on the stems. Flowers and fruits are largely unimportant.

Viburnum tinus (Laurustinus; Zones 8–10) is a 6- to 12-foot-high, upright evergreen shrub, grown in southern and western gardens for its dark green foliage, pink-turning-to-white flowers, and bright, metallic-blue fruit. Its clean, dense foliage hugs the ground, making it an excellent choice for screens and hedges; and it responds well to formal pruning. While well adapted to shade, it will flower more profusely in full sun. Native to the Mediterranean region of Europe.

Viburnum trilobum (American cranberry bush viburnum; Zones 3–9) is quite similar in all respects to *V. opulus*. Since it is hardier and much more resistant to aphids, it makes an excellent substitute. 'Compactum' is a fine dwarf form, about half the size of the species, and produces excellent flowers and fruits. The fruits of *V. trilobum*, unlike those of *V. opulus*, make excellent jams and jellies. Native from New Brunswick to British Columbia, south to New York and Oregon.

Viburnum × rhytidophylloides

Weigela florida (Old-fashioned weigela). Deciduous. Zones 5–8.

Out of bloom, the old-fashioned weigela is a coarse, usually rangy shrub that requires considerable pruning to keep it even halfway presentable. In bloom it is spectacular. From late May to early June it is heavily laden with clouds of rosy-pink bloom. Use *Weigela* in the shrub border, in mass plantings, and in groups, where its awkward form and coarse texture can be hidden when it's not in bloom. Many cultivars and hybrids are available, with white to deep red flowers. While *Weigela* prefers well-drained soil and a sunny location, it is nevertheless quite adaptable and pest free. Expect considerable dieback each year; prune after flowering to clean up the shrub's appearance. The variety *venusta* is the hardiest *Weigela* (Zone 4), with finely textured leaves and rosy-pink flowers. Native to northern China and Korea.

Weigela florida

Xylosma congestum (Shiny xylosma). Broadleaved evergreen. Zones 8–10.

Valued for its clean, shiny, yellow-green foliage in all seasons, shiny xylosma will grow slowly to be an 8- to 10-foot-high and -wide, rounded, loose shrub or small tree. Some forms are spiny and make useful barriers. Xylosma responds well to pruning and can easily be trained into an espalier. Also use it in a shrub border, as a container plant, as a formal or informal hedge, or for a high bank or ground cover. Plant it in any soil. It will tolerate heat and drought, but looks best when it has adequate water. Native to southern China.

Xylosma congestum

Index

Italicized page numbers refer to illustrations.